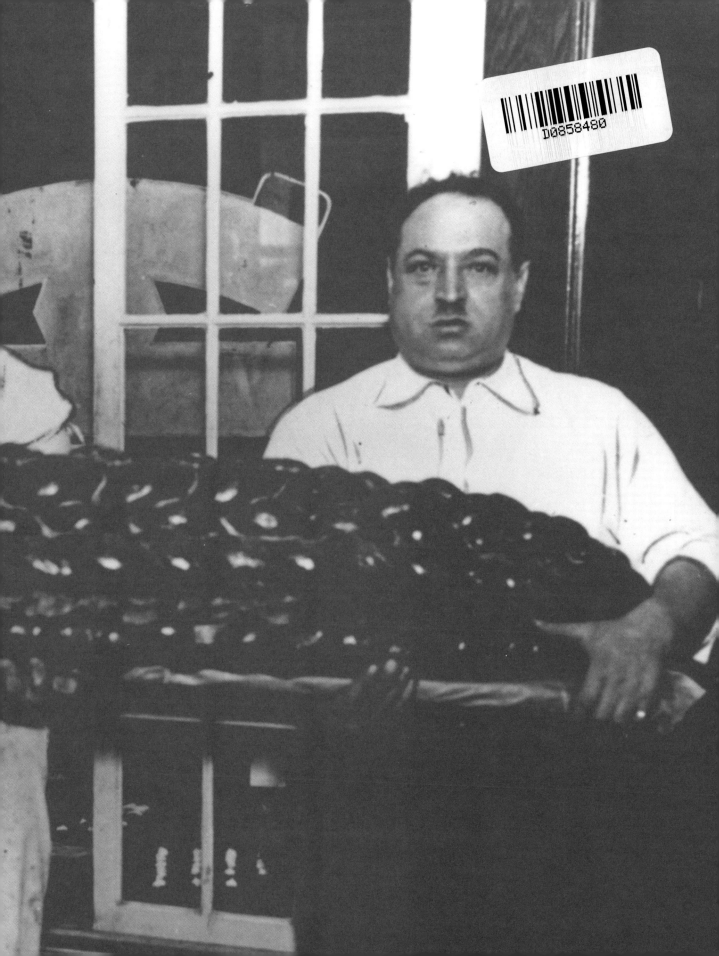

The Bathurst St. Kitchen

UJA Women's Philanthropy
UJA Federation of Greater Toronto

Published by UJA Federation of Greater Toronto
4600 Bathurst Street
Toronto, ON M2R 3V2
www.JewishToronto.com

Library and Archives Canada Cataloguing in Publication

The Bathurst St. kitchen.

Includes index.
Includes vintage photographs courtesy of the Ontario Jewish
        Archives which document early and mid 20th century
        Toronto Jewish life.
ISBN 978-0-9881551-1-4 (pbk.)

        1. Jewish cooking. 2. Cooking—Ontario—Toronto. 3. Jews—
Ontario—Toronto—History. 4. Cookbooks—I. UJA Federation of
Greater Toronto, issuing body II. Title: Bathurst Street kitchen.

TX724.B38 2015   641.5'676   C2014-908001-8

Indexer: Heather Ebbs
Front cover photo: TTC 4546 streetcar on Bathurst Street, immediately to the north of its intersection with Dundas Street West. Toronto, Ontario, Canada, 1968

First printing
Printed and bound in China

We apologize in advance for any errors or omissions regarding text, attribution and matters of food preparation and kashrut. Please let us know of any issues at www.JewishToronto.com/BathurstStreetKitchen so that we may address them and post corrections.

Produced by Callawind Book Publishing
(a division of Callawind Publications Inc.)
3551 St. Charles Boulevard, Suite 179
Kirkland, Quebec H9H 3C4
www.callawind.com
Publishing manager: Marcy Claman

contents

The History of Our Community

Today was Built Yesterday,
Tomorrow will be Built Today.

To those who came from far and wide
and helped build Toronto's Jewish community,
we celebrate your vision by sharing
your family's recipes and stories.

Dedicated to the mothers, wives, daughters and sisters
of our community and their families who will benefit
from the proceeds of this cookbook.

welcome

Welcome to *The Bathurst Street Kitchen!* Maybe you are flipping through these pages because you or your cousin contributed a recipe, or maybe you want to support UJA, or maybe you are simply curious about the title, or maybe . . . your friend made you buy a copy. Whatever the reason, chances are that you are connected to our wonderful Toronto Jewish community in some way and that you will feel a connection with some of the hundreds of home cooks and chefs, and their recipes and personal words that are featured here. If you read on, you will learn much about the history of our community, the incredible diversity of its background and the culinary traditions and trends that we have embraced. Jewish food in Toronto today extends way beyond bagels, blintzes and brisket! Indeed, you may be surprised and amused at the extent of our culinary diversity as you find recipes for gefilte fish alongside tuna tartar and ceviche; liver and onions rubbing shoulders with vegan lentil loaf and smoked tofu dip. There are simple, quick dishes sharing space with sophisticated gourmet fare and healthy high fibre, low glycemic trendsetters next to proudly traditional and decadent throwbacks!

As diverse as they are, these recipes share a central feature that is the theme of this cookbook: they are "our community's favourite, go-to dishes". The tremendous diversity of our cooking styles, traditions and tastes is the essence, authenticity and charm of this wonderful community cookbook that is really "for cooking, not just for looking"; there is something here by and for everyone.

About the title . . . *The Bathurst Street Kitchen* was named in honour and recognition of that vibrant area of Jewish settlement in Toronto known as the Bathurst Street corridor. For over a century, beginning at Queens Quay and now extending north past Richmond Hill, Bathurst Street and its surrounding areas have been home to Jewish immigrants from all over the world and to many born here as well. Today, about 80% of Toronto Jews live within a mile of Bathurst Street and the corridor is lined with our community's restaurants, synagogues, schools, businesses and homes as well as 3 incredible community campuses. At its heart is 4600 Bathurst Street and the offices of UJA Federation of Greater Toronto and many of its agencies; all dedicated to serving our incredible community. Speaking of UJA, the cookbook project that became The Bathurst Street Kitchen was inspired by a recent past Chair of UJA Women's Philanthropy, Lori Rosenthal, who was searching for a meaningful, hands-on, broad-based community project that supports and funds the wonderful work that UJA and its agencies do in Toronto, Israel and worldwide. We hope you agree that *The Bathurst Street Kitchen* achieves these ambitious goals! To take advantage of all the extras that the cookbook offers, please see the section entitled "More Than Just a Cookbook; The Extras!"

We wish you "Be-te- avon", "Es Gezunterheyt" and "Bon-Appetit"!

Karine Krieger & Elisa Morton Palter
Chairs, Bathurst Street Kitchen Cookbook

a recipe for a strong community

UJA Women's Philanthropy
UJA Federation of Greater Toronto

You know the one about the Catskills restaurant . . . Four Jewish women have been dining for about an hour when their visibly shaken waiter hesitantly returns to their table and asks, "Ladies, is anything alright?!" Let's face it, when it comes to food, we as a people can be pretty demanding, which is why our wonderful volunteer cookbook committee reached out to all sectors of the Toronto Jewish community asking for your "Go-to Recipes", your absolute best, the ones you make when your new in-laws are coming for Shabbat dinner. And the committee got an overwhelming response! You have contributed favourite generations-old recipes that you or your families brought from different countries, as well as completely new favourites, using ingredients and techniques that our ancestors did not dream of. You could say "The Bathurst Street Kitchen" is co-authored by hundreds of members of the Toronto Jewish community.

We welcomed this outstanding initiative to support the efforts of UJA's Women's Philanthropy because, like our talented home chefs, UJA knows the importance of bringing together the ingredients needed to achieve a successful recipe, a recipe for a strong, vibrant and caring Jewish community. Almost a hundred years after UJA was founded, our community has learned that we can do more, make profound advances, raise millions of dollars, allocate in a strategic way and build community ONLY through a collective fund. And that is UJA! In cooking parlance, it's putting our community's resources into one pot while together, we all stir. Whether it's UJA's incredible ability to galvanize the community on behalf of Israel in mere minutes, or its capacity for seeing to the needs of our community's vulnerable seniors, UJA continues to transform lives daily in Toronto, Israel and across the globe.

I was going to include here my own mother, Shirley Jackson's (z"l) go-to recipe, Beige Weekly Dinner. I decided not to because, although my mom was a talented educator known for many things, culinary savvy was not one of them. Everything she made was beige! This cookbook is not a beige cookbook. It, like our community, reflects variety, and history and a melding of cultures (into something that is significantly greater than the sum of its parts.)

We thank all of our chairs, committee members and contributors who helped make this cookbook a legacy for the Toronto Jewish community.

Susan Jackson
Executive Director, Women's Philanthropy
UJA Federation

"more than just a cookbook"; the extras

The Bathurst Street Kitchen is truly more than just a cookbook. In addition to its wonderful recipes, you will find:

The History of Our Community: Trailing along the bottom of the cookbook's pages, you will find a whimsical footnote being carried by a horse and carriage, a streetcar or a vintage Bathurst street bus, depending on the era. This footnote tells the story of Jewish settlement in Toronto from the mid-1800s until today; ✿ indicates Toronto's Jewish population size. We hope that you will take a moment or two to read it and learn more about our community's interesting evolution; some of it may surprise you.

A UJA Agency Listing: At the end of the book you will find a resource section listing many of the agencies that UJA Federation funds, the services they provide and their contact information. We encourage you to browse through this list and see how UJA agencies might be able to support you, your family and friends. Look too for the "did you know" notes sprinkled throughout the book that provide more interesting facts about UJA and its agencies.

Best Borrowed Recipes: Towards the back of the cookbook, you will find the Best Borrowed Recipes section with favourite recipes that have been published by other chefs and which our community is recommending. Those whose favourite recipes were not their own creations had the opportunity to participate in the project by submitting recipes found in cookbooks or online. The Best Borrowed recipes provide you the opportunity to discover wonderful new recipes in cookbooks that you may already own or websites that you can easily access.

Vintage Photos: Also throughout the book are fabulous vintage photographs courtesy of The Ontario Jewish Archives and private collections, which document early and mid 20th century Toronto Jewish life. You can access these and many more photos directly by visiting the OJA website at: www.ontariojewisharchives.org.

recipe feedback

Throughout the book you will find reminders to go online to the UJA website where you can read and submit reviews and photos of the recipes you made from the cookbook; your input will enrich the cookbook and add value to its recipes and its use by the community. It will also help us rectify any mistakes that we may have made!

www.JewishToronto.com/BathurstStreetKitchen

Esther Fine with cow
at Smith family farm
(Cedar Valley, ON), ca. 1925

we couldn't have done it without you

Thank you so much *to all those who assisted in any way, from helping with the history, to editing, to reaching out to the community for recipes, to inputting stories, to assisting with design, social media and much more! There were never too many chefs in The Bathurst Street Kitchen; this project could not have succeeded without you all and especially to the Vice-Chairs Lissie and Naomi, whose incredible dedication, skill sets and humour were indispensable! Thank you to Susan Jackson and the whole UJA team for their invaluable support. And, thank you to Marcy Claman of Callawind Book Publishing for all of her assistance above and beyond the call of duty. We know that others, not mentioned here, will be involved after the printing of this book, and we thank them here in advance.*

The Kitchen Cabinet
Co-Chairs:
Karine Krieger
Elisa Palter

Vice-Chairs:
Naomi Oelbaum
Lissie Sanders

Sales & Marketing Chair:
Brenlee Gurvey Gales

Recipe Review Chairs:
Bonny Reichert
Carolyn Tanner-Cohen

Recipe Collection Chair:
Daniella Kuhl

Illustrator:
Kathryn Klar

Archivists:
Cyrel Troster
Brooky Robins

Committee Members
Julie Albert
Sharon Appleby Hussman
Marlene Bedzow-Weisleder
Cindy Berg
Sharon Bizouati
Sophie Berg
Danielle Bizouati-Abrams
Miriam Blumstock
Jennifer Brodlieb
Andrea Bronstein
Jessica Bronstein
Carainn Buchalter
Rona Cappell
Ellen Cole
Brenda Cooper
Michelle Factor
Robin Farb-Eckler
Susan Fremar
Allison Frilegh
Randi Garbas
Harriet Goodman
Debbie Gorman-Sadja
Sara Gottlieb
Liza Gutfrajnd
Leanne Hazon
Michele Henry
Alison Himel
Cayla Hochberg
Deborah Hoffnung
Susan Jackson
Marlene Jaegerman
Wendy Kay
Julie Keshen
Wendy Klein (Goldhar)

Sarena Koschitzky
Vivian Kuhl
Julie Levin
Ellen Levine
Leanne Matlow
Lisa Matthews
Lesley Matthews
Illana Morton
Karen Morton
Judy Naiberg
Daphna Rabinovitch
Robin Recht
Rochelle Reichert
Anita Robins
Edith Rosemberg
Lori Rosenthal
Brooke Sacks
Lesley Sas
Rhonda Sheff
Adell Shneer
Deborah Siegel
Shari Silverstein
Dara Solomon
Kathy Spiro
Vivian Souroujon
Judy Steiner
Linda Waks
Sheri Wang Kagan
Hildi Weiman
Lindsay Weiner
Nina Wine
Daphna Zacks
Paula Zivot

our home cooks, chefs & contributors

We gratefully acknowledge *the contributions of everyone who submitted a recipe to* The Bathurst Street Kitchen. *Some submitted their own recipes and some submitted recipes on behalf of others, some recipes were original and some "Best Borrowed", but all are equally valued and appreciated. The complete list of contributors can be found below. Hundreds of recipes, many more than we could use, came from across Toronto's Jewish community; from people whose family origin was Mexico, Peru, Russia, Iraq, Israel, the Caribbean, Czechoslovakia, Venezuela, India, South Africa, France, England, the Philippines, Romania, Poland, the US, Chile, Hungary, Morocco, Tunisia, Italy, Cuba and more! We greatly appreciate the time and effort it took to submit these wonderful go-to recipes and apologize that we did not have space to publish them all. We hope to make use of unused submissions in future newsletters, on our website www.jewishtoronto.com/ BathurstStreetKitchen and/or perhaps, in future editions. Thank you all!*

Shai Abraham	Andrea Bronstein	Ruby Ettedgui	Mollie Gold z"l
Serri Abraham	Rena Buckstein	Michelle Factor	Shari Goldberg
Jennifer Haccoun Abramson	Marnie Burke	Robin Farb-Eckler	Ida Goldfarb z"l
Marlowe Ain	Dianne Cadesky	Ashley Farnell	Karen Goldhar-White
Shirley Albright	Ingrid Camhi	Gail Fenwick	Sara Goldman
Shelley Allen	Eric Cappell	Tamara Fine	Bonnie Goldstein
Julie Albert	Max Cappell	Lois Friedman Fine	Tiffaney Klein Goodman
Kathy Alpert	Rona Cappell	Valerie Fish	Debbie Gorman-Sadja
Lillian Alvin z"l	Dafna Carr	Michelle Fishman	Marilyn Gotfrid
Rae Appleby	Judy Feld Carr	Phyllis Flatt	Aviva Gottlieb
Margie Arosh	Rochelle Chester	Lauren Fleischmann	Ruth Gottlieb
Marla Askenasi	Marcia Cilevitz	Madeleine Fleischmann	Renee Gozlan
Lillian Alvin	Eva Citrin	Michele Frankel	Peter Graben
Debbie Bank	Gloria Clamen	Adele Freeman	Diane Grafstein
Elly Barlin-Daniels	Andrea Cohen	Susan Fremar	Kathy Green
Lauren Barrett	Annette Cohen	Linda Friedlich	Helene Green
Allan Barsky	Hilda Cohen	Judith Gabor	Pearl Greenspan
Rebecca Barsky	Ellen Cole	Brenlee Gurvey Gales	Stephanie Greenwald
Paula Barsky	Karen Cole	Ilexa Gales	Elise Stern Gropper
Randi Bass	Brenda Cooper	Corrie Gancman	Bessie Grossman
Leah Bhastekar z"l	Lou Dale	Nancy Gangbar	Ellen Grossman
Cindy Berg	Elly Barlin-Daniels	Ruth Garbe	Phyllis Grossman
Eveline Berger	Larry Dankoff	Norene Gilletz	Miriam Grunwald
Sally Berman	Etty Danzig	Karen Gilman	Bunny Gurvey
Pearl Gropper Berman	Madelin Daviau	Kevin Gilmour	Liza Gutfrajnd
Elle Bienenfeld	Max Daviau	Bronna Ginsburg	Emma Haccoun
Sharon Bizouati	Susan Devins	Celia Gitter z"l	Elie Haccoun
Rudy Bloom	Suzanne Eiger	Shirley Gladstone z"l	Pam Handelsman
Melanie Bogoroch	Sylvia Eilath	Donna Glassman	Sandra Hausman
Karen Bookman	Anna Ekstein z"l	Barbra Gluck z"l	Leanne Hazon
Sara Bornstein	Ruth Ekstein	Lisa Gnat	Sandra Frydman de Helfant
Michelle Brandes	Yona Elishis	Judy Godfrey	Ruth Henry
Leigh Ann Brenman	Suzanna-Lee Engels	Sharon Goelman	Jane Herman
Janis Breslin	Bubby Esther	Pearl Lottman Godfrey	Marla Hertzman

Alison Himel
Lorraine and Aubie Himmel
Cayla Hochberg
Deborah Hoffnung
Shelley Hornstein
Elana Carr Horowitz
Goldie Howard z"l
Sharon Appleby Hussman
Luna Igelman
Rebecca Isenberg
Bunny Iskov
Susan Jackson
Eileen Jadd
Fritzi Jaegerman
Marlene Jaegerman
Barbara Jerome
Karen Jesin
Sheri Kagan
Ilsa Kamen
Estee Kafra
Rhoda Katz
Sheryl Katz
Joy D. Kaufman
Nora Kaufman
Wendy Kay
Julie Keshen
Rachel Keshen
Esther Kirshenblatt
Wendy Klein
Mazel Tov Kolatkar z"l
Natalie Kopman
Genevieve Korman
Helene Korn
Ann Wieskopf Kornbluth z"l
Sarena Koschitzky
Leelah Koschitzky
Julia Koschitzky
Ruby Kreindler
Rachel Krengel
Karine Krieger
Ahuva Krieger
Davida Kugelmass
Daniella Kuhl
Vivian Kuhl
Pamela Kuhl
Nathan Ladovsky
Raquel Landau
Madame Laracine
Judy Laxer
Melanie Levcovich
Julie Levin
Myrna Levin z"l
Eleanor Levine
Ellen Levine
Terri Levy
Etica Levy
Hilda Libman z"l
Loren Lieberman
Susan Lindzon
Toba Lipman z"l
Paul Litwack

Emma & Sam Lottman z"l
Cherie Lubelski
Frances Mandell-Arad
Leslie Marcus
Eran Marom
Gav Martell
David Matlow
Esther Matlow z"l
Nira Mayer
Mark McEwen
Karen Medina
Molly Melul
Leslie Mendelson
Naomi Mendelson
Seth Mersky
Theresa Mersky
Mark Milgram
Bess Miller z"l
Henza Miller
Rivi Miller
Judy Moncik
Beck Morton z"l
Illana Morton
Julie Morton
Karen Morton
Sinnora Moses
Rosy Moses
Ellen Moss
Esther Tivoli Mucher
Debbie Myers
Judy Naiberg
Sharon Naiberg
Lorraine Neumann
Hana Nidbach
Naomi Oelbaum
Ronnie Oelbaum
Carole Ogus
Michael Ogus
Penny Offman
Safta Ora
Tabala Oreck z"l
Fern Orzech
Laura Orzy
Shawna Page
Adam Palter
Dani Palter
Elisa Palter
Elsie Palter z"l
Esta Palter
Syd Palter
Ann Phillips
Annette Metz Pivnick
Nina Politzer
Blanche Posen
Sadie Praiser
Daphna Rabinovitch
Debbie Rabinovitch
Orit Raf
Derek Ratcliffe
Kathy Reen
Bonny Reichert

Rochelle Reichert
Toby Reichert
Rose Reisman
Hailey Remer
Nira Rittenberg
Anita Robins
Brooky Robins
Helaine Robins
Natalie Roebuck
Mireille Roffe
Bella Rolnick
Edith Rosemberg
Anthony Rose
Bertha Rosen
Ellen Rosenthal
Eva Rosenthal
Lori Rosenthal
Marilyn Rotenberg
Sherryn Roth
Michele Rotman
Patti Rotman
Erica 'Buni' Rubinger
Esther Sachs
Sheryl Salter
Johanna Samuel
Fern Sanders
Emily Sanders
Lissie Sanders
Vera Sanders
Galina Sandler
Galya Sarner
Lesley Sas
Randi Satok
Lorraine Schacht
Karla Schaus
Laurenn Schecter
Ellen Schneidman
AJ Schur
Marla Schwartz
Michael Schwartz
Roz Schweber
Shelley Sefton
Susan Segal
Carol Seidman
Aunt Selma
Marlene Shapiro z"l
Roni Shaw
Anita Shedletsky
Laurie Sheff
Goldie Sheftel z"l
Helaine Shiff
Arlene Shillinger
2014/2015 Shinshinim
Adell Shneer
Shari Silverstein
Hinda Silber
Myrna Hurwich Silver
Peggy Silver z"l
Sandi Silver
Sylvia Silverberg z"l
Susan Silverberg

Helen Silverstein
Shari Silverstein
Rebecca Simpson
Gail Skopit
Hadassa Slater
Marilyn Slatter
Fannie Slonim z"l
Shayne Snaiderman
Sonny Sneid
Heidi Solomon
Reeva Solomon
Fran Sonshine
Shirley Steinberg z"l
Judy Steiner
Joyce Strauss
Jacquie Strauss
Rose Strauss z"l
Perlita Stroh
Reesa Sud
Sharon Sussman
Ruthy Tanenbaum
Carolyn Tanner-Cohen
Sarah Taradash
Danielle Thérien
Sheryl Traber
Cyrel Troster
Judi Urowitz
Stephanie Valentine
Dianna Vaturri
Linda Waks
Kimberley Walters
Devra Wasser
Sylvia Wasserman
Marni Wasserman
Shiffy Wasserman z"l
Lynda Weinrib
Shari Wert
Risa Goldenberg Wexler
Lis Wigmore
Lauren Wilner
Shari Wilson
Carole Winberg
Lou Winer
Barb Wiseberg
Sandrine Wizman
Betty Young
Joy Young
Ellen Zabitsky
Daphna Zacks
Melanie Zeldman
Dolly Zieper z"l
Maureen Zieper
Kathy Zilbert
Jackie Zimmerman
Paula Zivot

We apologize for any omissions of z"l, or of any contributors.

MILK STORE
CREAM CHEESE
BUTTER & EGGS
FRESH DAILY

Trachter's Milk Store,
71 Kensington Avenue,
Toronto, May 1925

breakfast, brunch & breads

nut-free granola

Sandi Silver *My children have severe nut allergies and it was difficult to find a nut-free granola in the stores. I tried several recipes but ended up devising my own after a bunch of recipes didn't get great responses from my gang. This is delicious as a cereal with milk or as a topping over fresh fruit and Greek yogourt.*

6 cups rolled oats, not quick cook oats

1 cup whole wheat flour

½ cup buckwheat flour (if none on hand, use whole wheat again)

1 cup brown sugar, packed

¾ cup orange juice (add a couple of tablespoons more if mixture seems dry)

6 tablespoons ground flax seed

6 tablespoons pure maple syrup

6 tablespoons canola or grapeseed oil

3 teaspoons cinnamon

Preheat oven to 300°F. Line two baking sheets with parchment paper. In a large mixing bowl, combine oats, flours, sugar, orange juice, flax, maple syrup, oil and cinnamon. Spread out mixture onto baking sheet and bake for about 25 minutes. Using ovenproof spatula, chop and toss baking mixture every few minutes to prevent burning. Remove from oven when desired consistency is reached. Some people like it crunchier than others. Let cool on sheets and then store in an airtight container.

TIPS & ADVICE: If you like dried fruit, you can add any kind to the mixture before it cools. Granola keeps in an airtight container for about 2 weeks.

NUMBER OF SERVINGS: 15–20

did you know?
Over 65,000 GTA students, educators and community members visit the Sarah and Chaim Neuberger Holocaust Education Centre every year.

golden granola

Marni Wasserman *I always loved granola growing up and ate it out of a box. As I became more knowledgeable about the ingredients harboured in those boxes, I knew that I needed to make my own version. Now, I always have it on hand for breakfast and snacking. It also makes a great gift, packed into glass jars during the holidays! Everyone loves it—I have tested it on kids, family and friends and granola seems to be a favourite all around!*

¾ cup maple syrup

¼ cup coconut oil

1 tablespoon rice milk

4 cups rolled oats

1½ cups oat bran

1 cup coconut flakes

1 cup chopped almonds

¾ cup sesame seeds

½ cup sunflower seeds

1 teaspoon sea salt

1½ cups raisins, dried cranberries or dried apricots, unsulphured

Preheat oven to 300°F. In a large saucepan over medium-high heat using wooden spoon, stir together syrup, coconut oil and rice milk until well combined. Set aside.

In a large bowl, using clean wooden spoon, mix oats, oat bran, coconut, almonds, sesame seeds, sunflower seeds and salt. Toss well. Add the oil/maple syrup mixture to the dry ingredients and stir together really well.

Pour granola mixture into 2 shallow baking pans or baking sheets lined with parchment. Bake 15 minutes, stir and bake an additional 10 minutes until light golden brown. Remove granola from oven and stir in dried fruit. Once cooled, store in glass, airtight containers. Serve in ½ cup portions with rice milk, almond milk or coconut yogourt or eat as a snack, like trail mix.

TIPS & ADVICE: Store bought granola is loaded with refined sugars, flour and poor quality oils. It also lacks flavour and that personal touch. You can make it yourself easily and feel good about eating it. You can make it nut free and school-safe by adding other seeds instead of almonds.

NUMBER OF SERVINGS: 12+

as the 1760s but only made Toronto a permanent home in the 1830s. Most of the →

baba sarah's buttermilk pancakes

Rochelle Reichert *Sarah Taradash was just "Baba" to us, but everyone at work called her "Mrs T." She was an immigrant from Russia, a mother, and a widow from a young age who needed to make a living. She put her talents as a superb cook and baker to good use by working for my dad, Saul Reichert, at his Edmonton restaurant. It was only later that my dad met Sarah's daughter, Toby, whom he married (and is my mom.) Baba was adored by her grandchildren and nothing gave her more pleasure than cooking for us. We loved everything she made, savoury and sweet, but one of our favourites was her buttermilk pancakes. She made them at home and they were on the restaurant menu, too. These have become a staple at my family's Sunday brunches, whether in the city or the cottage. We love them with honey butter.*

2⅔ cups all-purpose flour

3 tablespoons sugar

2 teaspoons baking powder

¾ teaspoon baking soda

½ teaspoon salt

2⅔ cups buttermilk

3 large eggs

3 tablespoons butter, melted

butter for frying

blueberries, sliced bananas, chocolate chips, optional

Honey butter:

Mix equal parts creamed honey and soft butter.

In a large bowl, mix together flour, sugar, baking powder, baking soda and salt. In another bowl using wire whisk, whisk together buttermilk, eggs and melted butter. Pour wet ingredients into dry ingredients and, using wooden spoon, combine until just mixed.

In a large, non-stick frying pan or griddle over medium high heat, melt a small chunk of butter, being careful not to let the butter burn. Drop spoonfuls of batter onto pan, leaving ample room to flip the cakes. Place toppings, such as fruit and chocolate chips, on uncooked side, if desired. Flip pancakes when you can see a few bubbles on top and underside is golden brown. Continue cooking on the second side. Add more butter to the pan each time you cook more pancakes. Serve with sour cream, honey butter, maple syrup or plain.

TIPS & ADVICE: Pancakes can be kept warm in a 300°F oven but they're best straight from the frying pan. Leftovers can be refrigerated and reheated in the microwave; they'll lose some of their fluffiness but none of their deliciousness.

YIELD: 6-7 pancakes

earliest settlers were British or German merchant families, and came from established Jewish →

serri's scrumptious phoot

Shai Abraham *Phoot is a specialty of my great-grandmother, Mazel Tov Kolatka, who passed it down to my mom, Serri Abraham, who lovingly makes it for our family each Passover. We all look forward to this special annual treat served at breakfast or as a dessert. Growing up in Mumbai, India, and then later in Be'er Sheva, Israel, as Bene Israel (Jews of India), we enjoyed a broader variety of 'kosher' for Passover foods than our Ashkenazi and even our Sephardic friends. Living in Toronto, I miss my mother's Phoot but am reminded of it when I make our traditional Bene Israel Charoset, which simply involves mixing together the last three ingredients of the recipe. The rest of the family is still enjoying Phoot back in Israel. Phoot is Kosher L'Pesah for Edot HaMizrah (East Asian Jews).*

2 cups water

2 cups rice flour

2 cups dates, chopped

2 cups nuts, chopped (your choice of nuts)

3 cups coconut, shredded (preferably sweetened)

In a medium-sized pot, heat water until hot but not boiling. Remove pot from stove and stir in rice flour. When a dough forms, place on flat surface and knead until the dough is fairly smooth. Divide into three equal balls. Using a rolling pin, roll out one ball of dough at a time into a circle approximately one centimetre thick (the dough may not be quite even or smooth due to the nature of the rice flour).

In a clean, medium-sized bowl, combine dates and nuts. Place one piece of flattened dough into a steamer basket. Arrange one third of the date-nut mixture on top, then sprinkle over it a layer of shredded coconut. Place second circle of dough overtop and repeat layering with date-nut mixture and shredded coconut. Do the same with the third layer, ending with shredded coconut on top.

In a pot with tight fitting lid, place steamer basket over water. Steam the dough (phoot) for about 15–20 minutes, until the dough looks shiny and moist. Serve immediately while still fresh and warm.

NUMBER OF SERVINGS: 8

matzah laddoo

Shai Abraham: *Matzah Laddoo is the other traditional Passover dish that my mom lovingly makes for us and which brings back great memories of growing up.*

½ cup margarine

1¾ cups matzah meal

½ cup chopped walnuts (or other nuts of your choice)

½ cup sugar (or to taste)

¼ cup raisins

In a medium-sized pot over medium heat, melt the margarine. Add matzah meal and nuts and, using wooden spoon, stir well. In another frying pan over medium-high heat, melt sugar until it forms a syrup. Pour sugar syrup into nut mixture and, with wooden spoon, mix well. When cool, form into balls with your hands.

TIPS & ADVICE: Serve at breakfast or as a dessert.

NUMBER OF SERVINGS: 12–15

'pancake house' apple oven pancake

Elisa Palter *Everyone from Winnipeg knows of the Pancake House, one of the best all-day breakfast places in town. They are famous for their puffy, delicious apple pancakes and this is a take on that recipe.*

2 tablespoons butter; and more for greasing pan

3 apples peeled, cored and cut into wedges

3 tablespoons brown sugar

¼ teaspoon cinnamon

4 large eggs

1 cup milk

1 cup all-purpose flour

1 teaspoon sugar

pinch salt

Preheat oven to 425°F. In an oven-proof skillet over medium-high heat, melt butter. Add apples, brown sugar and cinnamon. Cook until apples are tender. Set aside. In large bowl using electric mixer, beat together eggs and milk. Add flour, sugar and salt. Beat until smooth. Pour batter into butter-greased baking dish. Spoon apples overtop. Bake at 425°F for 20–30 minutes, until puffy. Serve hot, with syrup.

YIELD: 4 pancakes

(that do not include wives, children and those who didn't state their religion) show that in 1846 →

buttermilk waffles

Adell Shneer *I searched and searched for a good waffle recipe, testing a bunch of them. This one was adapted from an old Gourmet magazine recipe. It is my go-to recipe. I have taken this "on the road" when invited to a cottage by assembling the dry ingredients in a ziptop bag, and bringing the other ingredients and my waffle iron. It makes an easy, fast and welcome addition to a weekend menu.*

1 cup all-purpose flour

2 tablespoons sugar

1 teaspoon baking powder

¼ teaspoon baking soda

¼ teaspoon salt

1 cup buttermilk, well shaken

1 large egg

¼ cup unsalted butter, melted

In a large bowl, whisk together flour, sugar, baking powder, baking soda and salt. In a separate large bowl using clean whisk, whisk together buttermilk, egg and melted butter. Using wooden spoon, stir wet ingredients into dry ingredients until just combined and no flour appears.

Cook waffles one at a time in heated waffle iron, according to manufacturer's instructions, about 2 minutes per waffle. Serve immediately with your choice of fresh fruit, such as blueberries, sliced strawberries, or bananas and sprinkle with icing sugar or drizzle with maple syrup.

TIPS & ADVICE: You can stir chopped nuts, fresh blueberries, diced bananas or chocolate chips into the batter before cooking in waffle iron. You need about ½ cup fruit or chips per recipe. To freeze, first cool waffles on a rack. Before placing waffles into ziptop bags, place parchment paper between individual waffles so they don't stick together when frozen. To serve, remove from freezer and toast or bake at 350°F until hot.

YIELD: 3 Belgian waffles

'united bakers' dairy restaurant blintzes

Nathan Ladovsky *When our grandparents first opened their restaurant, their goal was to produce the same traditional dairy dishes whose wondrous flavours they remembered from family kitchens 'back home.' This blintz recipe, passed down from our Bubbie Sarah and followed in our kitchen to this day, is a tribute to the success of their idea.*

Crepe batter:

5 large eggs

1 tablespoon vegetable oil

1 cup milk (preferably whole)

¾ cup all-purpose flour

unsalted butter, for frying

Filling:

1½ pounds (680g) cottage cheese (preferably pressed dry cottage cheese and/or 4% milk fat)

4 large egg yolks

½ cup sugar

To serve:

butter for frying

To make the crepes: In a large bowl using electric mixer, beat eggs and oil until fluffy. Add milk. Beat until evenly blended. Gradually add flour, beating out all lumps. Strain crepe mixture through a fine sieve set over a bowl. Cover and refrigerate for up to one day (if made in advance).

Heat a lightly buttered 7" crepe pan or a non-stick frying pan over medium-high heat until almost smoking. Lift pan from heat and pour ¼ cup batter quickly into centre. Immediately, tilt pan in all directions to make thin film of batter over entire bottom of pan. Pour excess batter back into bowl. Return pan to burner and cook crepe until edges brown and lift away from pan, about 45–60 seconds. Turn out crepe onto a clean tea towel.

To make filling: In a medium-sized mixing bowl, break up cottage cheese by hand or by beating with a rubber spatula. Add egg yolks and sugar. Mix until blended. Cover and refrigerate for up to one day.

Rolling: Divide filling among crepes, forming filling into a log shape in the centre of each (about ¼ cup of filling in each). Working with one crepe at a time, fold the bottom of crepe over filling, then fold in sides. Roll from the bottom up to form neat cylinders. Blintzes can be covered and refrigerated for several hours or up to one night.

To serve: In a large frying pan over medium-high heat, melt butter and fry blintzes in batches (about 3 minutes per side). Serve with cinnamon-spiced applesauce or sour cream.

YIELD: 10 blintzes

gluten-free orange cheese blintzes

Davida Kugelmass *Blintzes will forever remind me of my Bubby. In addition to enough bagels and lox to feed a small village, my Bubby always had blintzes in the house. The blintzes were usually potato-based but then my life was changed forever when I tried the cheese blintzes at Katz's Deli in New York. It was like a Bar Mitzvah in my mouth! Here is my own (gluten-free) twist on a classic cheese blintz recipe.*

Crepes:

1 cup brown rice flour

1 cup water

1 cup unsweetened almond milk

4 large eggs

1 tablespoon plus 2 teaspoons coconut oil

Filling:

2 cups 0% fat cottage cheese

juice of ½ an orange

1 tablespoon brown sugar or coconut palm sugar

1 teaspoon orange zest

1 teaspoon vanilla extract

To serve:

coconut oil spray

orange slices, powdered sugar and maple syrup for topping

For crepes: Preheat oven to 375°F. In a large bowl, combine brown rice flour, water, almond milk and eggs. Whisk until well combined and all clumps are gone. In a large frying pan (or crepe pan), melt coconut oil over medium-high heat.

Add ½ cup of batter to pan and, using a tablespoon, spread the batter into a circle (like a crepe). Cook for about one minute. Using spatula, flip to the other side and cook for 20 seconds. If batter starts to brown, the pan is too hot, so decrease heat. Slide cooked crepe onto plate lined with paper towel. Repeat until all batter has been used. This should make the wrapping for about 10 blintzes.

For filling: In a large mixing bowl using wooden spoon, mix together cottage cheese, juice, brown/palm sugar, orange zest and vanilla. Divide filling evenly between the crepes (about 2 tablespoons each). Working with one crepe at a time, fold crepe over filling like an envelope, by first folding in left and right sides and then folding over the top and bottom.

To serve: Using coconut oil spray, coat a 9 x 11" baking dish. Place blintzes seal-side down in dish and bake in preheated 375°F oven for 10 minutes. Top with sliced oranges, powdered sugar and maple syrup.

TIPS & ADVICE: Feel free to use regular all-purpose flour instead of brown rice flour if gluten is not a problem!

YIELD: 5 blintzes

baked french toast

Marnie Burke *This is a great recipe. It is loved by anyone who enjoys French toast, especially because the prep work is done the day before. My friend, Judy Moncik, gave me this recipe and it has become a staple when I make brunch in my home.*

1 cup brown sugar

½ cup unsalted butter

2 tablespoons maple syrup

1 loaf challah, sliced

6 large eggs

1½ cups milk

1 teaspoon vanilla extract

In a large saucepan over medium-high heat, stir together sugar, butter and maple syrup and bring to a boil. Pour sauce into a greased 9 x 12" baking dish.

Once sauce is cool, arrange challah slices over top. Cover with second layer of challah slices.

In a large bowl using wire whisk, mix together eggs, milk and vanilla and pour over challah.

Cover challah mixture with plastic wrap and chill overnight in refrigerator.

When ready to serve, remove plastic wrap and bake in preheated 350°F for 40 minutes until browned on top. Cut and flip over to serve.

TIPS & ADVICE: Crust can be removed from the challah slices. Banana slices or berries can be added and sprinkled between challah slices.

Another way to make the same dish is to combine the same egg mixture and torn or cubed challah slices in a bowl and then place in greased pyrex and put sugar/syrup mixture on top. Leave overnight as before and bake as indicated. The casserole made this way can be served in the dish, instead of flipping it over to cut.

NUMBER OF SERVINGS: 8–10

cheese pie

Karen Morton *This is a recipe that we made in Winnipeg and we brought it with us when we moved to Toronto. It is always a hit and is usually served at our Yom Kippur Break Fast or any other time I need a great dairy meal or side dish.*

Crust:

2½ cups all-purpose flour

1½ cups milk

1 cup margarine; more for greasing pyrex

½ cup sugar

4 large eggs

2 teaspoons baking powder

¼ teaspoon salt

margarine to dot top with

Filling:

1 (500 g) container cottage cheese (squeeze out most of liquid and just use curds)

1 package LANA dry cottage cheese

6 tablespoons all-purpose flour

4 tablespoons margarine

4 large eggs

4 teaspoons sugar

Preheat oven to 350°F. To make crust: In a large bowl using electric mixer, beat together flour, milk, margarine, sugar, eggs, baking powder and salt until smooth. Set aside.

Filling: In a separate large bowl using wooden spoon, stir together cottage cheeses, flour, margarine, eggs and sugar.

Assembly: Place ½ of crust recipe in 9 x 12" pyrex greased with margarine. Spoon filling on top. Cover with remaining crust. Dot top with margarine. Bake in preheated 350°F oven for 30 minutes.

TIPS & ADVICE: Serve hot. Cut into squares and serve with sour cream or yogourt and berries, if desired.

NUMBER OF SERVINGS: 12–15

visit our website
www.JewishToronto.com/BathurstStreetKitchen

lox and bagel cheese strata

Norene Gilletz *This recipe is dedicated to the memory of my dear friend, Shirley Jackson, mother of Susan Jackson, Executive Director of Women's Philanthropy at UJA Federation of Greater Toronto. Shirley Jackson was a shining star in life and had a starring role in a play called "Golda's Lox and the Three Bagels." It was a community service project of Mount Sinai Chapter, B'nai B'rith Women of Montreal (now renamed ACT to End Violence Against Women). At our last visit, shortly before she passed away, Shirley and I reminisced about our youth, and then sang this silly, funny song from our play, to the tune of "Sunrise, Sunset" from Fiddler on the Roof: "Where is that bagel that I yearn for, where is that bagel I want hot . . ." I will always hold this truly special memory close to my heart and will think about Shirley when I eat bagels and lox. This do-ahead brunch dish is perfect fare for any special occasion. It's "dill-icious!" (Adapted from Norene's Healthy Kitchen by Whitecap)*

cooking spray

5–6 whole-wheat or sesame bagels, cut in bite-sized pieces (about 8 cups)

8 ounces (250 g) lox (smoked salmon), cut in bite-sized pieces

8 ounces low-fat Swiss and/or havarti cheese (about 2 cups grated)

2 green onions, chopped

2–3 tablespoons fresh dillweed, minced

6 large eggs (or 4 eggs plus 4 egg whites)

2 cups milk (skim or 1%)

1 cup light sour cream or plain yogourt

½ teaspoon salt (optional)

¼ teaspoon freshly ground black pepper

Spray a 9 x 13" baking dish with cooking spray. Spread the bagel pieces evenly in the dish. Top with lox and sprinkle with the grated cheese, green onions, and dillweed. In a medium-sized mixing bowl, combine the eggs, milk, sour cream, salt and pepper; blend well. Pour evenly over the bagel-cheese mixture. Cover and refrigerate for at least 1 hour. (If desired, you can prepare the recipe up to this point and refrigerate for 24 hours).

Preheat the oven to 350°F. Bake uncovered, for about 1 hour or until the mixture is puffed and golden. Remove from the oven and let it stand for 10 minutes for easier cutting. Keeps for 2–3 days in the refrigerator; reheats well.

VARIATIONS: Use sun-dried tomato, spinach, multi-grain, or all-dressed bagels, or use whole wheat or multigrain bread, cut in 1" pieces. Instead of lox, use 2 cans (7½ ounce/213 g each) of sockeye salmon or tuna, drained and flaked. You could also use 1½ cups of leftover cooked salmon. Try Monterey Jack, cheddar, Jarlsberg, or a mixture, or add ½ cup crumbled feta or goat cheese.

NUMBER OF SERVINGS: 12

Toronto Hebrew Congregation established in 1856 and renamed Holy Blossom Synagogue

→

gramma muffins

Karen Morton *These muffins are always in my fridge—my grandchildren always know they are there—that's how they came to be known as Gramma Muffins.*

2 cups All-Bran cereal

1 cup hot water

4 cups baking bran

2 cups brown sugar, packed

1½ cups canola oil

1 litre buttermilk (use low fat)

¾ cup sugar

4 large eggs

4 cups all-purpose flour

5 teaspoons baking soda

1 teaspoon salt

3 cups dried fruits (raisins, dates)

non-stick cooking spray for muffin pan

Preheat oven to 350°F. In medium-sized mixing bowl, combine All-Bran cereal and hot water. Set aside.

In another medium-sized mixing bowl using a wooden spoon, combine baking bran, brown sugar, oil, buttermilk, sugar and eggs and mix well.

Stir together baking bran mixure, baking soda, salt, All-Bran mixture and dried fruit. Pour batter into greased muffin tins, filling each tin about ¾ full. Bake in preheated 350°F oven for 20–30 minutes. Baked muffins freeze well. Unbaked batter can be refrigerated and baked later.

YIELD: 12 muffins

did you know?
Approximately 150 small business, education, or startup loans were distributed last year by Jewish Free Loan Toronto

in 1871. The congregation, then Orthodox, held its first service in a room over →

healthy energy muffins

Karen Goldhar-White *These muffins are tasty, filling and filled with great ingredients.*

1½ cups oat bran

3 x 30 g scoops vanilla protein powder

⅓ cup mini semi sweet chocolate chips

¼ cup stevia baking formula

1 teaspoon baking soda

1 teaspoon cinnamon

¼ teaspoon sea salt

1 cup unsweetened applesauce

4 large egg whites

1 teaspoon vanilla extract

non-stick cooking spray

Preheat oven to 350°F. In a large mixing bowl using wooden spoon, combine oat bran, vanilla protein powder, chocolate chips, stevia, baking soda, cinnamon and salt. In another mixing bowl using clean spoon, combine applesauce, egg whites and vanilla. Pour wet mixture into dry mixture and stir with a fork until the batter is well blended. Spray muffin pan with non-stick spray and scoop batter in. Bake 15–16 minutes at 350°F.

TIPS & ADVICE: I use a whey-based protein powder but any protein powder should work as well. The muffins freeze well and are most delicious if you toast them for a few minutes before eating.

YIELD: 10 muffins

butter horns

Bunny Gurvey *On our 60th wedding anniversary, my children presented my husband Gerry and me with a cookbook of our family's favourite recipes called "Beyond Butter Horns." This recipe holds a special place in our hearts and stomachs! The greatest joy is watching our grandchildren and little great granddaughter Sienna gobble them up.*

1 package traditional yeast (8 g)

3¼ cups all-purpose flour

3 tablespoons sugar

1 teaspoon salt

½ pound butter

2 large eggs

¼ cup milk

½ cup sugar mixed with 4 teaspoons cinnamon

Dissolve yeast as per package instructions. In a large mixing bowl, sift together flour, sugar and salt. Cut butter into dry ingredients. Using wooden spoon, stir in eggs and milk, and then yeast mixture.

Cover and let dough rise on countertop for about 1 hour, then divide it into 4 parts. Sprinkle a board with ¼ of the cinnamon-sugar mixture. Roll out 1 part of dough into a circle. Cut into 12 wedges. Roll each wedge from the wide end to the pointy end. Place on a parchment lined baking pan. Repeat 3 more times. Cover and let rise. Bake in preheated 350°F oven for 20 minutes or until lightly browned.

YIELD: 4 dozen

Coombe's drug store at Yonge and Richmond with a borrowed Torah scroll and 100 people in →

south african cape whole wheat bread

Melanie Bogoroch *I grew up in South Africa and my mom, Maureen Zieper, always made this homemade bread so it was very much a part of my childhood. When I became a mom, I started baking this for my children and hope to pass this recipe along to many future generations in my family. When I smell the bread baking in my home, it makes me think of my wonderful childhood back in South Africa and of all the times I baked this bread with my mom. This is a quick and easy recipe that uses ingredients that most of us would have at home. The bread is really delicious and has a beautiful crispy top once baked. It is nice to have a homemade, healthy bread that is free of all preservatives.*

2½ cups whole wheat flour

2 cups plain yogourt

1 cup oats

1 tablespoon honey or sugar

1 tablespoon oil

2 teaspoons salt

2 teaspoons baking soda

cooking spray for greasing pan

handful raw sunflower seeds, optional

Preheat oven to 375°F. In a large mixing bowl using wooden spoon, mix together flour, yogourt, oats, honey, oil, salt and baking soda.

Line a large loaf pan with tin foil or parchment. Spray with non-stick cooking spray or grease lightly with oil. Place dough into loaf pan. Sprinkle raw sunflower seeds on top. Place into a preheated 375°F oven on the middle rack and bake for about 1 hour.

Turn out onto a cooling rack and remove foil from the bread if it sticks. Leave the bread to cool completely before slicing.

TIPS & ADVICE: An option for this bread is to use ½ cup of oats instead of a full cup and make up a ½ cup mixture of flax seeds, wheat germ, bran, raw sunflower seeds and sesame seeds. Raw sunflower seeds, once baked, turn a slight green colour but the taste is the same. This bread bakes into a dense delicious loaf. Once cooled, slice thinly and wrap in foil to keep fresh out on the counter. Don't store in the refrigerator. It freezes well and then I always have slices available.

YIELD: one large loaf

baba's porridge bread

Bonny Reichert *During the dark and strangely beautiful winters of my Edmonton childhood, when my parents went on vacation, Baba Sarah would come to take care of us. It seemed like she never slept—when we'd get up in the morning, there were always these incredible smells. Some were pretty and some were really quite pungent, and we could quickly tell whether she was making cookies or liver or, once or twice, shockingly, cow lung in a huge pot on the stove. Our hands-down favourite was this porridge bread—a dark sweet loaf made with oatmeal and molasses. My sisters and I would get out of bed and swoon from the smell, running down to the kitchen in our nightgowns where Baba would cut us thick steamy slices, heavy with melting butter.*

2 cups boiling water

1 cup old fashioned (large flake) rolled oats

½ cup molasses

1 tablespoon + 1 teaspoon butter

2 teaspoons salt

1 large egg, beaten

1 teaspoon sugar

½ cup warm water

1 package (1 tablespoon) yeast

1 cup whole wheat or graham flour

3½–4 cups all-purpose flour

butter for greasing

In a large bowl, pour boiling water over oatmeal and let stand 1 hour. When water has been absorbed, mix in molasses, butter, salt and beaten egg.

In a separate bowl, dissolve sugar in warm water. Sprinkle yeast over top and let stand, covered, until yeast is foamy, about 10 minutes. Add yeast mixture to oatmeal base. Gradually add flour, continuing to add until dough is smooth and elastic, kneading as you go.

Grease a large bowl with butter and turn dough around in bowl so it is greased on all sides. Cover with greased plastic wrap and set aside in a warm place for approximately 3 hours or until dough has doubled in bulk. Turn dough out of bowl and divide into two equal pieces. Shape into loaves and place into buttered loaf pans. Allow to rise again for ½ hour. Bake at 375°F for 50–55 minutes. Test for doneness by turning bread out onto wire rack and gently tapping the bottom. Bread will sound hollow when it's done. Cool, then slice thickly and serve with butter and jam.

TIPS & ADVICE: This bread is heavenly but it doesn't stay fresh long, so enjoy it the day it's made and freeze leftovers, if you have them.

YIELD: 2 small loaves

challah

Shari Goldberg *I found this recipe in my son's nursery school recipe book many years ago. I have been making it for almost 10 years. It is so easy and delicious! The recipe yields two challahs. We usually stand around the kitchen on Friday afternoons and eat some warm challah after it has come out of the oven. We serve the uneaten one (which is usually still warm) at Shabbat dinner. The remainder of the challah is eaten over the course of the weekend!*

8 cups all-purpose flour, divided

2¼ cups warm water, divided

½ cup sugar

2¼ teaspoons quick rise yeast

3 large eggs, beaten

½ cup oil

1 teaspoon salt

Egg wash:

1 egg beaten

1 teaspoon salt

1 tablespoon water

sesame or poppy seeds for topping

In large mixing bowl using electric mixer with paddle attachment, combine 3 cups flour, 1¼ cups water, sugar and yeast. Once mixed together, add eggs, oil, salt, 4 cups flour, and 1 cup warm water. Mix well. Gradually add last cup of flour and mix until smooth and not sticking to the sides of the bowl.

Roll out dough onto a floured surface and knead until smooth and not sticking to hands.

Separate dough into two balls and place each ball into its own greased bowl. Cover with a damp towel and let rise for 1½–2 hours. Separate each ball into 3 or 4 strands and braid. Place each loaf onto a cookie sheet lined with parchment paper. Cover and let rise for another 30 minutes. Preheat oven to 350°F. Make egg wash by mixing together egg, salt and water. Use pastry brush to paint egg wash on challahs. Be generous. Sprinkle with seeds. Bake for 30 minutes until golden brown at 350°F. Remove from oven and place loaves on wire baking rack to cool.

TIPS & ADVICE: Recipe can be made with whole wheat flour but it will be very dense. Let rise for longer (3–4 hours) before braiding for fluffy challahs. I add more yeast to make really lovely, large challahs. Can add raisins and cinnamon sugar when rolling out strands for sweet challah for Rosh Hashanah and can be braided round as well.

YIELD: 2 challahs

had trouble finding and keeping good ministers and did not have an 'ordained' minister until →

multigrain challah

Daniella Kuhl *My sister, Rachel, has a challah baking business in my hometown of Miami Beach. She delivers 400 challahs on a weekly basis to the Jewish day schools throughout South Florida. She was my inspiration! I will also tell you that this recipe only works with Toronto water! I've tried baking this challah in the exact same way with the exact same hands and techniques in both Miami and New York with no success!*

4 packets quick rising active yeast

4 cups warm water

1 tablespoon sugar

14 cups Robin Hood multigrain bread flour

1¾ cups sugar

1½ tablespoons sea salt

3 eggs

1½ cups canola oil

Place first 3 ingredients into bowl and leave on top of open oven door with oven set to 350°F until mixture starts to bubble. If there is no bubbling, then yeast is not good and you need to start over. In large bowl, mix flour, sugar, and salt together by hand and make a well in the middle. Add 2 eggs, oil and yeast mixture into well. Knead by hand (or use mixer with dough hook) until dough comes away from bowl easily. Cover bowl with plastic wrap and a dish towel and let rise for 2 hours.

After 2 hours, preheat oven to 350°F. Separate dough into 3 balls. Separate each ball in 3 strands (ropes) and braid. Place each braided challah on a parchment lined cookie sheet and let rise uncovered for 30 minutes. You can also take the 3 balls of dough and place them in separate greased loaf pans if you don't wish to braid them.

Mix one egg and brush tops of challahs before baking in oven at 350°F for 25-30 minutes depending on oven. Challahs should be golden brown once baked.

TIPS & ADVICE: Feel free to add anything you like as a topping. I use a medley of poppy seeds, a mix of white and black sesame seeds, sunflower seeds and flax seeds, which I generously scatter on top of egg wash before baking.

YIELD: 3 large challahs

1890. In 1876, Holy Blossom built a permanent synagogue accommodating 400

gold medal challah

Andrea Bronstein *This bread is worth the effort!*

Challah:

1 teaspoon sugar

½ cup warm water

1 package yeast

3¾–4 cups flour (start with 3¾ cups and add the remaining ¼ cup only if necessary)

¼ cup sugar

2 teaspoons salt

½ cup oil

½ cup water

2 large eggs

¾ cup raisins, optional

1 large egg yolk beaten with 1 teaspoon water

Poppy seeds, sesame seeds, sea salt or streusel topping (streusel recipe to follow), optional

Streusel topping (optional):

2 tablespoons flour

1 tablespoon oil

2 tablespoons icing sugar

Rinse measuring cup with hot water, then dissolve sugar in ½ cup warm water in cup. Sprinkle yeast into sugar-water mixture and let stand for 8-10 minutes. Stir to dissolve. Using electric mixer with dough hook, combine 3¾ cups flour, sugar and salt in bowl. Pour dissolved yeast mixture over flour mixture and mix.

While mixer is running, add oil, water and eggs and continue blending until dough gathers and forms a mass. If using raisins, add them now.

Let mixer knead dough for 3–4 minutes, then turn dough out onto floured surface and knead with hands until the dough is smooth and elastic, using flour to prevent dough from sticking. Place rounded dough in a large oiled bowl. Cover it with a clean tea towel and let the dough rise in a warm place until it doubles (1½–2 hours). Once it rises, punch it down, then allow it to rise again until doubled (45–60 minutes). Punch it down and let the dough rest for 10 minutes.

Shape dough as desired. For a round braided challah, roll dough into 1 long rope, flatten to remove air bubbles, then roll again into a rope and coil up like a snail, starting with the centre and working outwards. Place dough on a parchment lined baking sheet. Cover with a tea towel and let it rise until doubled in size (45 minutes). Combine streusel topping ingredients if using. Brush challah with egg yolk/water and sprinkle with streusel or other topping. Bake at 350°F for 30 minutes in the lower third of oven, until golden brown and challah sounds hollow when tapped.

YIELD: 1 challah

people on Richmond St East, financed mainly by local Christians and American Jews. — — — — — — — — — — — →

chocolate challah

Vivian Kuhl *This chocolate challah is a staple at the Shabbat table on Briar Hill. Everyone who tastes this challah says how delicious it is and how it would be perfect with coffee for breakfast. It's magical when the leftovers are used for French toast. However, don't expect to have any left over!*

1½ packets active dry yeast

2 cups warm water, divided

½ cup sugar plus a pinch

7 cups all-purpose flour, divided

½ cup canola oil

1 tablespoon salt

2 large eggs

1 cup chocolate chips

additional oil for oiling dough

1 egg for egg wash

Dissolve yeast in 1 cup warm water with a pinch of sugar until foamy. Add 3 cups flour, mix and then add remaining 4 cups of flour and all other ingredients except for one egg to be used for the egg wash before baking. Knead mixture for 10 minutes, then rub oil onto the dough and grease a bowl as well. Put dough into bowl and cover with plastic wrap. Let it rise to double for approximately 2 hours. Preheat oven to 350°F. Divide dough into 6 equal logs and use 3 pieces to braid each loaf. Brush with egg and bake for 15–20 minutes.

TIPS & ADVICE: This challah freezes beautifully.

YIELD: 2 challahs

cornmeal bread ("mealie bread" in South Africa)

Marcia Cilevitz *This easy, delicious recipe is about 40 years old. My father-in-law was a cornmeal miller and cornmeal is the staple food of Africans. As this comes out of the microwave, the aroma is amazing. The pots of jam come out, as does a good cup of tea served in a china cup and saucer, with matching cake plate and cake fork, teapot, milk jug and sugar bowl.*

1 cup all-purpose flour

1 cup cornmeal

1 can creamed sweet corn

¾ cup 1% milk

2 large eggs

5 teaspoons sugar

3 teaspoons baking powder

½ teaspoon salt

butter for greasing

In a large mixing bowl using wooden spoon, stir together all ingredients. Pour mixture into a well-greased glass or microwaveable container or ring mould. Microwave on high for 9 minutes. Allow to stand a few minutes.

TIPS & ADVICE: Enjoy this with a bit of margarine or butter or delicious jam . . . as a breakfast, or for brunch. You can also make them into muffins. They freeze well.

YIELD: 1 loaf or 10–12 muffins

Members had the benefits of burial ground admission, ministerial services and a →

english kuchen

Judy Feld Carr *This kuchen is my husband, Donald Carr's, grandmother's recipe. When he grew up in Leeds, England, his mother made this loaf to break the fast on Yom Kippur. It was given to me by my late sister-in-law in Leeds. It can be made any time of the year and can be eaten with ice cream and fruit or on its own. Enjoy!*

For batter:

2 large eggs

2 cups of self-rising flour, sifted

1 cup sugar

pinch of salt

handful of sultana raisins (if desired)

¾ cup oil

1 cup 2% milk

butter or margarine for greasing pan

Crumble topping:

¼ cup all-purpose flour

3 tablespoons sugar

⅛ cup butter or margarine, cut in small pieces

Batter: In a large mixing bowl using electric mixer, beat the eggs until fluffy. Slowly add flour, sugar, salt, raisins, oil and milk. Pour batter into a greased loaf pan.

Topping: In a medium-sized mixing bowl, combine flour, sugar and butter. Crumble mixture over batter in loaf pan.

Place the loaf in a cold oven. Do not preheat the oven. After the loaf is placed in the oven, turn the oven to 350°F for 1 hour and 20 minutes or until the cake tester or toothpick comes out clean.

TIPS & ADVICE: Because every oven is different, I heat my oven to 335°F for the same length of time.

YIELD: 1 loaf

did you know?
In 2014/15 UJA's Israel Engagement ShinShinim program brought 22 young Israelis to work in our Jewish Day Schools, synagogues and summer camps to help promote a love of Israel, connecting our Toronto Community to our Homeland.

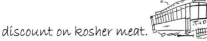

discount on kosher meat. *Until at least the 1880s, Holy Blossom was the center of*

apple crumble granola brunch cupcakes

Julie Albert and Lisa Gnat *While I'd like to take credit for our recipes, as always, all props go to Lisa, the sweet (as opposed to the salty) sister with the bionic palate and extreme taste buds. She's an expert feeder while I remain, as always her faithful eater.*

Cupcakes:

non-stick cooking spray

2½ cups all-purpose flour

1 teaspoon baking soda

½ teaspoon kosher salt

½ teaspoon cinnamon

2 small Granny Smith apples, peeled and diced

1¼ cups brown sugar

1 cup buttermilk

½ cup vegetable oil

1 large egg

1 teaspoon vanilla extract

Cream cheese frosting:

1 (4 ounce) package cream cheese

¼ cup butter, softened

¼ teaspoon vanilla extract

2½ cups icing sugar

1 tablespoon whole milk

Crumble topping:

1 cup all-purpose flour

½ cup sugar

½ cup granola cereal

pinch each cinnamon, kosher salt

⅓ cup butter, softened

Cupcakes: Preheat oven to 350°F. Line 16 muffin cups with cupcake liners and coat lightly with non-stick cooking spray. In a large bowl, combine flour, baking soda, salt, cinnamon and diced apples. In a medium-sized mixing bowl, whisk brown sugar, buttermilk, vegetable oil, egg and vanilla. Gently stir sugar mixture into flour mixture, until just combined. Spoon batter into prepared muffin tins, dividing evenly. Bake for 20 minutes. Cool completely before frosting.

Frosting: In a large mixing bowl, using an electric mixer, cream together the cream cheese and butter until well combined. On low speed, add vanilla, icing sugar and milk. Mix to combine, increasing speed to medium until a smooth spreading consistency.

Topping: In a large mixing bowl using wooden spoon, combine flour, sugar, granola, cinnamon and salt. Add butter and crumble in with your fingers until mixture looks like coarse meal. Spread onto a parchment-lined baking sheet and bake in a 350°F oven for 10 minutes. Stir and continue to bake 10 minutes more, until crumble is golden. Set aside and let cool completely before using as garnish. Spread frosting on cooled cupcakes and garnish with crumble topping.

YIELD: 16 cupcakes

Jewish religious practice and community life in Toronto (our story continues on page 36 . . . read on) →

starters, snacks, sauces & spreads

Daiter's, circa late 1930s. Faye Daiter ran the store while Harry Daiter ran Daiter's Silverthorn Dairy Ltd.

phyllo with goat cheese and smoked salmon

Daphna Rabinovitch *I rarely put out a lot of nibblies before a meal because I don't want my guests to fill up before they even sit down. Perhaps that's classic projection as that's what happens to me. I love to try the various dips and crackers and then find my appetite has waned considerably. So I prefer a sit-down appetizer course. I developed this recipe for a magazine a long time ago after they asked for an article on phyllo. I actually love working with phyllo as it's so versatile and quite forgiving, despite its reputation to the contrary. I also love the combination of the goat cheese with the smoked salmon. Substitute arugula for the spinach if you prefer.*

6 sheets phyllo pastry, thawed

⅓ cup unsalted butter, melted

¾ cup roasted red pepper, julienned

3 garlic cloves, minced

4 ounces smoked salmon, sliced

1 cup baby spinach leaves (about 12)

4 ounces fresh goat cheese, crumbled

¼ teaspoon each salt and pepper

Preheat oven to 375°F. Place one sheet of the phyllo pastry on a work surface; keep the remaining phyllo sheets covered with a piece of plastic wrap and then a damp paper towel to prevent them from drying out. Starting at the edges, lightly brush some of the melted butter over the phyllo. Lay a second sheet of phyllo on top of the first so that the edges match. Brush lightly with the melted butter. Repeat with the remaining phyllo and melted butter.

Place the roasted red peppers in a thin line about 2" from one long end of the stack of phyllo. Layer with the garlic, smoked salmon, spinach and goat cheese. Sprinkle the pile with the salt and pepper.

Starting at one long end, tightly roll up the phyllo into a log, tucking in the ends. Place, seam side down, on a parchment-paper lined rimmed baking sheet. Brush with the remaining melted butter. Bake in the center of the preheated oven until golden brown, 15–20 minutes. Cool the phyllo strudel on the pan on a wire rack for 10 minutes. Slice into diagonal slices.

NUMBER OF SERVINGS: 8

including welfare efforts through the Anglo-Jewish Association and the Ladies Montefiore →

stuffed mushrooms

Gav Martell *Stuffed mushrooms are one of my wife's favourite dishes to order when we go out for Italian food. The combination of flavours and textures is really delicious. The crispy Japanese panko breadcrumbs, the flavourful spinach, the cheese mixture and the earthiness of the mushrooms make every mouthful delightful. Every time I make these mushrooms, they get gobbled up quicker than I can plate them. This is the best compliment a home chef can have! These are a crowd-pleasing appetizer; there are never any leftovers.*

12 large white mushrooms, stems removed

4 tablespoons extra virgin olive oil, divided

¼ teaspoon pepper

½ teaspoon salt

1 garlic clove, minced

10 ounces fresh spinach

1 cup unsalted butter, softened

1 tablespoon fresh basil, chopped

1 tablespoon fresh parsley, chopped

¼ teaspoon granulated garlic

¼ teaspoon dried oregano

1½ cups panko breadcrumbs

salt and pepper, to taste

1 cup fontina cheese, grated

paprika to coat

Preheat oven to 350°F. Place mushrooms in a mixing bowl, add 2 tablespoons of olive oil, salt and pepper. Place on a baking tray with gills up and roast in the oven for 15 minutes. Remove, and allow mushrooms to cool slightly. Turn over mushrooms onto paper towel to allow the liquid to drain. Heat 2 tablespoons of oil in a pan on medium heat. Add minced garlic and lightly brown. Add spinach and salt and pepper to taste. Stir until reduced in volume, about 3 minutes. Remove from heat, drain, cool, and coarsely chop. Set aside.

In a large mixing bowl, combine butter, basil, parsley, granulated garlic, oregano, panko breadcrumbs, salt and pepper. Using your hands, form into 12 small discs or patties. In a separate mixing bowl, combine cooked spinach and fontina cheese. Place 2–3 tablespoons of the spinach-cheese mixture into each mushroom cap. Top the mushrooms with disc/patty mixture and sprinkle with paprika. Bake until golden brown, about 15–20 minutes.

TIPS & ADVICE: Gruyere, Edam, Gouda or provolone can be substituted for the fontina.

NUMBER OF SERVINGS: 4

veggie fritters

Karine Krieger *This is a recent Daviau family favourite and part of a repertoire of healthier vegan dishes that I serve which are enjoyed by all. The only downside is that they are very filling and sometimes leave people too full to eat their dinner.*

1 cup frozen peas

1 cup frozen corn

1½ cups chickpea flour (aka gram, besan, garbanzo flour)

1 cup water

1 teaspoon mild curry powder (optional but nice)

1 teaspoon salt or to taste

2 tablespoons canola or other oil for frying

½ cup thai chili pepper sauce (mild or spicy)

½ cup vegennaise/aioli

3 teaspoons fresh dill, minced

1 tablespoon fresh lemon juice

Pour frozen peas and carrots into colander, rinse under tap until defrosted and set aside to drain. Using wooden spoon, stir water into chickpea flour until well mixed and no lumps. Stir in curry powder and salt. Pour frozen peas and carrots into chickpea batter and mix. (Batter will be fairly thick and consist mainly of peas and carrots with just enough chickpea to hold the fritter together once cooked.) Heat small amount of oil in large frying pan; I use cast iron. When pan/oil is hot, drop tablespoons of veggie batter onto pan, leaving room between fritters to allow for easy removal. Begin with a fritter or 2 and taste for flavour, then adjust seasoning accordingly. Panfry fritters for up to 3 minutes until sides have slightly hardened and underside is tan colour. Flip over and fry for another couple of minutes. Re-oil the pan as necessary. As each batch is ready, place fritters onto serving platter and serve with thai chili pepper sauce and/or aioli/vegennaise mixed with dill and lemon juice.

TIPS & ADVICE: This is a flexible 'base' recipe that can be made with different vegetables and spices. Instead of peas and carrots, I have used sautéed mushrooms and caramelized onions; also delicious. Make the fritters close to mealtime and serve warm or earlier and serve at room temperature. Keeping them hot in a warming drawer or reheating in a microwave tends to dry the fritters out a bit. They are also fine to be refrigerated and served even a few days later.

NUMBER OF SERVINGS: about 30 (2") fritters

zucchini tahini dip

Joy Young and Laurenn Schecter *We started Joy Foods because we both love healthy, high quality, vegetarian food. This vegan dip is creamy, delicious and nutritious.*

2 zucchinis

6 garlic cloves, skin on

⅓ cup white onion, diced

4 tablespoons lemon juice

3 tablespoons olive oil

3 tablespoons water

1 tablespoon apple cider vinegar

1 teaspoon Braggs sauce or soy sauce

pinch mustard seed powder

7 dashes black pepper

pinch salt

Preheat the oven to 350°F convection setting. Slice the zucchini in half lengthwise and, together with garlic, place on a cookie sheet lined with parchment paper. Bake 30 minutes, turning zucchini over once. Remove zucchini and garlic from oven. When cool enough to handle, peel the garlic. Place zucchini, garlic and the rest of the ingredients in a blender or food processor and puree until you have a smooth consistency. Add additional salt and pepper to taste.

YIELD: about 1 cup

vegetarian ceviche

Ingrid Camhi *I was born in Mexico City. Our family vacationed in Acapulco every December, where my mom made fish ceviche, and everyone loved it—but I didn't like fish. So, my mom created this vegetarian version just for me.*

1 can hearts of palm, drained and sliced

1 can sliced mushrooms, drained

¼ onion, chopped

1 tomato, chopped

1 avocado, cubed

3 tablespoons fresh cilantro, chopped

½ cup ketchup

1 lime, juiced

2–3 drops Tabasco

Mix all ingredients in a glass bowl. Let all of the ingredients sit for a few minutes to marinate. Enjoy!

TIPS & ADVICE: Add green jalapeno peppers for a spicier version and more lime or cilantro to suit your own taste.

NUMBER OF SERVINGS: 4

predominantly English speaking, middle class, residentially integrated and even socially →

leeks with warm thyme vinaigrette

Daphna Rabinovitch *The leeks are French inspired and a lovely way to start a meal. I like this dish because of its simplicity, which belies its sophisticated taste. Leeks themselves are under-appreciated, in my opinion, and this is a delicious way to introduce them to your entertaining. I am extremely partial to thyme, and the earthiness of this herb pairs especially beautifully with the subtlety of the leeks.*

8 leeks

2 teaspoons extra virgin olive oil

½ cup water

Vinaigrette:

¼ cup extra virgin olive oil

1 tablespoon red wine vinegar

1 teaspoon Dijon mustard

1 teaspoon freshly squeezed lemon juice

1 teaspoon dried thyme leaves

½ teaspoon each salt and pepper

Cut off the dark green tops of each leek, so that only the white and very light green parts are left; trim the root end. Cut each leek in half lengthwise. Rinse well under cold running water to wash away any sand. Pat dry.

In a large non-stick skillet, heat the oil over medium-high heat. Add the leeks, arranging them so that they are in a single layer. Cook, turning once, until they just start to turn golden, 3 to 5 minutes. Pour in ½ cup of water. Reduce the heat to medium-low. Cover the skillet and cook until the leeks are tender, about 15 minutes.

Meanwhile, in a small bowl, whisk together the olive oil, vinegar, mustard, lemon juice, thyme, salt and pepper. Warm in a microwave at High (100% power) for 45 seconds or just until warm. Whisk to recombine. Arrange two leek halves on a small plate. Pour warm vinaigrette over.

NUMBER OF SERVINGS: 8

did you know?

Since its inception in 2008, the One Happy Camper incentive program has awarded grants to over 2,436 children. 75% of these children went back to Jewish overnight camp the next year.

assimilated with minimal overt anti-Semitism. *The Jews of mid 19th century Toronto* →

crispy barbecued wings

Hailey Remer *My family lives all over the world: Miami, Israel, California, Toronto, and Barbados. We try to congregate together over the Jewish Holidays and during the summer. In the summer, we just hang out, relaxing by the pool and barbecuing. No one wants to go out and pick anything up, so we usually walk into the kitchen at the last minute and try to find something that goes together. One day, it was my brother-in-law's turn to get dinner ready and chicken wings are a family favourite. He put a little bit of this and a little bit of that and voilà, yummy chicken wings! We spent that dinner trying to guess what the sauce was made out of. This recipe is my re-creation of that great sauce. I'm not 100% sure if that's what he put in it, but this one is so good.*

Marinade:

¼ cup honey

¼ cup barbecue sauce

2 teaspoons soy sauce

2 teaspoons garlic powder

1 teaspoon paprika

1 teaspoon fresh lime juice

1 teaspoon ground ginger

½ teaspoon cumin

2 drops sesame oil

small amount of water to dilute mixture

2 pounds chicken wings

Mix all the ingredients for the marinade in a blender/processor. Use half to marinate the wings for 2–3 hours or overnight. Place the other half of the marinade in the fridge. Turn the barbeque on high and once it is hot, turn the temperature to medium-low. Put the wings on the grill and cook until crispy, about 20–30 minutes. Halfway through, before the wings are turned over, dunk them in a small amount of the reserved marinade. When done, pour the rest of the marinade on top of the wings and serve.

TIPS & ADVICE: The marinade can be made ahead of time and stored in the fridge. If you put the barbeque on lower heat and move all the chicken wings into the middle, they get crispy, but you need to leave them on for awhile.

NUMBER OF SERVINGS: 4–6

were merchants dealing in jewellery, tobacco, optical supplies, hardware, insurance and various

galya's stuffed fig balls

Galya Sarner *Food has always had a central place in my life. I was born in Jerusalem and in my early years, grew up near Machane Yehuda, the city's main outdoor food market. I often went there with my mother and I got to know the market well. In my early 20's, my husband and I moved to Paris and our first apartment was above the Rue Montorgueil Market, one of the oldest markets in Paris. During the five years we lived in Paris, I took a few French cooking lessons. I love spending time in the kitchen, inventing new recipes that combine my childhood memories of Israel with my experience in Paris. I frequently run culinary workshops in Toronto, specializing in Israeli food with a French twist. This recipe is an example of my cooking style. I refer to it as "when Jerusalem and Parisian markets meet".*

Marinade:

¼ cup olive oil

⅓ cup balsamic vinegar

1 tablespoon maple syrup

1 tablespoon Dijon mustard

1 tablespoon dry rosemary

1 tablespoon fresh tarragon

1 cup sun-dried tomatoes, chopped

200 grams feta cheese, cut into small cubes

20 dried figs

¼ cup za'atar

fresh arugula

2–3 fresh endives, leaves separated

½ cup strawberries, finely sliced

½ cup candied pecans

Combine all ingredients for the marinade in a bowl and add the sun-dried tomatoes. Cover and keep in a cool place for about 24 hours. Remove tomatoes, reserving the marinade for later. Combine chopped tomatoes with feta cheese and mix well. Remove the stem from each fig and make a cut width-wise, being careful not to cut through the fig completely. Place a small amount of the cheese mixture inside each fig and roll into a ball. Sprinkle with za'atar.

To create a flower design, spread the arugula on a round serving plate and place the endive leaves in the shape of a flower. Place the fig balls in the endive leaves and pour the reserved marinade over them. Place strawberries along border of plate and decorate with the pecans.

NUMBER OF SERVINGS: 6–7

retail endeavors. *Their leadership and respect in the community was such that in*

liver ecstasy (liver and onions)

Joyce Strauss *This recipe was given to me by my late mother-in-law, Rose Strauss, our family's matriarch. It is a family favourite for every occasion. If you like liver, it is sure to be your favourite too.*

6 slices raw calves' liver

1 Spanish onion, diced

2 tablespoons chicken soup powder

3 tablespoons olive oil

2 tablespoons sugar

salt and pepper to taste

Preheat oven to 350°F. Carefully clean the liver and bake at 350°F in a baking dish for approximately 10 minutes. Liver should still be soft to touch. Be careful not to overcook. Cut the liver into small cubes. Add the onion to the liver. Mix together soup powder, olive oil, sugar, salt and pepper. Toss lightly with liver and onions. Put the mixture into a glass bowl and refrigerate for at least 30 minutes. Serve with sliced challah, crackers or rye bread.

NUMBER OF SERVINGS: 8

mini mushroom quiches

Ellen Rosenthal *Every time I make a brunch, I make these mini quiches. They are always a hit and are devoured before anything else on the table! A close colleague gave me the recipe, which she had received from her daughter-in-law.*

6 eggs

1 pound Swiss cheese, shredded

1 pint sour cream

2 (10 ounce) cans sliced mushrooms drained, or sautéed fresh mushrooms

2 (3 ounce) cans French fried onion rings (Durkees)

1 teaspoon Worcestershire sauce

1 dash Tabasco sauce

sea salt and pepper to taste

Preheat oven to 325°F. With an electric mixer, beat eggs and gradually fold in all other ingredients. Spoon into lightly greased muffin tins. Bake until golden brown (approximately 30–35 minutes). Cool on rack.

NUMBER OF SERVINGS: 12

1897, they were able to thwart the Anglican Church's proposal for the introduction of religious →

ceviche à la mexicana

Sandra Frydman de Helfant *Ceviche is a wonderful dish to serve guests in the summer. It is very healthy. When you eat it, you can imagine you are in Mexico.*

1 pound halibut, cut into ½" cubes

2 cups fresh lemon or lime juice

1 white onion, chopped

1 hot green chili, finely chopped (optional)

½ bunch coriander, chopped

½ pound ripe tomato, chopped

1 tablespoon orange juice

1 teaspoon salt

1 large avocado (for decoration)

Place the fish and lemon/lime juice in a glass bowl. Cover and marinate for a minimum of two hours or overnight in the refrigerator. Pour into colander and drain juice. In a large bowl, mix fish with all remaining ingredients except the avocado. Taste and adjust salt as necessary. Cover and refrigerate for two more hours. Serve in a large bowl or in individual bowls and decorate with slices of avocado.

TIPS & ADVICE: When marinating, make sure the pieces of fish are completely covered with the lemon/lime juice. They should be floating in the juice, so that all sides 'cook'; this is the term we use in Mexico.

NUMBER OF SERVINGS: 6–8

fritzi jaegerman's baked gefilte fish

Marlene Jaegerman *This is my mother in-law's recipe. It has been passed down from generation to generation. It is absolutely delicious!*

2 pounds grouper or snapper, ground

7 eggs, separated

2 onions, ground

5 tablespoons matzah meal

2 tablespoons sugar

1½ teaspoons salt

¼ teaspoon ground pepper

¾ cup water

¾ cup canola oil

Preheat oven to 300°F. With an electric mixer, beat together the fish, egg yolks, onion, matzah meal, sugar, salt and pepper. Add the water and oil slowly. Beat everything for 20 minutes. In a separate bowl, beat the egg whites and carefully mix with the above fish mixture. Place combined mixture into a rectangular 9 x 13", well-oiled pan. Bake at 300°F for approximately 1 hour.

TIPS & ADVICE: Please . . . if you really want it to taste delicious, stick to the recommended fish. I have used white fish (cheaper) but it doesn't taste as good.

YIELD: 1 loaf

emma and sam lottman's gefilte fish

Robin Farb-Eckler for the Lottman/Grossman/Godfrey Family *Katie (Lottman) Grossman was our neighbour growing up in Forest Hill Village and her younger sister, Pearl (Lottman) Godfrey has always been a close family friend. Pearl got the recipe from her daughter Jodi, who was lucky to have received it from her late Aunt Katie.*

Lottman's Bakery was a favourite landmark in Kensington Market, Toronto's Jewish Neighbourhood. Emma and Sam Lottman owned the large bakery that was on Baldwin Street for many years. As landmarks disappear, these recipes, and the memories that go with them, remain and can be shared across generations. This is easy to make with children and a Yiddish favourite of Ashkenazi Jews.

For Stock:

3 quarts Fish Stock:

Fish bones and heads, washed well, with bones cleaned, and gills, blood and eyes removed

3 quarts water

4 carrots, sliced

2 onions

9 tablespoons sugar

1 teaspoon white pepper

1 teaspoon salt

For Fish:

3 pounds assorted white fish, pickerel, lake trout, and pike, ground

10 tablespoons sugar

5 extra large eggs

3 carrots, grated

2 large onions, finely chopped

1 cup cold water

3 tablespoons salt

1½ teaspoons white pepper

Make stock by adding all stock ingredients to large soup kettle and cooking for 30 minutes. To make the fish, add sugar, eggs, carrots, onions, water, salt and pepper to chopped fish and mix well. Using an ice cream scoop, drop fish balls into boiling fish stock. Cook for about 3 hours, adding water as needed.

Gently shake the pot to prevent the fish balls from sticking to each other. Strain through slotted spoon. Cool on platter. Strain the stock, reserving the carrots for topping as garnish.

NUMBER OF SERVINGS: 12–15

visit our website
www.JewishToronto.com/BathurstStreetKitchen

increased dramatically over the last two decades of the 19th century as large numbers of eastern →

gramma pidgey's sweet and sour salmon

Karen Morton *Gramma Pidgey was my mom; her name was Tabala, which means pigeon in Yiddish, so my dad always called her Pidgey. That is what my kids and grandkids called her too. This was one of her specialties. It is great to serve at 'break the fast' as it can be prepared in advance and also keeps for a week or more after.*

3-4 pounds salmon, butterflied and skinned, and cut into 2" chunks

3 or 4 onions, chopped and lightly sautéed

1 cup ketchup

1 large bottle Heinz chili sauce

1 (15 ounce) jar sweet pickles

¼ cup vinegar

6 or 7 gingersnaps, broken up

4 tablespoons brown sugar

Mix all ingredients except fish. Bring sauce to a boil and stir to combine (gingersnaps will melt into the sauce). Reduce to a simmer and add fish. Gently combine so that fish is covered in sauce but don't stir after as the fish will break into small pieces. Cover and simmer for 30-40 minutes. As an option, you can also put all ingredients in a roasting pan in the oven at 350°F for 45 minutes instead of cooking on stovetop. This option allows you to make a larger quantity if desired. This dish keeps well for 2-3 weeks in the refrigerator.

NUMBER OF SERVINGS: about 10

marlene's pickled salmon

Sandra Hausman *This recipe is a favourite from my late girlhood friend, Marlene Shapiro, from Montreal. She made it every year as we left on our girls' road trip. We started the trips when we turned 70; there were 7 of us then. Although she was already in poor health, Marlene made it on three trips. We carry on the trips in her memory. She would be proud to be included in the cookbook. This year, we are going to the Berkshires.*

3-5 pound salmon fillets, skinned and boned

1 cup water

1-2 bottles Heinz chili sauce

1 cup white vinegar

½ cup sugar

2-4 tablespoons pickling spice

1 large Spanish onion, sliced

Cut salmon into 2" cubes and place in one layer in a pyrex. Cover with one cup water and microwave on high uncovered for 5-10 minutes, turning once until salmon is just cooked. Drain. Combine remaining ingredients and pour over salmon. Cover and refrigerate turning every day or two. Keeps for two weeks or more. I find for the larger amount of fish, I use 1½ bottles of chili sauce, keeping the rest of the ingredients the same.

NUMBER OF SERVINGS: about 10

European Jews escaped pogroms, persecutions and economic hardships. ✿ By 1891, →

spicy raw tuna or salmon tacos

Shari Wert *This recipe is a big hit every time I make it. Someone always asks for the recipe.*

¾ pound sushi-grade tuna or salmon or a mixture of both, diced or cubed

½ cup cucumber, diced

¼ cup green onion, chopped

2 tablespoons soy sauce

1½ teaspoons fresh lemon juice

1½ teaspoons sesame oil

1 teaspoon crushed red pepper flakes

1 tablespoon light mayonnaise

¼ teaspoon Sriracha sauce or to taste

5½ tablespoons sesame seeds, toasted

1 avocado, diced

Place fish in a large bowl. Add cucumber, green onion, soy sauce, lemon juice, sesame oil and crushed red pepper. Mix gently. In a separate small bowl, add ¼ teaspoon Sriracha sauce to the mayonnaise. Mix well and taste. Add more Sriracha as desired. Set aside. Toast the sesame seeds in a dry skillet over medium heat for about 3 minutes. Stir often to prevent burning. Let cool. Add Sriracha/mayonnaise mixture and sesame seeds to fish and mix to combine. Add diced avocado and toss gently.

To serve, heat 8–10 small flour tortillas on a plate in microwave for 22 seconds and serve warm with tuna/salmon mixture spooned onto each.

TIPS & ADVICE: This recipe can also be served with hard taco shells or corn tortillas. Top each serving with tobiko (fish roe) if desired.

NUMBER OF SERVINGS: 9

did you know?
UJA's investment in Israel strategically leverages an additional $7 million through local municipalities, the Israeli government, private foundations and Israeli philanthropists.

Toronto's Jewish population was 1,425. ✡ By 1901, the population more than doubled →

shiffy wasserman's pickles

Pam Handelsman *Shiffy's pickle recipe has been handed down from my mom, Shiffy, to me, as well as to other friends and neighbours, such as our cottage neighbour, Esther Burnett. My mom would be so proud that her recipe is in a Jewish community cookbook; I can see her smiling! Every fall, my dad would go to Kensington Market and bring my mom home 2 bushels of cucumbers. Since her birthday was around then, he always said "happy birthday" as he walked in with the bushels. My mom made sure that everyone who visited left with a jar of pickles. She said they would stay good and delicious until Passover.*

Brine:

½ cup coarse salt

2 cups hot water

14 cups cold water

In each 1 gallon jar:

2 whole chili peppers

4 garlic cloves

2 bunches dill

2 tablespoons pickling spice

20-24 small pickling cucumbers (approximately)

2 celery stalks

To make the brine, mix together the salt and the 2 cups of hot water. Stir until the salt is dissolved. Then add the 14 cups of cold water. At the bottom of each clean gallon jar, place 1 whole chili pepper, 2 garlic cloves, 1 bunch of dill and 1 tablespoon pickling spice. Add small cucumbers and some celery sticks to fill jar (celery is supposed to keep the pickles crispy) and on top, place another layer of 1 chili, 2 garlic cloves, 1 bunch dill and 1 tablespoon pickling spice. Add brine to top and close lid. If using smaller jars, put same first layer, but only top off with a second chili pepper, not another layer of garlic, dill and pickling spice. Seal the jars.

You can keep them at room temperature or in a cool place. I think Shiffy had a cold cellar in her house as was popular in her day. I usually keep my pickles at room temperature for two weeks. Once you put them in the refrigerator, the pickling process slows down. So you can be the judge of how new or old your family likes their dill pickles.

TIPS & ADVICE: Best to make these pickles with fresh local pickling cucumbers that are available in late summer to early fall.

YIELD: 15–20 one gallon jars

again to 3,090. Toronto's Jewish immigrants arriving in the late 1800s consisted →

dankoff's dills

Randi Satok *My father Larry Dankoff has been making pickles since I was a little girl, and my brother and I would help. He makes gallons every year for Rosh Hashanah and gives them away to family and friends with a homemade label, "Dankoff's Dills, Cures all ills."*

1 head garlic, peeled and minced

⅓ cup salt

2 heaping tablespoons pickling spices

5 crushed chili peppers

pickling dill

2 pounds fresh firm #2 cucumbers to fill gallon jar, washed

celery (optional)

Place ¾ of garlic in bottom of a sterilized gallon jar. Add salt, pickling spices, peppers, and 4 sprigs of dill to bottom of jar. Pack cucumbers firmly standing up. Before you add a second row of standing cucumbers, add remaining garlic and a little dill. On top of this layer, place a few more cucumbers on their side, leaving 2" at top of jar. Add water to cover and two more sprigs of dill. Close securely and shake to dissolve salt. Store at room temperature for 10–12 days. For ½ sours, reduce salt to 3 tablespoons, add 1 tablespoon vinegar, 1 tablespoon prepared mustard and omit chilis. Store for 4–5 days. Best to make in August.

YIELD: one gallon jar

orange and rosemary baked olives

Ellen Grossman *A great tasting dish without too much work.*

3½ cups mixed olives, drained

¼ cup dry white wine

2 tablespoons fresh orange juice

2 tablespoons olive oil

2 garlic cloves, minced

2 sprigs fresh rosemary and/or 1 teaspoon toasted fennel seeds

2 tablespoons fresh parsley, chopped

1½ tablespoons fresh oregano, chopped

4 teaspoons grated orange zest

¼ teaspoon crushed red pepper flakes

Preheat oven to 375°F. Stir the whole olives with the wine, orange juice, olive oil and garlic in a 9 x 13" baking dish. Stir in toasted fennel if using and/or nestle in the sprigs of rosemary under the olives. Bake for 15 minutes, stirring halfway through the baking. Discard the rosemary sprigs, stir in the parsley, oregano, orange zest and red pepper flakes. Serve warm or cold.

NUMBER OF SERVINGS: Can't tell as they are eaten up so quickly!

of largely destitute, Yiddish speaking Russians, Galicians and Poles. Unlike Jewish

honey bran crunch

Brenda Cooper *More than 30 years ago, I went to Leawood, Kansas for a family bar mitzvah. At the Saturday night party, they served bowls of this crunch. One taste and I was hooked! This yummy snack was made by the bar mitzvah boy's grandmother, my great aunt by marriage. She was thrilled to hand down the recipe and excited that I was "bringing it to Toronto"! It's a wonderful remembrance of Aunt Sonny.*

3 cups corn bran cereal

1 cup oatmeal

1 cup broken pecans and/or walnuts

1 cup raisins

2 teaspoons cinnamon

¼ teaspoon salt

1 cup brown sugar

½ cup honey

½ cup margarine

In large bowl, combine cereal, oatmeal, nuts, raisins, cinnamon, and salt. In a small saucepan, combine brown sugar, honey, and margarine and cook over low heat, stirring constantly until margarine is melted and everything is well blended. Pour over the cereal mixture and mix until thoroughly coated. Spread evenly in shallow baking pan sprayed with non-stick cooking spray. Bake the mixture in preheated oven at 325°F for 20 minutes, stirring occasionally, until golden brown. Cool completely and break into chunks.

TIPS & ADVICE: Store in an airtight container.

NUMBER OF SERVINGS: 6–8

roasted pecans with honey and cinnamon

Naomi Oelbaum *I like my kids to eat nuts and look for new ways to serve them. I keep a bowl of nuts on hand for easy nibbling and add ingredients to keep my kids coming back for more.*

½ stick (¼ cup) unsalted butter

½ cup light brown sugar, packed

1 tablespoon honey

1 tablespoon water

⅛ teaspoon cayenne pepper

⅛ teaspoon cinnamon

⅛ teaspoon black pepper

3 cups raw pecans

Melt butter in a medium saucepan over medium low heat. Add brown sugar, honey, water, cayenne, cinnamon, and black pepper. Stir until sugar is dissolved. Turn up heat to medium high and add pecans. Continually stir the mixture until caramel turns deep brown, bubbles vigorously and nuts are fully coated, about 3 minutes. Pour onto a baking sheet lined with parchment paper. Cool for about one hour.

TIPS & ADVICE: If any of these spices don't appeal to you, simply omit. Ginger or nutmeg can be added or interchanged. Cashews, almonds or walnuts can be used instead of or with the pecans.

YIELD: 2 cups

communities in many US cities which, fearing increased anti-Semitism and economic hardship, →

homemade breadsticks

Naomi Oelbaum *This is a very easy recipe to make and I usually have all the ingredients in the house. They're great for an after school snack or for pick-up in the car. These are also perfect for a brunch and they go really well with a bowl of fresh tomato soup.*

⅓ cup all-purpose flour

¼ cup whole wheat flour

¼ cup Pecorino Romano cheese, grated

¾ teaspoon baking powder

¼–½ teaspoon black pepper

5 tablespoons water

1 teaspoon olive oil

Preheat oven to 450°F. Combine flours, cheese, baking powder and pepper in a medium bowl. Add water and oil, stir until dough forms. Knead the dough gently (4 or 5 times) on a floured surface. Divide into 18 pieces and roll each piece into a 10 cm rope. Place on a lightly greased cookie sheet and bake for 10 minutes or until the bottoms are golden. Place on a wire rack and cool.

NUMBER OF SERVINGS: 6

cranberry sauce

Helaine Robins *This is so easy and so much better than canned cranberry sauce.*

1 lemon

1 orange

1 cup sugar

1 cup water

1 bag fresh cranberries

1 apple, peeled, cored and cut into small pieces

Grate rind from lemon and set aside. (Use the lemon for another purpose.) Grate rind from orange. Remove remaining peel as well as membranes from orange. Cut flesh into small pieces. Put sugar and water in pot and bring to a boil. Rinse bag of cranberries, drain, add to pot and bring back to boil. Simmer uncovered for 10 minutes. Add lemon and orange rinds, orange and apple pieces. Turn off heat, cover and let thicken.

YIELD: 1½ cups

tried to exclude the new immigrants, the Toronto community welcomed them and made efforts

sauce for smoked trout or smoked salmon

Judy Godfrey *This is so easy and makes smoked salmon or smoked trout more festive for an appetizer.*

½ cup mayonnaise

2 tablespoons grainy Dijon mustard

1 tablespoon white horseradish

Mix all ingredients together in a bowl until well mixed.

TIPS & ADVICE: Serve in a pretty dish beside smoked salmon on a platter. Garnish with lettuce, small red onion slices and capers.

YIELD: ¾ cup—enough for a side of smoked salmon

world's best tomato sauce

Marla Schwartz *This sauce is very easy to make and very adaptable. It is a great basic and can be used as a base for other recipes including lasagna and eggplant Parmesan. I often make a double batch and freeze it in containers.*

½ cup olive oil

1 large white onion, chopped

3 garlic cloves, finely chopped

1 teaspoon chili flakes

2 (28 ounce) cans plum tomatoes

¼ cup tomato paste

1 tablespoon white sugar

¼ cup olive oil

1 tablespoon kosher salt

Warm olive oil in large stainless steel pot. Add onion, garlic, and chili flakes and cook over medium heat until soft but not brown. Add tomatoes, tomato paste and sugar. Cook over medium heat until sauce thickens, about 20 minutes. Remove from heat and allow mixture to cool slightly. Puree with a handheld blender, add olive oil, and salt.

TIPS & ADVICE: For additional flavour, add chopped black olives or feta cheese.

YIELD: 6 cups

to integrate them. But the eastern Europeans felt uncomfortable in the modern

romanian eggplant salad

Anita Robins *My mother, Etica Levy, lived in Israel for seven years before emigrating from Romania to Canada. This eggplant is a very Romanian take on an Israeli staple.*

1 large purple eggplant

2 tablespoons canola oil

½ teaspoon salt (or to taste)

½ teaspoon pepper (or to taste)

1 medium tomato, chopped

1 bell pepper, chopped

½ medium cooking onion, chopped

Cut eggplant in half lengthwise and place flesh down on a tin foil-lined baking pan. Broil for approximately 30 minutes in the middle of the oven. Place the eggplant on a tilted cutting board for at least 30 minutes so that juices drain out. Scoop out the flesh with a wooden spoon and chop on a board using a wooden chopper so that flesh remains as white as possible. Put chopped eggplant into mixing bowl and add oil to mix well. Add tomato, pepper, onion, salt and pepper and chill in fridge until serving.

TIPS & ADVICE: The eggplant looks nice when decorated with whole black olives and additional bell pepper. Serve as an appetizer.

NUMBER OF SERVINGS: about 6

guacamole

Rebecca Barsky *In San Antonio, it is popular to serve tableside guacamole at restaurants; I decided to continue the tradition at home. This recipe is also great for the cottage. It is quick to make and it goes really well with Scotch and the sunset. The most amazing thing about this recipe is that it's kosher for Passover! We serve it before we sit down for the Seder with matzah crackers and veggies.*

1 avocado, diced (not too finely)

2 tablespoons orange juice

1 tablespoon lime juice

1 plum tomato, diced

1 jalapeno, (or to taste), minced finely

1 tablespoon red onion, minced

kosher salt to taste

fresh coriander (optional)

Mix all the ingredients together gently. Serve with tortilla chips (unless it's Passover).

NUMBER OF SERVINGS: 4–5

Holy Blossom setting and quickly established their own synagogues in their neighbourhood →

salad cuite

Judy Steiner *Salad Cuite is a staple you will find on every Moroccan family table. You can heat it in a pan and crack eggs into it until cooked, or spread it on bread or crostini. This is one of the first Moroccan dishes that I learned to make from my mom, Annette Cohen. It's the easiest thing to throw together, with great results.*

1 (28 ounce) can diced tomatoes, drained

1 green pepper, diced

2 garlic cloves, minced

1 teaspoon paprika

½ teaspoon black pepper

dash turmeric

dash cayenne pepper

salt to taste

Put all ingredients into a medium pot and bring to a boil. Reduce heat and simmer on low for about 1½ hours, stirring occasionally. Cook until mixture is thick. Taste and add more salt, if needed. Once cooled, place in a Mason jar. It will last for about 1 week in the fridge.

TIPS & ADVICE: Omit the cayenne if you do not want the Salad Cuite to be spicy.

NUMBER OF SERVINGS: 6

baldrock smoked tofu dip

Karine Krieger *The basic recipe was given to me (minus any measurements) by our Baldrock Island, Lake Muskoka cottage neighbours from Kentucky. I often serve it as a brunch item. People love it and assume it's smoked whitefish. It is vegetarian and great for people with fish or dairy allergies and, if you use the vegennaise, the dish becomes vegan.*

1 block (210 grams) smoked tofu

3 tablespoons mayonnaise, vegennaise or aioli

2 teaspoons Dijon mustard

¾ teaspoon hot pepper sauce

¼ teaspoon soy sauce

sliced vegetables or crackers for dipping

Finely grate the smoked tofu block into a bowl and use a fork to mix in the mayonnaise (or vegennaise/aioli), Dijon mustard and hot pepper sauce until well blended. Adjust ingredients to your taste. Serve in a small bowl (it looks nice over lettuce leaves) with cut vegetables and/ or crackers for dipping.

TIPS & ADVICE: If you can't find smoked tofu, you can substitute regular tofu and add a teaspoon of liquid smoke; but it won't be as good. I use Soyganic smoked tofu, by Sunrise Soya Foods.

YIELD: 1 cup

at Richmond and York including Goel Tzedec in 1883 and Beth Hamidrash Hagadol Chevra
——→

mock chopped liver

Rivi Miller *I got this recipe from my mother, Bess Miller, who loved to make healthy alternatives to traditional dishes. We have several vegetarians in our family and so I often make it for holiday meals as an appetizer. Even the non-vegetarians love it!*

1 cup dried green lentils

2 cups water

2 large Spanish onions, chopped

3 tablespoons canola oil

3 large eggs

⅓ cup pecans or walnuts (can toast or roast for extra flavour)

salt and pepper to taste

Place lentils and water in saucepan and bring to a boil. Cover, reduce heat, and simmer until tender, 20-25 minutes, adding more water if necessary. Sauté onions in oil over medium heat until golden brown, about 20 minutes. Hard-boil the eggs. In a food processor fitted with a metal blade, process nuts until finely ground. Remove and set aside in a bowl. Add eggs to processor and pulse until coarsely chopped. Add eggs to ground nuts. Add lentils to processor and purée for 10 seconds. Add onions, salt and pepper and pulse until well combined. Add to other ingredients, mix well by hand and adjust seasonings. Keep refrigerated.

YIELD: 2½–3 cups

eggplant dip

Galina Sandler *My daughters and I share a fondness for eggplant. Whenever they come back home from Montreal, they ask if I've made 'my eggplant'. This recipe is homage to the eggplant appetizers or 'zakuski' of Jewish families from the Former Soviet Union.*

2 large eggplants, peeled and halved

½ sweet onion, chopped

2 tablespoons light olive oil

1 large tomato, roughly chopped

1 garlic clove, minced

3-5 fresh basil leaves

1 tablespoon balsamic vinegar

1 teaspoon salt

1 teaspoon freshly ground pepper

Cook eggplant in microwave oven for 20 minutes or roast in the oven at 375°F for 40 minutes. Cool and scoop out the seeds. (This prevents bitterness). Mix the chopped onion with the oil and microwave for 8 minutes. Add tomatoes and garlic to the cooked onion and microwave for 5 minutes. In a food processor, combine cooked mixture with basil, balsamic vinegar, salt and pepper and process until smooth. Before serving, add an extra dash of balsamic vinegar and some chopped basil. Serve warm or cold.

TIPS & ADVICE: This dip is perfect on crackers or with vegetables or as a side dish with fish. It can also be used as a spread for sandwiches.

NUMBER OF SERVINGS: 6–10

T'Hillim in 1887 (merging in 1947 to form Beth Tzedec) and Shomrei Shabbos in 1889.

→

fat pasha base hummus

Anthony Rose *Fat Pasha chef, Kevin Gilmour, showed me how to make his hummus. The restaurant makes hummus several times a day from scratch but since home cooks often prefer the ease of canned chickpeas, I'm giving both methods. Some people swear by removing the chickpea skins. It's up to you. I cook a lot of Jewish food because it brings me back to my roots and reminds me of my family. There's also an incredible amount of cultural significance to it.*

4½ ounces dried chickpeas (½ cup + 2 tablespoons)

½ teaspoon baking soda

or

1 (19 ounce) can chickpeas, drained

2 garlic cloves, peeled, chopped

½ cup well-stirred tahini

¼ cup extra virgin olive oil

¼ cup ice water

2 tablespoons fresh lemon juice

1½ teaspoons kosher salt, or to taste

If using dried chickpeas: Place chickpeas in large bowl of cold water. Let stand on counter overnight or up to 24 hours. Drain. Rub off and discard skins, if desired. In medium, heavy saucepan over medium-low heat, combine drained (but still wet) chickpeas and baking soda. Cook, stirring constantly, 5 minutes. Fill pot with cold water (remember chickpeas will double or triple in size) and bring to a boil over high heat. Reduce heat to medium or medium-low and simmer until chickpeas are very tender (45–90 minutes depending on age of chickpeas and how long they soaked). While they're cooking, discard any skins that float to top. Drain.

If using canned chickpeas: Place chickpeas in bowl. If desired, rub off as many skins as possible. Place in a medium pot and cover with water. Bring to a boil and then reduce heat to medium-low; simmer 10 minutes. Drain.

Transfer drained chickpeas to food processor. Add garlic. Purée 3 minutes until a thick paste forms. Scrape down sides with rubber spatula. With motor running, slowly drizzle in tahini, oil, ice water, lemon juice and salt to taste. Purée until very creamy, 1–2 minutes. Taste; adjust salt, lemon. Thin with water if desired. If you've used hot chickpeas, let hummus cool to room temperature, about 30 minutes. If you've used canned chickpeas, the hummus can be eaten immediately. Refrigerate in sealed container for several days, but return to room temperature before eating.

TIPS & ADVICE: To serve, top with either braised chickpeas or baked chicken skin.

YIELD: about 2 cups

By 1897, when Holy Blossom moved to its new and larger Bond St building, →

ikra

Ahuva Krieger *Almost 60 years ago in Israel, my husband Moshe, originally from Romania, taught me to make Ikra; a classic Balkan dip (much tastier than its Greek cousin, Taramasalata.) It is commonly found in Israeli grocery stores and delicatessens. Called the 'poor man's caviar', this dip/spread is a favourite of my entire family and friends.*

1 cup raw carp roe (you purchase it by weight, so get enough to equal 1 cup after removing it from the sac)

2-4 tablespoons lemon juice

1½ teaspoons salt

1½-2 cups vegetable oil (canola, sunflower, etc.)

3 tablespoons lemon juice or to taste

½-1 onion, finely diced

1 teaspoon salt, or to taste

crackers or cut vegetables for dipping

Cleaning the carp roe: Rinse the roe sac under cold water, peel off the outer pocket of skin, and discard. With a fork, gently scrape away the pink membranes that hold the eggs/roe together; a messy job. Transfer the clean roe to a small stainless steel or glass mixing bowl.

Curing the carp roe: Add up to ¼ cup lemon juice and 1½ teaspoons of salt to the roe and mix with an electric or manual hand mixer at the lowest speed until well blended. Remaining membranes will stick to the beaters. The Ikra can be made now, but will have a better consistency if the roe is refrigerated, or better yet, frozen for a day or two. Divide cured roe into 1 cup or smaller portions and freeze in zip top bags up to a few months. The cured roe may turn light pink, stay brownish or be a combination of both.

Preparing the Ikra: Remove cured roe from fridge or defrost from freezer. In a small bowl, beat the roe with an electric mixer on the lowest speed for a minute. Slowly drizzle the oil in, allowing it to be absorbed after each drizzle until you have added half the oil. Continue drizzling the oil, now alternating with the lemon juice until the roe achieves a thick mayonnaise-like consistency and is a whitish colour with pink flecks. Mix in the chopped onion. Add salt and possibly more lemon juice to taste. Refrigerate immediately and allow time to set. Wait 3 hours before serving.

TIPS & ADVICE: Carp roe may hard to find. Try fish counters that sell carp (eg. Longos in spring). The amounts of salt, lemon juice and onion can be adjusted to your taste. If you use less oil, the consistency and flavour might not be as good. It can stay in the fridge for at least a week.

YIELD: about 3 cups

the new Eastern European arrivals far outnumbered the established English and German →

matbucha

Hadassa Slater *This recipe comes from a Jewish Iraqi family who were friends of ours years ago. On erev Shabbat they would occasionally drop off some delicious homemade fresh pitas and Matbucha. When they moved, they gave us the recipe and we have been making it for Shabbat ever since.*

1 green pepper

1–2 tablespoons olive oil

3 garlic cloves, minced

1 small can diced tomatoes

¼ teaspoon chili flakes

Slice the green pepper in half and roast in the oven until the skin darkens. Cool and slide the skin off. Cut into cubes about the same size as the diced tomatoes. In pot or frying pan, heat the olive oil on low and add tomatoes. Once the liquid has evaporated (15 minutes), add the green peppers and cook for 5 more minutes. Add the minced garlic and cook an additional 2 minutes. Season to taste with chili flakes. Serve cold or at room temperature.

TIPS & ADVICE: This delicious dip lasts 2 weeks in the fridge in an airtight container.

NUMBER OF SERVINGS: 8

bean and onion spread

Esther Kirshenblatt *A Kirshenblatt family favourite!*

2 cups dried lima beans

¼ cup Vidalia onion, finely chopped

1 teaspoon olive oil

salt

Soak the lima beans in warm water for a half hour. Rinse, strain, and put into a pot. Cover with water, add a little salt and simmer on low heat for at least an hour. The beans should be soft. Drain and mash them. At this point, you can freeze half of the bean mixture in a plastic container. Add chopped onions, olive oil and a pinch of salt. The mixture should be spreadable. If not, add some more olive oil.

TIPS & ADVICE: Serve this dip with crackers or challah on Friday nights.

YIELD: 2½ cups

beet gravlax

Ashley Farnell *This is my twist on the popular Scandinavian dish I saw at a food festival in Tromsø, Norway. It can also be made with golden beets for a colourful vibrant contrast.*

2 cups beetroot, grated

¼ cup kosher salt

¼ cup fine sugar

¼ cup vodka

2 pounds salmon, skin on

Peel and grate beetroot, keeping pulp and any juice together in a bowl. Stir in kosher salt, sugar and vodka. Spread out ⅓ of the mixture in a thin layer on a baking tray and place salmon fillet on top, skin side down. Cover salmon with remaining beetroot preparation and wrap the whole tray tightly with plastic wrap. Let it cure in the fridge for about 48 hours. Then scrape off beetroot mixture and discard. Wipe off excess salt on salmon with paper towel. Starting at the tail end, hold a sharp, flexible-bladed knife at a 20 degree angle and cut the cured salmon flesh into thin slices, taking care not to cut through the skin. The edges of the gravlax will be bright red. Lift salmon slices off the skin and serve with toast and crème fraiche.

NUMBER OF SERVINGS: 16

gramma morton's hot mustard

Dani Palter *This recipe was my great-grandmother's who for years never gave her family the recipe, saying they'd get it in her will. One day as a joke, she handed my grandfather and his sister a standard will and testament from a stationary store, and on it was her famous hot mustard recipe. However, this standardized will also stated that 'this document supersedes all my previous wills and testaments' so my grandfather (a lawyer) freaked out, because her real will had just became invalid, and all she was officially passing on now was a hot mustard recipe!*

1 (113 g) container Keene's dry mustard

2–3 tablespoons sugar (to taste)

1 teaspoon salt

approximately ½ cup water

1–2 tablespoons vinegar

1–2 tablespoons oil

Mix mustard, sugar, and salt together. Boil water and allow it to cool a bit. Gradually add water to mustard, sugar, and salt, stirring. Add vinegar and oil. Taste. If too strong, add more sugar. This keeps for months in a sealed container in the fridge and is good on everything!

YIELD: about 1 cup

Toronto increased more than any other immigrant group. ✡ By 1911, the Jewish →

erica 'buni' rubinger's zacusca

Deborah Hoffnung *This traditional Romanian spread or appetizer is a family favourite. Our Buni (Romanian for grandmother) has made it her own. Zacusca is low fat, vegetarian and has great taste and colour. It's easy to make and can be doubled or tripled.*

8 red bell peppers, stems and cores removed

1–2 tablespoons olive oil

2 yellow onions, thinly sliced

2 carrots, thinly sliced

5 Roma tomatoes, seeds removed

4 garlic cloves, crushed

3 tablespoons ketchup

1 teaspoon sugar

salt, pepper and red pepper flakes, to taste

Broil or grill peppers until the skins are blackened. Cool and remove the skin. Slice into 1" pieces. Heat a large deep skillet over medium heat, add oil and sauté onions until translucent, about 5 minutes. Add the carrots and continue to cook until softened and onions are lightly caramelized, about 15 minutes more. Add the roasted peppers, tomatoes, garlic, ketchup, sugar, salt, pepper and red pepper flakes. Lower heat and simmer uncovered for about an hour until the liquid has evaporated. Stir frequently. Cool and serve at room temperature .

TIPS & ADVICE: This recipe can be stored in the fridge for a month. You can grill and add eggplant, different peppers and increase or decrease the sweetness or spiciness. It can be pureed, canned and stored, and served hot or cold. This dish is great with BBQ meat, chicken or fish or add canned tuna for a great lunch dish.

YIELD: about 2 cups

mémé's (emma haccoun's) tunisian quince jam

Jennifer Haccoun Abramson *We use this jam to break the Yom Kippur fast. It was my Grandmother Emma's recipe as told to me by Tonton Lilou, Élie Haccoun. I added the cloves. The way the colour goes from pale yellow to deep rust is symbolic of how with time and patience, things can change for the better.*

2–3 quince fruits

about 1 cup sugar

juice of ½ lemon

⅓ cup water

2 cinnamon sticks

3 whole cloves

Peel the quince, remove the core and slice thinly. Use a food scale to weigh the slices. Weigh out an amount of sugar equal to 70% of the weight of the fruit. In a small pot, combine the quince, sugar, lemon juice, and water. Add the cinnamon sticks and cloves. Cook over low heat, stirring occasionally, until the colour turns a deep rusty red. Remove from heat and discard the cloves and cinnamon stick. Keeps well in the refrigerator for several weeks.

YIELD: about 1 cup

population reached 18,237, six times its size in 1901.   (our story continues on page 62 . . . read on)

Joseph Gary's Groceries,
420 College Street,
Toronto [ca. 1935]

selma's salad dressing (pareve)

Carol Seidman *My aunt Selma gave me this recipe over 40 years ago when I got married. I have also used it on occasion as a basting sauce for turkey and chicken. Enjoy!*

1 cup vegetable oil

⅔ cup white vinegar

4 large garlic cloves

2 heaping tablespoons light or regular mayonnaise

2 teaspoons salt

1½ teaspoons sugar or 2 packages of Splenda

1 teaspoon dry mustard powder

½ teaspoon pepper

Blend all ingredients together either manually or in a blender and store in a tightly covered container.

TIPS & ADVICE: It lasts for months in the refrigerator.

YIELD: 1½ cups dressing

thick and yummy caesar salad dressing

Janis Breslin *Everyone raves about this easy and delicious dressing.*

6 tablespoons vegetable oil

4 tablespoons Hellman's light mayonnaise

2 tablespoons Parmesan cheese, grated

2 tablespoons red wine vinegar

1 egg

1 garlic clove, crushed

salt and pepper to taste

dash of Worcestershire sauce

dash of Tabasco sauce

Parmesan cheese shavings

Whisk all the ingredients together, except for the Parmesan cheese shavings. If the dressing is too thick, add more oil and if it's too thin, add more mayonnaise. I enjoy a thicker consistency. Caesar Salad is usually made with romaine lettuce and often contains croutons as well. Add the Parmesan shavings after the salad has been tossed.

NUMBER OF SERVINGS: 6

 ✡ Two years later, it reached 32,000 and represented over 7% of the city's population.

caesar salad dressing

Sharon Naiberg *This recipe is an amalgamation of the best Caesar salad recipes I have come across since the early 1970s and is still a family favourite.*

½ cup olive oil

1 egg yolk

2 tablespoons white wine vinegar

2 tablespoons lemon juice

1 garlic clove, sliced

½ tablespoon Dijon mustard

1 teaspoon Worcestershire sauce

½ teaspoon anchovy paste

¼ tablespoon salt

¼ teaspoon pepper

½ cup Parmesan cheese shavings

Whisk all the ingredients together, except the Parmesan cheese. Taste the dressing for seasoning. If necessary, add more salt and pepper to taste. Remove garlic slices from dressing. After salad is dressed, top with Parmesan cheese.

TIPS & ADVICE: Boxed croutons will not do it justice. I recommend making your own by toasting day-old baguette cubes with garlic and olive oil in a frying pan on medium heat until golden brown.

NUMBER OF SERVINGS: makes enough dressing for a large salad

did you know?
Over 4500 families in the GTA (about 6500 kids) receive Jewish children's books each month to their home with the PJ Library.

Most Jews arriving in Toronto after 1900 settled in St. John's Ward or "the Ward".

creamy caesar salad (pareve)

Elise Stern Gropper *My cousin, Orit Raf, came to Canada for my brother's Bar Mitzvah from Israel 40 years ago and never left. Along with gaining a sister, we also benefitted from her amazing cooking abilities. She gave me this creamy pareve Caesar salad dressing recipe that we translated from Hebrew. It is a crowd pleaser for all ages. We never fail to get questioned if it is REALLY pareve.*

salads

Dressing:

1 cup olive oil

¼ cup red wine vinegar

1 raw egg

5 pieces anchovies

3 garlic cloves

1 teaspoon lemon juice

1 teaspoon salt

¾ teaspoon black pepper

½ teaspoon Dijon mustard

¼ teaspoon mustard powder

¼ teaspoon sugar

Salad:

3 heads romaine lettuce, chopped

3 mini English cucumbers, diced

2 hard boiled eggs, sliced

non dairy croutons

Combine all dressing ingredients in a blender on high speed. Blend until creamy. Cool in fridge. Combine the salad ingredients. Add the dressing. Garnish with croutons, if desired. There will be more dressing than you need so you can enjoy it the next day.

TIPS & ADVICE: I double the recipe so that I can use a whole container of anchovies at the same time. I use a bit less oil than is called for when I double it, although when my mom doubles this recipe, she combines one cup olive oil and one cup canola oil. Either option works.

NUMBER OF SERVINGS: 12–14

This infamous immigrant slum adjacent to the garment district was bounded by

thai salad with beef

Karen Cole *This is an easy dinner for two. You can leave out the meat for a vegetarian option and you can increase the salad ingredients for a buffet meal.*

Dressing:

3 tablespoons fish sauce*

3 tablespoons lime juice

2 tablespoons canola oil

1 garlic clove, minced

1 tablespoon light brown sugar

1 tablespoon water

1½ teaspoons chili paste

½ teaspoon sesame oil

Salad:

1 carrot, julienned

1 bunch scallions, thinly sliced

½ cup mixed cilantro, mint and basil, chopped

½ pound flank steak, seasoned with salt and pepper

1 large handful dried rice noodles

1 large handful mesculin or chopped lettuce

1 large handful cabbage, shredded

3 radishes, thinly sliced

⅓ cup cucumber, seeded and diced

⅓ cup mango, diced

⅓ cup tomato, diced

2 tablespoons crushed peanuts to garnish

For the dressing, whisk all ingredients together and let it sit at room temperature while you prepare the rest of the recipe. Add the carrot, scallions and herb mixture to a hot skillet with seasoned beef. Sear the beef, 2–3 minutes per side for medium rare. Let meat rest a few minutes and then slice on the bias. Toss the beef with 2–3 tablespoons of the dressing. Soak the rice noodles in boiling water until soft. Cut into small pieces and chill. Mix noodles with remaining salad ingredients, except peanuts, in large bowl. Add dressing until well coated. Divide salad between 2 plates, and place beef in a mound on top. Sprinkle with toasted peanuts.

EDITORIAL NOTE: It is a custom, not a law, in Kosher homes not to mix fish and meat on the same plate. If this is your custom, you can substitute 2 tablespoons of Bragg's Liquid Aminos and 1 tablespoon of Shiro miso in lieu of fish sauce.

NUMBER OF SERVINGS: 2

Yonge, University, Queen and College streets and contained all the amenities of a shtetl.

arugula salad with berries and feta cheese

Melanie Bogoroch *I make this salad a few nights each week and still hear from my family that it's one of their favourite salads every time I serve it. It is always requested when there is a family gathering, potluck meal, or barbeque. It goes well with everything. I love making this salad as it's so colourful and looks beautiful served on a platter.*

Dressing:

equal parts of white wine vinegar, maple syrup, grapeseed oil

large handful arugula or small pre-washed package of mixed greens

2 mini cucumbers, diced

1 red pepper, diced

½ orange pepper, diced

1 can drained mandarin oranges, cut into small pieces

1 cup feta cheese, crumbled

½–1 cup candied pecans, chopped

½ pint container of fresh strawberries, sliced

½ pint container of blackberries cut in half

Mix the vinegar, maple syrup, and grapeseed oil together and shake well. Dressing may be prepared a day or two ahead to allow the flavours to meld. Toss the arugula, all the vegetables, and half of the mandarins, feta, candied pecans, strawberries and blackberries with the dressing and place in low flat bowl or onto a platter. Arrange the remaining mandarins, feta, candied pecans, strawberries and blackberries on top of the salad and serve.

TIPS & ADVICE: This salad can be made with any greens instead of the arugula. It's also delicious when you add either grilled chicken (omit feta) or salmon and serve as a main course. It's tasty without the nuts if allergies are an issue. You can also add a touch more maple syrup to your dressing if you like it a little sweeter. Adjust the amount of greens, peppers, cucumbers, berries, mandarins, feta and nuts to your liking.

NUMBER OF SERVINGS: 5

In 1911, it had the highest density in the city with 80 people per acre and an average

baby kale and apricot salad

Rose Reisman *Baby kale is such a powerhouse of nutrition. One cup cooked contains only 36 calories, but provides 350% of daily vitamin A, 90% of vitamin C, and 1,000% of vitamin K.*

8 cups baby kale leaves

1 cup red onion, sliced

½ cup dried cranberries

½ cup toasted almonds, sliced

Dressing:

2½ tablespoons apricot jam

2 tablespoons olive oil

1 tablespoon cider vinegar

1 tablespoon lemon juice

pinch salt and pepper

Place the baby kale, onion, cranberries, and almonds on a serving platter. To make the dressing, mix the jam, oil, vinegar, lemon juice, salt, and pepper together and pour over top of the salad.

TIPS & ADVICE: I love this dish as a side salad, but I also make it a main meal by adding some protein such as grilled chicken or tofu.

NUMBER OF SERVINGS: 8

salads

asian salad

Debbie Rabinovitch *My late mom, Toba Lipman, made this salad at the cottage when we were expecting a large gang. It's easy and light and everyone always enjoys it.*

Dressing:

½ cup organic coconut sugar

½ cup grapeseed oil

¼ cup apple cider vinegar

3 garlic cloves, minced

2 tablespoons soy sauce

2 tablespoons canola oil

1 package instant ramen noodles, broken up

½ cup slivered almonds

¼ cup sesame seeds

1 bag ready-to-eat romaine lettuce

Boil the sugar, grapeseed oil, apple cider vinegar, garlic and soy sauce for 3 minutes and then refrigerate for 1 hour. Heat oil in a frying pan on medium-low heat. Add noodles, nuts, and seeds until they are lightly brown. Let cool. Put the romaine lettuce into salad bowl. Toss in the cooled noodles, seeds and nuts. Add dressing. Enjoy!

TIPS & ADVICE: Cut up pieces of clementine may be added to salad as an option.

NUMBER OF SERVINGS: 4

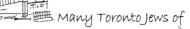

of 6 to 8 people per building; often just a small cottage or room. Many Toronto Jews of

zvoorech, zichel, farmer's salad

David Matlow *Farmer's salad is a traditional springtime treat in Polish and eastern European Jewish traditions. My mother, Esther Matlow, referred to it as Zvoorech although I don't know the origin of that word. As a young fan of farmer's salad, I renamed it Zichel, for no other reason than I liked the sound of that word better. My name caught on, so much so that after a while the family thought that Zichel was what this delicious dish was called in the outside world.*

As one who experiences the calendar through his taste buds, I associate certain foods with different times of the year. A chocolate bar heralds the beginning of the school year. Ice cream is for September 11. Turtles (the kosher kind, with pecans and caramel) on my birthday. Zichel is so special that it has two places on the calendar: in the meal that breaks the fast after Yom Kippur and on Shavuot. Serving Zichel at those meals is a family tradition; although not all the family members like to eat it, they all like to know it is there. It is a constant in a world that is always changing.

Two months before my mother passed away, at my request, she taught me how to make it. The key, said my mother, is to put in lots of vegetables. Keep chopping and slicing. For the radishes, cut in parallel lines one way, then the other way, and then across the circumference so that the radish crumbles into a hundred mini radish cubes. For the green onions, cut and throw it all in, even when you get to the end where it looks like tasteless leaves. For the cucumbers, slice, slice and slice again, all 30 centimeters of it. And then do it again with another cucumber. Like all of my mother's dishes, don't skimp, fill it to the brim, go all in. Every Shavuot and after Yom Kippur, I close my eyes to take a bite of Zichel, and I remember my mom.

2 packages of pressed cottage cheese

1 (16 ounce) container of light sour cream

1 bunch of large radishes

2 bunches of green onions

2 English cucumbers

Mix the cottage cheese and sour cream together, and add as much of the radish, green onion and cucumber (sliced and chopped as described above) as is humanly possible. Then, season with lots of pepper and a little bit of salt. It is not necessary, but it is a nice touch to add a few leaves of parsley on top. Spread high on fresh bread or a bagel. Take a bite. Enjoy.

NUMBER OF SERVINGS: 12

chicken salad

Leelah Koschitzky *I grew up in Toronto, went to college in New York where I married, and then moved to Israel with my husband and 2 year old daughter. My mother-in-law lives in New Jersey. She's a great cook and I'm always stealing her recipes. This is one of them.*

Chicken marinade:

½ cup sesame oil

½ cup soy sauce

2 boneless chicken breasts

Dressing:

1 cup olive oil

1 small onion, chopped

¾ cups sugar

⅓ cup apple cider vinegar

1 garlic clove, crushed

1 teaspoon dry mustard

1 teaspoon salt

3 tablespoons sesame seeds

1 head romaine lettuce, torn into bite size pieces

2 peppers, sliced

1 cup dried cranberries

1 mango, cut into strips

1 bunch asparagus tips, blanched

Marinate chicken overnight in sesame oil and soy sauce. Blend all dressing ingredients, adding sesame seeds at the end. Grill chicken or broil in oven, then slice on the diagonal. Toss all ingredients for salad, adding chicken on top. Drizzle dressing and serve.

TIPS & ADVICE: Salmon works equally well with this marinade and salad.

NUMBER OF SERVINGS: 4

did you know?

Birthright Israel has brought over 14,000 young Torontonians to Israel on a life changing Jewish experience.

chickpea, artichoke and sun-dried tomato salad with balsamic tahini dressing

Liza Gutfrajnd *I love salads and I enjoy playing around with ingredients all the time. This one was given to me years ago in a much simpler version and I just added ingredients and got creative with it.*

2 cans (540 ml or 19 ounce) chickpeas, drained and rinsed

3 jars (250 ml) artichoke hearts in oil, drained and chopped

1 cup black olives, sliced

½ cup sliced roasted peppers cut into small pieces (such as Unico red peppers)

1 small jar (250 ml) sun-dried tomatoes in oil, drained and julienned

½ cup fresh parsley, chopped

Dressing:

2 tablespoons tahini paste

2 tablespoons balsamic vinegar

1 tablespoon freshly squeezed lime juice

⅓ cup extra virgin olive oil

salt and pepper to taste

In a medium bowl, combine chickpeas, artichoke hearts, olives, red peppers, sun-dried tomatoes, and parsley. In a small bowl, whisk together the tahini paste, balsamic vinegar, and lime juice until the tahini is well mixed. Add the oil slowly, whisking at the same time until all dressing ingredients are well mixed. Add salt and pepper to taste. Pour desired amount of dressing into the chickpea mixture. If there is leftover dressing, it can be refrigerated for a couple of days.

TIPS & ADVICE: Any leftover salad lasts 2–3 days in the fridge. You can also serve the salad on a bed of arugula and drizzle with balsamic and olive oil.

NUMBER OF SERVINGS: 6–8

competition from other immigrant groups, allowed them to observe Shabbat and holidays and

daikon radish and cucumber slaw

Bunny Iskov *This is vegan and diet friendly and perfect as a side dish for any main course.*

1 large daikon radish (long white radish), peeled

6" piece English cucumber, sliced

¼ cup olive oil or grapeseed oil

½ teaspoon parsley flakes

salt and pepper to taste

In a food processor, using the shredder blade, grate the daikon radish. Squeeze out the excess water from the grated radish. Drain and place in a bowl. Add the English cucumber to the radish. Pour in the oil and mix the ingredients. Chill for a half hour in a covered bowl and sprinkle on the parsley flakes just before serving.

NUMBER OF SERVINGS: 4–6

salads

delicious napa cabbage salad

Elise Stern Gropper *This recipe is quick and easy to prepare and is always a crowd pleaser! It's also a great side dish for barbeques.*

1 large napa cabbage, chopped

8 green onions, chopped

½ green cabbage, chopped

½ cup fresh parsley, chopped

1 cup slivered almonds

½ cup sesame seeds

noodles from 2 packages instant Oriental flavour ramen soup

Dressing:

1 cup canola oil

6 tablespoons white vinegar

4 teaspoons sugar

2 teaspoons salt

2 soup flavour packages from instant Oriental flavour ramen noodles

Combine the napa cabbage, green onions, green cabbage and parsley into a large bowl.

Toast the almonds, sesame seeds, and uncooked instant oriental noodles, broken into pieces, in a pan on medium-low heat. Let cool and add to the salad bowl. Combine oil, white vinegar, sugar, salt, and flavour packages from the ramen in a jar. Shake vigorously. Add to salad and enjoy!

TIPS & ADVICE: I like to make the dressing early in the day so the ingredients can blend together.

NUMBER OF SERVINGS: 8–10

ellen's tex mex salad

Ellen Zabitsky *I'm always searching for fresh, easy salad recipes for summer living, and this one does the trick. It's a family and friends' favourite, best served with everything!*

2 medium ripe avocados, peeled and diced

1½ cups corn kernels, cooked or canned

1 can (540 ml) black beans, drained and rinsed

½ red bell pepper, diced

¼ cup green onion, chopped

Dressing:

⅓ cup lime juice, freshly squeezed

3 tablespoons olive oil

1 teaspoon garlic, minced

¼ teaspoon salt

¼ teaspoon ground pepper

In a large bowl, mix salad ingredients and set aside. In a small bowl, whisk together dressing, and toss with salad. Enjoy!

TIPS & ADVICE: I prefer to use fresh ingredients whenever possible, so I usually steam the corn and squeeze the lime juice; I find everything tastes better that way!

NUMBER OF SERVINGS: 6

 As competition increased, Jews found work in other independent ventures as tailors,

fresh and simple orange almond salad

Sheryl Traber *I was looking for a delicious, fresh, easy-to-make salad that I could serve at my Shabbat table or throw together to take to friends or family . . . and this is it! Everyone loves this great go-to salad for any season.*

1 bunch lettuce of your choice, torn

3-4 green onions, chopped

1 small can orange segments, drained

¼–½ cup slivered almonds, toasted

Dressing:

¾ cup canola or sunflower oil

¼ cup white vinegar

4-6 tablespoons sugar

2 teaspoons Dijon mustard

2 garlic cloves, minced

dash paprika

Mix all the salad ingredients together in a large bowl. Mix all the dressing ingredients together. Add the dressing to the salad and toss. Use only the desired amount of dressing based on the size of the salad.

TIPS & ADVICE: Leftover dressing will keep in the fridge for up to 3 weeks and can be added to other salads.

NUMBER OF SERVINGS: 6– 8

salads

did you know?
Chaplaincy Services representatives provided spiritual and religious care to over 30,000 members of the Jewish Community last year.

healthy tasty tuna salad

Stephanie Valentine *This is a great new tuna salad recipe; super tasty with healthy ingredients. Store-bought salads may be yummy, but you don't know exactly what's in them.*

Dressing:

2 tablespoons oil from the tuna can (if you use water packed, substitute extra virgin olive oil)

2 tablespoons lemon juice, freshly squeezed

¼ cup raw unsalted sunflower seeds

1 medium garlic clove

1 tablespoon Dijon mustard

1 tablespoon raw honey

1 jar white tuna packed in olive oil (drain oil, reserving 2 tablespoons)

1 stalk celery, diced

Combine all of the dressing ingredients in a food processor. Run the processor for a couple of seconds until it becomes a dressing-like consistency. Add the tuna to the food processor and run for a couple more seconds to blend. This can also be done by hand in a mixing bowl. Add the celery to the tuna salad mixture.

TIPS & ADVICE: You can add onions or even chopped up peppers to the salad if you like.

NUMBER OF SERVINGS: 2

summer salad

Elana Carr Horowitz *I like to serve this salad during the summer when we are having a dairy brunch. Using chickpeas always reminds me of Israel!*

2 avocados, peeled and chopped

1 can chickpeas, rinsed and drained

⅓ cup cilantro, chopped

⅓ cup feta cheese, crumbled

2 tablespoons green onion, chopped

juice of one whole lime

salt and pepper to taste

In a medium bowl, combine all ingredients. Stir until well mixed. Season with salt and pepper. Serve and enjoy! I usually double this recipe.

NUMBER OF SERVINGS: 4

major appeal of the "shmatte" or garment industry was that earnings were directly related to →

kale salad with peanut dressing

Yona Elishis *This recipe has made its way to my Shabbat lunch every week. It is my friend, Daniella's, three year old daughter's favourite!*

1 bunch kale, sliced in ribbons

½ cup peanuts, crushed

Dressing:

½ cup olive oil

¼ cup rice vinegar

1 garlic clove

1 teaspoon sugar

½ teaspoon sea salt

Place dressing ingredients into food processor and process until smooth. Massage the kale ribbons with dressing to coat and then sprinkle the crushed peanuts on top.

TIPS & ADVICE: You can add dried cranberries to this recipe for a sweeter taste or add roasted sliced beets to add some colour. It is delicious on its own as well. This salad can be dressed in advance . . . it does not get soggy!

NUMBER OF SERVINGS: 4

maple tahini kale salad

Eva Rosenthal *This was an attempt, on my part, to create something different for my family. None of us had ever tried kale before, but it seems to be the "in vogue" ingredient. I looked in my fridge, pulled together a few things, and came up with the following recipe. It is quick and easy to prepare and my family loves it!*

1 bunch of kale, torn into bite sized pieces

3 ripe avocados, peeled and sliced

1 red pepper, julienned

1 (311 g) can mandarin oranges, drained

Dressing:

5 tablespoons prepared tahini, not in paste form

1 tablespoon maple syrup

1½ teaspoons orange juice

1 teaspoon extra virgin olive oil

Arrange salad ingredients in bowl. In a small bowl, combine the dressing ingredients. Stir well. Spoon the dressing over the salad and toss to coat.

NUMBER OF SERVINGS: 4–6

individual effort. The industry also attracted off-season Jewish workers from New York,

roasted fall salad

Jackie Zimmerman *Anytime I make this salad and serve it to company, it is a big hit and I get a lot of requests for the recipe. The salad adds beautiful colour to the table or buffet.*

5–6 very ripe Bartlett pears, sliced in wedges, unpeeled

3 tablespoons olive oil, divided

1 teaspoon ground ginger

1 small butternut squash, peeled and diced

kosher salt, to taste

2 Vidalia onions, diced or thinly sliced

2 tablespoons balsamic vinegar

1 tablespoon white sugar

1 cup pecans, whole or chopped

½ cup icing sugar

¼–½ teaspoon chili powder, optional

1 large bag organic spring mix or baby spinach

Dressing:

½ cup good quality olive oil for salad

⅓ cup white wine vinegar or cider vinegar

2½ tablespoons honey

1½ tablespoons Dijon mustard

½ teaspoon garlic, minced

½ teaspoon salt

¼ teaspoon fresh ground pepper

Preheat broiler or convection oven to 375°F–400°F. Lay sliced pears on parchment lined cookie sheet, brush with 1 tablespoon olive oil, and sprinkle with ginger. Broil or roast the pears until they are brown on top. Keep watch, as this can happen quickly. Sprinkle with kosher salt. Set aside. Toss the squash with 1 tablespoon olive oil, lay on parchment lined sheet, and roast until tender but not mushy, approximately 20 minutes. Sprinkle with kosher salt. Set aside. Sauté onions in 1 tablespoon olive oil on medium-low heat and cook until light brown, approximately 15 minutes. Add the balsamic vinegar and then add the white sugar. Allow onions to cook until brown and syrupy, approximately 10 minutes. Add dressing ingredients to a jar and shake to combine.

To candy the pecans, combine pecans, icing sugar and chili powder (if using). Sauté on medium low heat until brown and bubbly. Remove and cool on parchment lined cookie sheet.

Assemble all of the ingredients on a platter; dress and toss before serving.

TIPS & ADVICE: For a healthier option, use toasted pecans instead of candied. Use any greens you like. It works really well with arugula or kale.

NUMBER OF SERVINGS: 8

molly melul's roasted pepper salad

Luna Igelman *My mother, Molly Melul, gave me this Sephardic roasted pepper salad recipe and it has become a staple at every holiday meal. I have modified it by roasting the garlic to garnish the peppers, rather than crushing it into the dressing. It is quick and easy and it's a hit every time. Everyone looks forward to the peppers, especially with freshly baked bread or warm matzah. Enjoy!*

8 small Cubanelle peppers

2 tablespoons extra virgin olive oil, divided

Dressing:

1 whole head of garlic

⅓ cup extra virgin olive oil

juice of 1 lime

roasted garlic from above

salt and pepper to taste

2 tablespoons chives, finely chopped

Preheat oven to broil. Place oven rack on the second highest rack (⅓ of the way down from the broil element). Wash and dry peppers, brush them with 1 tablespoon of oil and place on flat pan or cookie sheet lined with foil. Place under broiler until slightly charred and then continue turning them until all areas are charred and the peppers are softened. Remove from the oven and place in a bag. Cool for about an hour. Peel off as much skin as possible. Discard any liquid. Slice into wedges or strips depending on size of pepper. Place on serving platter.

Slice off the top of garlic head, drizzle with some olive oil and wrap in foil. Bake in oven at 375°F until softened, about 40-45 minutes. Remove garlic head from oven and squeeze the cloves out of their skins. Slice each clove in half. Mix oil with lime, salt, pepper, and roasted garlic clove halves. Drizzle over peppers. Garnish with chopped chives and serve with fresh bread or flat bread.

TIPS & ADVICE: This recipe works beautifully with yellow, orange and red bell peppers. Does NOT freeze well.

NUMBER OF SERVINGS: 8

tabbouleh salad

Norene Gilletz *This nutritious Middle Eastern salad is packed with vitamins, minerals and flavour. For best results, dry parsley and mint thoroughly before chopping them in the processor. (Copyright © Norene Gilletz, September 3, 2014)*

½ cup bulgur (cracked wheat)

2 cups boiling water

1 large bunch flat-leaf parsley (about 1 cup chopped)

1 small bunch mint (about ¼ cup chopped)

4 firm, ripe tomatoes, cored and quartered

4 green onions, cut in chunks

¼ cup extra-virgin olive oil

¼ cup fresh lemon juice

Salt and freshly ground black pepper to taste

In a medium bowl, soak bulgur in boiling water for 15 minutes. Drain in a fine mesh strainer. Soak parsley and mint in cold, salted water for 10 minutes. Drain and dry well. Trim stems from parsley and mint. Using the steel blade in your processor, process tomatoes with on/off pulses, until coarsely chopped. Place in a large bowl. Add drained bulgur to tomatoes. Wipe processor bowl dry. Process parsley with mint until finely minced. Add green onions and process with on/off pulses, until chopped. Add to bulgur mixture along with remaining ingredients and mix gently. Refrigerate at least 1 hour before serving. Serve chilled. Leftovers will keep 1 or 2 days in the refrigerator.

TIPS & ADVICE: For a grain-based tabbouleh, increase bulgur to 1 cup. If you prefer a greener tabbouleh, use only ¼ to ⅓ cup bulgur. Couscous can be substituted, or you can replace the soaked bulgur with 1 cup cooked quinoa. If desired, add ½ cup sliced olives and sprinkle with feta cheese. Save the parsley stems and use them when making chicken or vegetable broth.

NUMBER OF SERVINGS: 6

visit our website
www.JewishToronto.com/BathurstStreetKitchen

Ward, hiring them within the factory and for piece-work. Despite Eaton's relatively

tex mex salad

Stephanie Greenwald *This recipe is from my roommate during freshman year at Stern College. As she was was from Los Angeles and I am from Miami, the two of us commiserated about the cold New York winters. We have stayed close. When my family visited Los Angeles in the summer, she made this recipe for us.*

Dressing:

1 package taco seasoning

⅛ cup mayonnaise

juice of 2 lemons

salt and pepper, to taste

Salad:

kernels from 8 ears of corn

olive oil, for drizzling

1 pint cherry or grape tomatoes, halved

1 small red onion, chopped

1 yellow pepper, diced

½ red pepper, diced

¼ cup cilantro, chopped

2 avocados, peeled and diced

4 grilled boneless chicken breasts, optional

Combine the taco seasoning, mayonnaise, lemon juice, salt, and pepper for dressing and set aside. Preheat oven to 400°F. Remove the corn from the cob and lay it out on a baking sheet. Drizzle olive oil, salt and pepper and roast the corn at 400°F until golden. Remove from oven and cool. Toss corn kernels with remaining vegetables and cilantro. Add grilled chicken, cut into small pieces, if desired, then add the avocado right before serving. Toss with dressing and serve.

NUMBER OF SERVINGS: 8–10

salads

decent conditions for the times, Jewish workers organized an unsuccessful strike in 1912. →

the crown jewels: massaged kale salad

Jennifer Haccoun Abramson *We joined a Community Supported Agriculture (CSA) project a few years ago and all of a sudden, kale became a big part of our diet. It grows well locally, has a long growing season and a long fridge life. This recipe uses kale and anything else that happens to be in the weekly box. This healthy, beautiful salad can easily be adapted; substitute pumpkin seeds for almond slivers for nut-free; edamame or diced leftover chicken for peas for high protein; diced peppers for dried cranberries for low carb.*

salads

1 large head of kale, finely chopped

juice of 1 lemon

⅓ cup olive oil

½ tablespoon salt

½ cup frozen peas

⅓ cup red onion, diced

¼ cup dried cranberries

¼ cup almonds, slivered

Clean kale, remove the tough stems and place in a large bowl. In a small bowl, combine lemon juice, olive oil and salt. Pour over kale. Using your hands, massage the lemon juice mixture into the kale until you feel the fibers breaking down. The kale will start to feel softer, almost as if it were cooked. Add the remaining ingredients and toss to combine. Serve at room temperature in a glass bowl.

TIPS & ADVICE: I sometimes add other items to this, such as canned mandarin oranges, sliced strawberries, and/or chopped apricots. The key is to use brightly coloured fruits and vegetables, preferably in jewel tones (deep ruby red, bright emerald green, vibrant orange) that look beautiful and complement the tartness of the lemon juice with their sweetness and/or crunchiness. It is also a great way to use leftovers, because pretty much anything would be good in this salad.

NUMBER OF SERVINGS: 6–8

Toronto Jews also began their own small, specialized garment operations servicing

tomato salad with bread

Karen Cole *This is a perfect summer salad, easy, and pretty for a buffet.*

5 cups assorted tomatoes, cut into small wedges

2 celery ribs, cut into bite size slices

1 cucumber, cut into chunks

½ red onion, diced

10–20 pitted olives, sliced

¼ cup capers, chopped

1 red pepper, sliced

1 yellow pepper, sliced

Dressing:

1 cup assorted fresh basil, rosemary, thyme combined or ⅓ cup each or to taste

¼ cup olive oil

1 tablespoon balsamic vinegar

½ cup Parmesan cheese, grated

½ cup Asiago cheese, grated

¼ cup skinned plum tomatoes, chopped finely

1 day old or toasted French bread cut into cubes

Lay out all the salad ingredients on a large platter. Combine dressing ingredients. Pour dressing on salad a couple of hours before serving. Add cheeses and extra tomatoes on top. Add bread cubes last, just before serving.

TIPS & ADVICE: Use as many varieties of tomatoes in assorted sizes and colours as possible. Slice some of the olives and leave some whole.

NUMBER OF SERVINGS: 10–12

salads

"armenian" salad

Cayla Hochberg *I discovered this recipe a few years ago when my Armenian friend and colleague, Taleen, brought it for lunch. Her family had been making it for generations and it was her go-to salad to bring to a potluck. It caught my eye because it was so colourful and had such an unusual combination of ingredients. When she offered me a taste, it was love at first bite. I assumed that the salad was Armenian and searched Armenian recipes to recreate it. Taleen later advised me that it's actually not a traditional Armenian recipe at all, just a recipe that her Armenian grandmother made up. Two years later, I still call it Armenian Salad . . . even though it's not really an Armenian Salad. It's vegan, pareve and gluten-free. I've made it for breaking of the fast, Passover, and everything in between. It's the perfect make-ahead dish as it tastes even better when the flavours have time to come together.*

1 small can black olives, drained, rinsed and sliced

1 small can green olives, drained, rinsed and sliced

1 red bell pepper, seeded and diced

1 green bell pepper, seeded and diced

1 cup walnut pieces

¼ cup green onions or chives, minced

Dressing:

2 tablespoons olive oil (or double the amount of the lemon juice)

juice of ½ lemon (about 1 tablespoon)

salt and pepper

¼ cup parsley, chopped

Place all salad ingredients in a big bowl. Whisk the olive oil and lemon juice together with about ½ teaspoon of salt and a few pinches of black pepper. Pour the dressing on the salad ingredients and mix well, adding more lemon juice, olive oil, or salt as you see fit. Cover and let sit for anywhere from 1 hour to overnight before serving. Mix again, adjust seasonings, and sprinkle with the chopped parsley just before serving.

NUMBER OF SERVINGS: 4–6 as a side dish

salads

moved westward to better accommodations, and other ethnic groups moved into the Ward, the

green and red salad

Rochelle Reichert *This salad is definitely NOT a dish that has been handed down through the generations of my Eastern European family. It's a more modern dish with Italian and Israeli influences which reflects the great abundance of interesting ingredients which are available in Toronto and which we have come to take for granted. As a dietitian, I am always looking for ways to use vegetables and make them super tasty. I was inspired to create this recipe by a salad I ate at a restaurant in Jerusalem.*

1 small head romaine lettuce, washed and torn into bite size pieces

1 bunch arugula, washed and torn

1 small head radicchio, washed and torn

1 red apple, chopped

½ bulb fennel, sliced

small handful fresh dill, torn or chopped

2 tablespoons fresh tarragon, torn or chopped (optional)

Dressing:

½ cup canola oil

3 tablespoons red wine vinegar

1½ teaspoons Dijon or grainy mustard

1 teaspoon sugar

⅓ cup toasted walnuts, left in large pieces

Place vegetables, apple and herbs into a large salad bowl. Combine oil, vinegar and other dressing ingredients in a glass jar and shake well. At the last minute, pour over salad. Add walnuts. Toss to coat well.

TIPS & ADVICE: I like to use a combination of mild and robust lettuces, so feel free to mix it up. Toasted sunflower or pumpkin seeds work well if you are concerned about a nut allergy or simply don't like walnuts. Once, I added some leftover cooked red quinoa and it added a nice visual touch and crunchy texture. For a bit of sweetness, maple syrup, honey or jam all work well instead of sugar in the dressing. Making a great salad dressing depends on just the right combination of sour, sweet and salty so be sure to taste the salad and adjust the flavours before serving.

NUMBER OF SERVINGS: 8

beet salad

Daphna Zacks *The ancient Jewish tradition of Simanim, blessing and eating foods that have symbolic meaning, is different in every Jewish household. Some people stick to apples dipped in honey, yet others embrace a range of symbols, some of which are either a play on words or translations from Yiddish or Hebrew. In our house, we have a whole Rosh Hashanah Seder, which is a series of symbolic foods that visually and deliciously embody our wishes and intentions for the New Year.*

Beets are one of those symbolic foods. We feel it's a fun way to make the holiday meal interactive.

2 pounds fresh orange beets

2 sprigs fresh rosemary, optional

1 tablespoon olive oil

Dressing:

¾ cup balsamic vinegar

2 tablespoons olive oil

1 teaspoon brown sugar

1 teaspoon kosher salt

¼ teaspoon black pepper

2 cups fresh radicchio or kale, sliced thinly

1 cup grape tomatoes, halved

⅓ cup golden raisins

⅓ cup dried cranberries or currants

2 tablespoons candied or toasted pecans

Preheat the oven to 450°F. With heavy-duty aluminum foil, completely wrap beets, rosemary, and the olive oil in an aluminum package. Seal with another piece of foil to prevent dripping in the oven. Place on a small roasting pan and bake in oven for about 55 minutes, or until beets are tender. Carefully open package to release steam, and cool completely. With a paper towel, remove beet skin and then cut into wedges. Discard rosemary. Pour balsamic vinegar into small saucepan and bring to boil. Reduce heat, and simmer, uncovered, for about 10 minutes or until vinegar is reduced to about ¼ cup. It will thicken as it cools. Whisk in 2 tablespoons olive oil, sugar, salt and pepper. Place radicchio or kale on a large serving platter. Scatter beets, tomatoes, raisins, cranberries and nuts. Drizzle dressing over top and serve.

TIPS & ADVICE: The recipe can be easily doubled. This beet recipe can be made with or without the nuts, as not everyone uses nuts on Rosh Hashanah.

NUMBER OF SERVINGS: 6–8

soups

UNITED

QUICK LUNCH

Rosie Lieberman, Rosie Haneford Green,
Aaron Ladovsky and Sarah Ladovsky
in front of United Bakers,
338 Spadina Avenue, 1920

harira

Sandrine Wizman *This soup is traditionally served to break the fast after Yom Kippur and is great and hearty on a cold day.*

1 cup dried chickpeas

½ cup dried brown lentils

3 tablespoons olive oil

2 onions, diced

5 tomatoes, peeled and diced

½ cup dried lima beans

3 stalks celery, diced

1 bunch coriander or parsley, chopped

1 pinch saffron

1 pound beef (chuck), cut into bite size pieces

11 cups water, divided

½ cup flour

1 lemon, juiced

salt and pepper to taste

¾ cup broken spaghetti, uncooked

Wash and soak the chickpeas and lentils overnight in a good amount of water. Before use, drain and rinse well. In a stockpot, heat oil over medium-high and add onions and tomatoes, sautéing until onions are translucent. Add chickpeas, lentils, dried lima beans, celery, coriander or parsley, saffron and meat. Add 10 cups water and bring to a boil, then reduce heat to medium and let simmer, covered, for approximately 1 hour.

Dissolve flour in 1 cup of cold water and stir into the soup with a wooden spoon until well mixed. Add lemon juice, salt and pepper. Add spaghetti and continue cooking for an additional 15 minutes. Adjust seasoning if necessary.

TIPS & ADVICE: This soup may be made vegetarian by eliminating the meat. Canned chickpeas, lentils and lima beans may be substituted, but add them when adding the spaghetti in the last 15 minutes. The soup is best made the day before as the flavours have a chance to develop. Reheat on a low heat.

NUMBER OF SERVINGS: 10–12

By 1914, 66% of Toronto's Jews had moved out of the Ward to the area bounded by

tata danielle thérien's harira soup

Jennifer Haccoun Abramson *My aunt Danielle used to make this on cold winter nights. It is simply the most delicious, hearty soup I have ever tried. I imagine it kept my ancestors warm in their unheated homes. It is also easy to make and a great way to use up leftover pasta bolognese: just add it, chopped up, when adding the rest of the ingredients.*

2 tablespoons oil (enough to cover the bottom of the pot)

1 large onion, diced

1 heaping tablespoon garlic, minced

1 cup dried lentils, soaked overnight

1 cup dried chickpeas, soaked overnight

1 bunch cilantro, chopped

1 bunch parsley, chopped

1 small can tomato paste

water to cover

1 lemon, sliced

Heat oil over medium heat in a large saucepan. Add onions and garlic and fry until onions are translucent, making sure garlic doesn't burn. Add lentils and chickpeas and fry for another 1–2 minutes. Add remaining ingredients except lemon, cover with water and stir until tomato paste is well dispersed. Bring to a boil. Reduce heat and simmer 15–20 minutes. Serve hot with lemon slices.

TIPS & ADVICE: DO NOT add salt to the water until the end, if at all. Lentils and chickpeas will not cook properly in salted water. In a pinch, a can each of lentils and chickpeas can be substituted for the dried and soaked lentils and chickpeas.

NUMBER OF SERVINGS: 6

soups

ann wieskopf kornbluth's cabbage soup

Eleanor Levine *This is a recipe that my mother Ann Wieskopf Kornbluth made during cold Montreal winters. I grew up eating and loving it but I always hated cooked cabbage. I was allowed to eat the soup and brisket and leave the cabbage behind! I still have my mother's 1962 handwritten instructions in my recipe binder. Today, at age 74, I continue to eat only the brisket and soup but not the cabbage. Everybody else likes the whole combination so this is a popular dish in my family.*

1 (5 pound) brisket

1 large can tomatoes, diced

5 cups water, divided

1 teaspoon salt

1 teaspoon pepper

¾ cup sugar

½ lemon, sliced, including skin

1 small cabbage, sliced

3 tablespoons toasted flour

Wash brisket and place whole into a 5 quart saucepan that has been heated on the stovetop. Sear on both sides. Remove from pan and let cool. Slice brisket, trying not to lose any of the juices. Without washing saucepan, add diced tomatoes and 4 cups water. Bring to a boil. Return sliced meat to saucepan. Add salt, pepper, sugar, lemon, and cabbage. Return to a boil, then reduce heat to low and cook for 2½ hours or until meat is tender. Taste as it cooks—you may want it sweeter. After 2 hours, combine toasted flour with remaining cup cold water. Mix until smooth and add to soup. If the soup is too thick, add a bit more water.

TIPS & ADVICE: This comfort-food recipe is better the next day. Letting it sit marries the flavours. It also freezes very well and makes a quick and satisfying meal.

NUMBER OF SERVINGS: 10–12

soups

market and a new Jewish neighbourhood had been created on and near Kensington.

asian chicken coconut soup

Dianna Vaturri *I moved with my husband and family to Japan for a couple of years, and this is a recipe I brought back home to Toronto.*

1 small onion, chopped

1½ cups pumpkin, cut into cubes

8–10 mushrooms, sliced

1 zucchini, sliced

2 carrots, cubed

3 sticks lemon grass, slit in half

1 can coconut milk

2 tablespoons chicken soup mix

1 tablespoon sugar

1 egg, beaten

2 tablespoons flour

1 tablespoon soy sauce

few drops water

1 chicken breast, cubed

oil for frying

Place all vegetables (including lemon grass) into a saucepan and cover with water. Bring to a boil. Simmer until vegetables are softened, about 30 minutes. Add coconut milk, chicken soup mix and sugar and let simmer for an additional 10 minutes. Meanwhile, mix together egg, flour, soy sauce and a dash of water to make coating. Add chicken breast and mix until well coated. Fry coated chicken in oil and then add to soup.

NUMBER OF SERVINGS: 8–10

soups

did you know?
UJA Federation allocates $12 million annually to Jewish education in Toronto.

Life in Toronto for the average Jewish immigrant arriving at the beginning of the 19th century

saftas ora and roni's chicken soup

Dafna Carr *I am 43 and my mother has been making this chicken soup all my life! She learned how to make it by watching her mom cook it. So Safta Roni learned from Safta Ora who learned from Safta Bat Sheva in Israel. This soup is served at all of our holiday celebrations and never ceases to please all; compliments are plentiful. If you are feeling sick, it always makes you feel better.*

soups

1 whole chicken

10½ cups water

3 carrots

1 onion

3 celery stalks with leaves

½ celery root, peeled

1 parsnip, peeled

1½ garlic cloves, peeled

1 bay leaf

salt and pepper to taste

1 handful dill

Place fresh chicken in a large saucepan. Cover with water and bring to a boil over medium heat, then reduce to a simmer. Using a large spoon, skim foam off the surface of the liquid for the next 15–30 minutes, until broth looks clear. Add all of the remaining ingredients except for the dill. Cook on very low heat with the lid slightly open. Simmer for 90 minutes. Remove soup from heat and let cool.

Once cool, strain broth into a fresh saucepan using a sieve. Discard all solids except the carrots. Refrigerate soup and carrots overnight. The next day, remove fat solids from the surface of the soup and bring it back to a boil. Add dill, simmer 10–15 minutes, then remove to avoid a bitter taste. Add carrots back into soup. Taste and adjust seasoning as necessary.

TIPS & ADVICE: For additional flavour, add a couple tablespoons of chicken soup base. Serve with matzah balls or noodles.

NUMBER OF SERVINGS: 8–10

chicken soup and wings appetizer all-in-one

Eva Citrin *I wanted to make my chicken wings less fatty tasting and crisper. I like chicken soup but I don't like boiled chicken. This is an excellent way to prepare both. If prepared ahead, the soup can be quickly reheated in the microwave and the chicken wings are just as good cold.*

12 chicken wings, tip removed and split

6 cups cold water

3 teaspoons powdered pareve chicken soup base

2 tablespoons vegetable oil

spices such as onion powder, garlic powder, celery powder, paprika

2 cooking carrots, chopped into chunks

2 stalks celery, cut into pieces

1 parsnip, cut into pieces

2 cups curly pasta or egg noodles, uncooked

Rinse chicken wings in cold water and place in saucepan with water and chicken soup base. Simmer over medium-low heat for 20 minutes. Do not discard soup water. Meanwhile, preheat oven to 350°F. Line a cookie sheet with aluminum foil and distribute oil evenly. Remove wings from the saucepan and place on cookie sheet. Sprinkle with spices, as desired. Bake wings in oven for about 30 minutes or until desired crispness. Allow to cool for about 5 minutes before serving.

Meanwhile, add carrots, celery and parsnip to soup pot and cook over medium heat for 10 minutes. Increase heat and bring soup to a rapid boil, add in the pasta and cook for about 8 minutes or until pasta is al dente. Skim fat from top of soup and discard.

TIPS & ADVICE: Serve the chicken soup with chicken wings on its own as an appetizer, or with a mound of salsa or hummus, carrots and celery sticks. Add a salad, and the soup and wings become a meal for two.

NUMBER OF SERVINGS: 4 servings as an appetizer plus soup

hilda libman's matzah balls

Karen Bookman *This was my mom's recipe. It makes the fluffiest matzah balls. Chicken soup and matzah balls are part of my family's collective memory. Cooking my mom's food keeps her spirit close to me! I feel her presence through making her recipes.*

4 eggs

¼ cup club soda

¼ cup oil

1 teaspoon salt

dash pepper

1 cup matzah meal

Beat eggs slightly. Add club soda, oil, salt and pepper. Add matzah meal and mix the ingredients. Cover and refrigerate for at least 45 minutes. Mix again. Moisten hands and form into balls. Drop into a saucepan of boiling water (for added flavour, add powdered chicken soup to the water). Cover and cook for 45 minutes. Remove with slotted spoon and serve with hot soup. This recipe can be doubled.

NUMBER OF SERVINGS: 10–12 matzah balls

 Jobs were scarce and the majority of Jews in Toronto were new to the city, had no

matzah balls

Phyllis Grossman *Schmaltz adds flavour and provides great texture. Adding the ground-up greven enhances the taste. These may not look as pretty as other matzah balls but the taste and texture make up for that. The highest compliment came from my mother-in-law who said I made the best knaidlach (matzah balls). I was truly honoured as she was an excellent cook.*

2 tablespoons schmaltz
(chicken fat—see tips & advice)

2 jumbo eggs

½ cup matzah meal

½ teaspoon salt

1–2 tablespoons ground greven
(rendered chicken skin—see tips
& advice)

2 tablespoons water

If making schmaltz and greven:

1 cup chicken skin, chopped

½ onion, finely chopped

salt

Mix melted and cooled schmaltz and eggs in medium bowl. Add matzah meal, salt and ground greven. Add water and mix well. Refrigerate for 1 hour. Bring large saucepan of salted water to boil. Roll dough into walnut-sized balls. Place in boiling water for about 40 minutes before draining carefully through a sieve. If freezing, place matzah balls on a parchment-paper-lined baking sheet, then transfer to a bag before returning to freezer.

TIPS & ADVICE: You can buy schmaltz and greven or make it yourself. To make shmaltz and greven: Place chopped chicken skin in a small saucepan over medium heat. Stir often as fat renders out, scraping bottom of pan. Stir in ⅛ teaspoon salt. When skin starts to get crisp, add onion. Continue cooking until skin is crisp and onion is golden brown. Remove skin and onions with slotted spoon and drain on paper towel. When cooled, grind greven until fine. Store leftover greven in fridge. Pour leftover schmaltz in jar and store in refrigerator for frying, etc.

NUMBER OF SERVINGS: 8–10 matzah balls

savings, lacked skills and did not speak English. *At least three Christian missions*

hana's fabulous lentil soup

Joy D. Kaufman *My cousin, Hana Nidbach in Israel, is an excellent cook. Whatever she makes is great, but she does not measure her spices, so I had to figure this out on my own. She kept telling me that "koorkoom" is the spice that gives it a kick. I asked her what "koorkoom" was and she showed me the spice, which I took home in a jar. When I took it to a shop here, they opened the jar, smelled and said "Oh, turmeric!" My older daughter told me that of all the soups I make, this is her favourite. You may adjust the seasonings according to your taste.*

2 tablespoons olive oil

2 large garlic cloves, crushed

3 large carrots, peeled and finely chopped

1 large celery stalk, finely chopped

1 large sweet onion, finely chopped

1 small potato, peeled and finely chopped

3 cups dried red lentils, soaked in water for ½ hour and drained

11 cups water

2 teaspoons salt

1 tablespoon pepper

1 teaspoon cardamon

1 teaspoon turmeric

Heat olive oil in a small pan over medium heat. Add garlic, carrots, celery, onion and potato and sauté for 10 minutes. Stir to prevent vegetables from sticking. In a large saucepan, combine sautéed vegetables with the drained lentils and water. Cook over high heat until soup boils; then reduce to a simmer and cook 45 minutes longer. Ten minutes before soup is done, stir in seasonings.

TIPS & ADVICE: You may substitute another colour of lentils for the red ones. Freezes well.

NUMBER OF SERVINGS: 12

did you know?
The Socialization Program at the Bernard Betel Centre serves over 3,000 seniors per year.

were established to assist and convert the Jewish newcomers with little success and much →

carrot and red lentil soup

Natalie Roebuck *My daughter is vegan. This soup is easy and healthy.*

2 tablespoons vegetable oil

l large onion, chopped

2 garlic cloves, minced

2–3 teaspoons curry powder

4 large carrots, sliced

1 red pepper, chopped

1 cup dried red lentils

6 cups water or vegetable stock

¼ cup parsley, chopped

2 green onions, chopped

pinch cayenne pepper

Heat oil in a large saucepan over medium heat. Add onion, garlic, curry powder, carrots and red pepper. Cook, stirring, for 5 minutes. Add lentils and liquid and simmer until lentils are tender. Stir in parsley, green onion and cayenne pepper. Freezes well.

NUMBER OF SERVINGS: 6–8

red lentil apricot soup

Sheryl Katz *Very quick, easy and delicious. Freezes well.*

3 tablespoons vegetable oil

1 medium onion, chopped

⅓ cup dried apricots, chopped

2 garlic cloves, minced

1 cup dried red lentils, rinsed

1 large can diced tomatoes

6 cups consomme or chicken broth

½ teaspoon salt

¼ teaspoon pepper

2 tablespoons lemon juice

½ teaspoon cumin (optional)

In a large saucepan, heat oil and sauté onion, apricots and garlic. Do not let them brown. Add lentils, tomatoes, broth and seasoning and bring to a boil. Reduce heat to low and simmer for 30 minutes, stirring occasionally. Using an immersion blender, blend until smooth.

TIPS & ADVICE: When reheating, add water or stock if soup is a bit too thick.

NUMBER OF SERVINGS: 10

resentment and protest. In response to the hardships and the threat of the missions,

cuban black bean soup

Roz Schweber *My Mom is a Cuban Jew and this is her recipe. Because I love Cuban food, this is a comfort dish for me. Also, this version is vegetarian and pareve, and unlike Mexican food, it is not spicy, so it appeals to many palates.*

Soup:

7 cups water

16 ounces black beans

½ bell pepper, in pieces

5 garlic cloves, minced

1 bay leaf

1 tablespoon olive oil

1 tablespoon kosher salt

Sofrito:

1 tablespoon olive oil

¼ onion, finely chopped

2–3 garlic cloves, minced

¼–½ green pepper, finely chopped

¼ cup white cooking wine

¼ onion, chopped for garnish (optional)

In a pressure cooker, combine water, black beans, bell pepper, garlic, bay leaf, olive oil and salt over high heat. When pressure cooker begins to whistle, reduce heat to medium and cook for 45–50 minutes. Let pressure cooker cool. In the meantime, in a skillet, heat oil over medium heat. Add onion, garlic, chopped bell pepper and white wine and cook, stirring until vegetables are soft and onions are translucent. This is called a sofrito. After pressure cooker has cooled, open and add sofrito and cook uncovered for another 10 minutes. Serve over white rice as a side dish or main dish. If desired, you can chop up another ¼ onion to serve over top.

TIPS & ADVICE: Don't open pressure cooker until it cools.

NUMBER OF SERVINGS: 6–8

soups

dozens of mutual aid and sick benefits societies were created to provide Jewish immigrants →

mexican tortilla soup

Edith Rosemberg *This is a very popular soup in Mexico and a favourite in our house. We often serve it at our Shabbos dinners, where it is common to see both Jewish and Mexican dishes. When our grandparents first arrived in Mexico City in the 1920s, they immediately added Mexican dishes to their repertoires. Some changes had to be made to the original recipes, as many Mexican recipes call for lard and the mixing of meat and dairy. This recipe is very easy to make once all the ingredients have been assembled and prepared. It can be doubled, too. However, do not double the number of chiles since it may be too spicy. You may want to use plastic gloves to handle the chiles.*

soups

2 tablespoons vegetable oil

½ cup onion, coarsely chopped

2 garlic cloves, chopped

1 dried pasilla chile, softened in hot water and seeded

1 dried ancho chile, softened in hot water and seeded

1 cup canned strained tomatoes

4 cups vegetable broth

2 cups water

1 teaspoon vegetable bouillon base

salt and pepper to taste

2 cups vegetable oil

12 corn tortillas, cut into thin strips

1 cup mozzarella cheese, grated

1 avocado, peeled and cubed

1 cup sour cream or crème fraîche

Heat oil in a large saucepan and fry onions for 5 minutes until translucent. Add garlic and fry until fragrant. Add chiles and fry for 2 minutes longer. (Be careful as they burn very easily.) Add strained tomatoes and heat thoroughly. Add vegetable broth and bring to a boil. Lower heat, and with an immersion blender, blend till smooth. Add water and bouillon, and season with salt and pepper. Simmer for 5 minutes.

To fry tortillas, heat oil in a deep saucepan. Add tortillas in batches and fry until lightly golden. Serve in bowls with tortilla strips, cheese, avocado and cream as garnish.

NUMBER OF SERVINGS: 6

with free loans, sick and death benefits, burial plots, and other vital support.

minestrone soup

Bronna Ginsburg *Refreshing, delicious and healthy!*

1 tablespoon olive oil

1 onion, chopped

5 garlic cloves, crushed

1 cup carrots, chopped

1 cup celery, chopped

1 cup zucchini, chopped

1 cup red pepper, chopped

2 teaspoons salt, divided

1 teaspoon dried oregano

1 teaspoon dried basil

2 bay leaves

1 (14 ounce) can chickpeas

2 cups tomato puree

4 cups chicken or vegetable stock

¾ cup each of tomato paste and dry red wine

1 cup fresh tomatoes, chopped

pasta, prepared al dente (optional)

parsley and grated cheese (can add if using vegetable stock)

In a large saucepan, heat olive oil and sauté onion and garlic for about 5 minutes. Add carrots, celery, zucchini, red pepper, 1 teaspoon salt, oregano, basil and bay leaves and mix well. Cover and cook on low for 5–8 minutes until vegetables are tender. Add remaining ingredients except tomatoes and cover and simmer for 15 minutes. Add tomatoes and 1 teaspoon salt. Simmer on low for approximately 1 hour. Add freshly ground pepper to taste. When ready to serve, pour soup into bowls and add some freshly cooked pasta. Garnish with parsley and freshly grated cheese if desired.

NUMBER OF SERVINGS: 10–12

soups

did you know?
Jewish Immigrant Aid Services (JIAS) Toronto helps 500+ new Toronto families each year with resettlement & integration into Canadian & Jewish community life.

Many ethnic congregations/synagogues and societies, "Landsmanshaft" were also

karen's kale tomato veggie soup or "hulk" soup

Karen Medina *I'm a trainer. I developed this recipe for some of my clients that don't love vegetables or don't like eating salad in the winter. It's delicious and nutritious! Even my kids love it. They call it "hulk" soup because it's green. I tell them it will make them grow big and strong. This is a fantastic way to get your greens and veggies in one bowl.*

1 white onion, chopped

4 carrots, peeled and chopped

4 stalks celery, chopped

2 garlic cloves

1 teaspoon sea salt

½ teaspoon black pepper

½ teaspoon red pepper flakes

1 tablespoon fresh rosemary

1 tablespoon fresh basil

24 ounces strained tomatoes, no salt or sugar

2 cups water or chicken broth

1 bunch kale, coarsely chopped

Place all ingredients in a saucepan and bring to a boil. Reduce heat and simmer for 45 minutes. Puree soup with immersion blender. Enjoy.

NUMBER OF SERVINGS: 6

did you know?
UJA Federation provides essential items to 168,000 Jewish elderly living in poverty in the former Soviet Union, many of whom are Holocaust survivors.

roasted vegetable and barley soup

Anita Shedletsky *This is a perfect soup for everyone but especially vegetarians. It is almost filling enough to be a meal.*

Non stick vegetable oil spray or oil

1 whole head of garlic

6 large plum tomatoes, halved lengthwise

3 large carrots, trimmed, peeled, halved and diced

1 large onion, diced in ½" pieces

1 red bell pepper, diced

2 medium zucchini, trimmed, halved then quartered, diced, (can use 1 green and 1 yellow)

1 pound butternut squash, peeled and cubed

salt and pepper, to taste

8 cups or more canned low sodium vegetable broth

3–6 sprigs fresh thyme (sprig is 1 branch)

1 bay leaf

1 cup pearl barley

cayenne, optional

fresh parsley, chopped

Preheat oven to 400°F. Spray large rimmed baking sheet with nonstick spray or use disposable tin foil pans. Cut top off a head of garlic, place in a piece of tin foil and drizzle with some oil, wrap and place in one of the pans. Arrange tomatoes on one pan and next 6 ingredients on another sheet. If using disposable pans, you will need 3 or 4. I usually put the squash and carrots in one, the tomatoes alone in one, the zucchini and red pepper in one and the onion in one. Drizzle with oil; sprinkle with salt and pepper. Roast until vegetables are tender and brown around edges, stirring occasionally, about 55 minutes. Coarsely chop any large pieces of vegetables, remove skins from the tomatoes and place half of all the veggies and their juices in a large soup pot and reserve other half and all the garlic.

Use half cup of broth to scrape up browned bits from pans; add to pot with vegetables. Add 7½ cups broth, thyme, and bay leaf to pot. Bring to boil. Reduce heat to medium; cover and simmer until vegetables are very tender, about 15–20 minutes. Puree reserved vegetables and 6 cloves of the peeled, roasted garlic in processor until smooth. Add barley to pot and bring to boil. Reduce heat to medium; cover and simmer until barley is tender, about 40 minutes. Remove bay leaf and thyme. Add reserved vegetable puree to pot; simmer until soup thickens and flavours blend, about 10 minutes. Season soup to taste with salt and pepper; add some cayenne pepper for a slight kick. Cool soup slightly, then cover and keep chilled. Reheat over medium heat, thinning with additional broth if desired. Ladle soup into bowls. Sprinkle with parsley and serve.

TIPS & ADVICE: If using 3 or 4 pans, 2 on upper shelf and 2 on lower, change them at about 30 minutes so they do not burn. It may take 60–75 minutes to roast if using 4 disposable pans. This soup can and should be doubled as it's time consuming; may as well do it once. Soup can be frozen.

NUMBER OF SERVINGS: 8–10

bonnie's gazpacho

Bonnie Goldstein *This is one of my favourite recipes. I often serve it at the cottage and when it is gazpacho season, I know summer is here!*

4 large tomatoes

1 English cucumber

1 large green pepper

3 ounces sweet pimentos

3 cups tomato juice

⅓ cup red wine vinegar

1 lemon, juiced

1 teaspoon salt

⅛ teaspoon pepper (to taste)

½ teaspoon Tabasco sauce

fresh herbs for seasoning

Using the steel knife blade of your food processor, dice each vegetable separately, leaving some texture. Combine in a large bowl. Add tomato juice, vinegar and lemon juice as well as seasonings and stir until blended. Add any desired fresh herbs (basil, dill, chives, etc). Adjust seasonings to taste. As garnish, I recommend a selection of diced cucumbers, diced green peppers, croutons, shredded cheddar and/or sour cream.

NUMBER OF SERVINGS: 4-5 bowls

zucchini soup

Lissie Sanders *This was inspired by the zucchini soup at a wonderful Italian restaurant.*

2 tablespoons olive oil

3 garlic cloves, chopped

1 Vidalia onion, chopped

10 medium zucchinis, peeled and chopped

1 package fresh organic spinach

1 teaspoon sea salt

1 teaspoon freshly ground pepper

2 litres organic vegetable stock

2 teaspoons fresh or frozen basil

In a large saucepan, heat olive oil over medium heat and add garlic cloves and onion. Cook until onion is soft and translucent. Be careful not to burn garlic. Add chopped zucchini and toss with olive oil, onions and garlic. Season with sea salt and pepper. Pour in vegetable stock and add basil.

Cook over low heat until zucchini is soft and then add spinach. Cook until wilted. Turn off heat and puree mixture with immersion blender. Serve with a drizzle of olive oil and some fresh basil. Add salt and pepper to taste.

TIPS & ADVICE: Spinach can be left out, but it makes the soup a bit greener! This is a low fat delicious soup that freezes well.

NUMBER OF SERVINGS: 10

services including medical care by Dr. Samuel Lavine, (our story continues on page 102 . . . read on)

grains, pastas, matzah & kugels

Etta Simon lighting
candles at Passover seder,
Toronto [1950s]

wild rice pancakes

Brenlee Gurvey Gales *My sister and I have been making these for 25 years based on two recipes. One came from Pam McDonald, a talented chef that I worked with at David Wood Food Shop. The other came from Bishop's Restaurant in Vancouver. This recipe amalgamates the two, for a very special dish with great texture.*

½ cup wild rice, uncooked

1½ cups cold water

1 cup flour

1½ teaspoons baking powder

1 teaspoon salt

1 teaspoon sugar

2 eggs

¾ cup milk

2 tablespoons butter, melted

2 tablespoons shallots, minced

2 teaspoons garlic, minced

½ cup carrots, grated

½ cup celery, finely diced

1 tablespoon fresh parsley, chopped

grains, pastas, matzah & kugels

Wash the rice thoroughly. Combine the rice with the water in a small heavy pot. Bring to a boil and then immediately reduce the heat to low. Cover with a tight-fitting lid and simmer for 40 minutes. Remove from heat and drain any excess water. Let cool. Combine flour, baking powder, salt and sugar in a bowl and set aside. In a large mixing bowl, whisk eggs and then add milk and melted butter. Mix the dry ingredients into the wet ingredients. Blend well. Add the rice, shallots, garlic, carrots, celery and parsley. Stir to form a chunky batter.

Ladle out ¼ cupful portions onto a medium-hot, lightly oiled, non-stick frying pan or griddle and cook until nice and brown. Turn with a spatula and cook about 2 minutes longer on the other side. To keep warm, place parchment paper between layers and place in a 200°F oven.

TIPS & ADVICE: Substitute pareve margarine and almond milk to serve with meat. This is a great dish to bring to a dinner, and can be warmed just before serving.

YIELD: 12 to 14 pancakes

red rice composed salad

Fern Sanders *This red rice salad is completely original as I just "discovered" red rice in Israel and had to figure out what to do with it when I brought it to a party.*

1 cup red rice (Sugat)

1 teaspoon oil

2¼ cups water

pinch salt

3 tablespoons brown sugar

1 teaspoon cinnamon

1 large onion, diced

1 tablespoon oil

⅓ cup raisins, rehydrated (pour boiling water over them and then drain once soft)

¼ cup toasted pecans

Toast rice for 1 minute in 1 teaspoon of oil. Add water, sugar, salt and cinnamon, following package directions for technique. Cook for about 30 to 35 minutes until done. In another pan, cook the diced onion in oil until golden. Mix into cooked rice. Rehydrate the raisins, then add to rice mixture and blend well. Taste rice mixture and adjust seasonings (sugar, cinnamon). Pour into serving bowl and top with toasted pecan pieces. Serve and eat.

TIPS & ADVICE: You can substitute cranberries, dried cherries or your favourite dried fruit.

NUMBER OF SERVINGS: 4

grains,
pastas,
matzah &
kugels

visit our website
www.JewishToronto.com/BathurstStreetKitchen

guarantee members' admittance. *Other important aid efforts by the community* →

wheatberry or barley salad with crunchies

Elisa Palter *We throw whatever veggies are in the house into this salad and by varying the grain (barley works well too) and substituting orange juice for lemon juice or oranges for dried cranberries, this salad can be changed in a variety of ways. It is great for vegetarians (or vegan if you omit the feta) and is a colourful and tasty salad for any meal. We often add arugula and cut up chicken into it (without the feta) and make it a meal.*

grains, pastas, matzah & kugels

Salad:

1 cup wheatberries or barley, rinsed and drained

1 cup cucumber, chopped

½ cup red pepper, chopped

½ cup feta, crumbled

3 green onions, chopped

1–2 mandarin oranges, separated into sections with each section cut in half

1 tablespoon fresh mint, chopped

Dressing:

3 tablespoons olive oil

3 tablespoons balsamic vinegar

1 tablespoon maple syrup

1 teaspoon fresh lemon juice

freshly ground black pepper to taste

Sweet spicy crunchies:

2 cups pumpkin seeds (raw, unsalted)

¼–⅓ cup maple syrup

a few shakes of chili powder, if desired (cayenne or chipotle chili powder)

1 package ramen noodles with ½ of seasoning package

Follow package instructions to cook wheatberries. Test after 25 minutes for "done-ness". Berries should be chewy, but not tough. It may take as long as an hour to cook. When berries are the desired consistency, drain and cool.

Meanwhile, make the dressing, chop the veggies, and prepare the "crunchies" as follows. Mix pumpkin seeds, maple syrup, and chili powder in a skillet over med-low heat. Stir often for about 7–8 minutes until seeds are coated and have soaked up almost all the syrup. Add broken up ramen noodles to seeds and add about half the package of the seasoning mix sprinkled on top (alternatively, just sprinkle some crunchy sea salt if you don't want to use the packet). Stir about 3–4 minutes more until everything is coated and no liquid remains. Spread crunchies on a parchment in a single layer to cool. Break up large pieces when crisp. These can be made up to 1 week ahead, and stored in an airtight container or ziploc bag.

Add dressing to the veggies and cooled wheatberries (or barley). Add oranges (may substitute dried cranberries), feta, mint and toss. Sprinkle crunchies on top right before serving so they stay crunchy.

TIPS & ADVICE: The salad sometimes soaks up too much dressing by the next day, so making extra dressing and crunchies is always a good idea.

NUMBER OF SERVINGS: 6–8

included a free outpatient clinic called the Jewish Dispensary and the many relief services of →

quinoa, zucchini, tomato and pine nut salad with mint vinaigrette

Raquel Landau *Fresh and crunchy!!! The mint vinaigrette is just outstanding.*

Salad:

1 cup quinoa

2 cups broth or water

½ teaspoon salt

2 zucchinis, julienned, 1" length

2 cups cherry tomatoes, halved

½ cup pine nuts, toasted

¼ cup cilantro, chopped

2 cups arugula

Mint vinaigrette:

1 cup mint, chopped

½ cup olive oil

3 tablespoons red wine vinegar

2 garlic cloves, minced

2 teaspoons Dijon mustard

½ teaspoon sugar

½ teaspoon salt

8 grinds black pepper

salt to taste

Prepare quinoa with broth/water and salt as per package instructions. When quinoa is cool, combine it with zucchini, tomatoes, pine nuts, and cilantro. Prepare vinaigrette in food processor until it is emulsified. Add salt and pepper to taste. Mix the vinaigrette into the salad ingredients and just before serving, add the arugula.

NUMBER OF SERVINGS: 8

grains, pastas, matzah & kugels

waldorf quinoa salad

Bronna Ginsberg *This recipe is a delicious dish that I have adapted for Passover. I typically serve it at my Seder and it is always a big hit. Quinoa is a great vegetarian source of protein and this dish makes for a tasty light lunch the next day. Enjoy!*

Salad:

1 cup raw quinoa, rinsed

2 Granny Smith apples, cored and chopped

½ cup celery, chopped

¼ cup dried cranberries

¼ cup raisins

3 tablespoons red onion, finely chopped

Dressing:

¼ cup rice vinegar

¼ cup orange juice

3 tablespoons canola oil

2 tablespoons honey

1 teaspoon salt

¼ cup pecans, walnuts or almonds, chopped and toasted

¼ cup cilantro or parsley, chopped

Cook quinoa according to package directions. Combine rest of salad ingredients. Combine dressing ingredients. Toss together. Refrigerate until ready to serve. Top with toasted nuts and cilantro.

TIPS & ADVICE: For Passover, use 3 tablespoons wine vinegar, 1 tablespoon white wine, 1 tablespoon sugar and ½ teaspoon salt to replace the rice vinegar, and substitute olive oil for canola oil.

NUMBER OF SERVINGS: 10-12

grains, pastas, matzah & kugels

orange quinoa salad

Randi Bass *This is my 'go-to' recipe for all occasions. A crowd pleaser!*

Dressing:

¼ cup fresh orange juice

2 tablespoons extra virgin olive oil

1½ tablespoons low fat buttermilk

2 teaspoons honey

½ teaspoon salt

⅛ teaspoon freshly ground pepper

Salad:

1⅓ cups uncooked quinoa

2¾ cups water

½ teaspoon salt

1 cup green onions, thinly sliced

1 cup dried cranberries

⅓ cup fresh parsley, chopped

3 tablespoons sliced almonds, toasted

Dressing: Combine ingredients in a small bowl. Stir with a whisk until blended.

Salad: Place quinoa in a large nonstick skillet; cook for 4 minutes over medium heat, stirring frequently. Place quinoa in a fine sieve; place sieve in a large bowl. Cover quinoa with water. Using your hands, rub grains together for 30 seconds; rinse and drain. Repeat procedure twice. Drain well.

Combine quinoa, water and salt in a large saucepan. Bring to a boil. Cover and reduce heat; simmer 20 minutes or until all of the liquid is absorbed. Remove from heat and cool to room temperature. Stir in dressing, onions and the remaining ingredients. Cover and chill.

NUMBER OF SERVINGS: 10 (around ½ cup per serving)

grains, pastas, matzah & kugels

spiced pomegranate quinoa

Reesa Sud *My husband, Avrum, has been a vegan for the past 20 years. When I found out that quinoa was a protein and kosher, I knew it would become a weekly staple in our home. It can be served as a side dish or main course for a vegan. It is easy to prepare and can stay in the fridge for 3 or 4 days.*

2 teaspoons olive oil

2 tablespoons ginger, freshly grated

1½ cups rinsed white quinoa

3 cups chicken broth or vegetable stock

1 cinnamon stick

½ teaspoon cumin

¼ teaspoon nutmeg

1 large bay leaf

½ cup pistachios, toasted

2 green onions, thinly sliced into strips

seeds from 1 pomegranate

Heat oil in a large pot over medium low. Add ginger. Stir often and add quinoa to combine. Add broth, cinnamon stick, bay leaf, cumin and nutmeg. Turn heat to high and bring to a boil. Cover, reduce heat and simmer gently until quinoa is tender; approximately 20 minutes. Remove seeds from pomegranate and set aside. When quinoa is finished cooking, fluff with fork. Discard cinnamon stick and bay leaf. Add pomegranate seeds, pistachios and green onions to cooked quinoa and toss to combine.

NUMBER OF SERVINGS: 10–12

Reorganized in 1938 to cope with the Depression, the Federation finally became what is →

quinoa chili

Patti Rotman *As a vegetarian, I could never enjoy chili. I devised this recipe so that it was filling, healthy and enjoyed even by real meat lovers.*

2 packages Yves ground round (substitute 1 pound ground beef for non-vegetarian version)

½ cup vegetable stock (substitute chicken stock for non-vegetarian version)

½ cup tomato sauce

1 (28 ounce) can diced tomatoes

1 (28 ounce) can kidney beans

1 can corn niblets

1 (28 ounce) can chickpeas

1 package shredded carrots

2 cups cooked quinoa

¼ teaspoon pepper

¼ teaspoon salt

½ teaspoon granulated garlic

Sauté ground round in stock. Add the tomato sauce, tomatoes, beans, corn, chickpeas, carrots and quinoa. Simmer on low heat for 30 minutes. Add garlic, salt and pepper to taste.

TIPS & ADVICE: Can be easily doubled and tripled. Even meat lovers will love the vegetarian version!

NUMBER OF SERVINGS: 8

grains,
pastas,
matzah &
kugels

now called the United Jewish Appeal of Greater Toronto in 1948. Despite the hardships,

pomegranate quinoa salad

Melanie Levcovich *I like this recipe because pomegranates make me think of Israel. It's a crowd pleaser, and my kids (who are very fussy) really enjoy it.*

Salad:

2 cups water

1 cup quinoa, rinsed

1 cup pomegranate seeds

1 cup cucumber, diced

¾ cup parsley, chopped

½ cup green pepper, diced

½ cup cilantro, chopped (optional)

¼ cup fresh mint, chopped

Dressing:

¼ cup lemon juice

¼ cup olive oil

salt and pepper to taste

¾ cup slivered almonds, toasted

Prepare quinoa in water according to package directions and let cool. Prepare all other salad ingredients (except nuts) and add to a bowl. Whisk lemon juice, pepper and olive oil for dressing and toss over salad. Add nuts before serving.

TIPS & ADVICE: Dress just before serving. Serve at room temperature.

NUMBER OF SERVINGS: 4

grains, pastas, matzah & kugels

greenest quinoa cakes with tahini

Carolyn Tanner-Cohen *This recipe is perfect for a light supper, a lunch box item served at room temperature or even for the freezer. It is tried and true in my house. Everybody loves these! If you are not in the mood to make the dip, serve the cakes without it alongside a salad with a light vinaigrette.*

Quinoa cakes:

1 cup dry quinoa, any color, cooked

3 eggs, beaten

½ teaspoon kosher salt

1 cup kale, any type, finely chopped

⅓ cup chives, chopped

⅓ cup dill, chopped

1 cooking onion, chopped finely

2 garlic cloves, minced

½ teaspoon cumin

1 teaspoon baking powder

1 cup panko breadcrumbs or any other breadcrumbs you like

½ cup Greek feta, crumbled (optional)

olive oil for light pan frying

Tahini (makes 1 cup):

½ cup tahini paste

juice from 1 lemon, more if needed

water

1 garlic clove, minced

2 tablespoons parsley leaves, finely chopped

¼ teaspoon cumin

½ teaspoon kosher salt

freshly ground pepper to taste

In a medium size mixing bowl, combine quinoa with eggs and salt; mix well. Add kale, chives, dill, onion, garlic, and cumin; mix well. Add baking powder and breadcrumbs and let sit for 10 minutes to absorb moisture. Test the mixture after 10 minutes; you should be able to form a patty that is a little moist and holds together. You can add more crumbs or a little water if necessary.

Add feta (if using), and gently stir. Form into patties the size of a small burger, and place on a platter. Heat the oil in a large, heavy skillet over medium-low heat. Add 6 patties, with some room between each, cover, and cook for 7 to 10 minutes, until the bottoms are deeply browned. Turn up the heat if there is no browning after 10 minutes and continue to cook until the patties are browned. Carefully flip the patties with a spatula and cook the second side for 7 minutes, or until golden. Remove from the skillet and cool on a wire rack while you cook the remaining patties.

Tahini: In a medium bowl, using a whisk, mix together the tahini paste and lemon juice until you have a very thick creamy consistency. Add water to thin it out to a consistency of loose cream. Add garlic, parsley, cumin, salt and pepper. Use more water if it thickens.

NUMBER OF SERVINGS: 10

grains, pastas, matzah & kugels

babi goldie's fried rice

Illana Morton *This is a side dish that my Babi Goldie Sheftel in Calgary and then my mom, Sheila Gurevitch, also in Calgary, made each Friday for Shabbat. It is truly a favourite and I love to eat the rice alongside meatballs. Babi made it so often that her serving dish, which I now have, has permanent stains. When I look at it, I smile.*

2 cups water

1 cup Uncle Ben's Converted Rice

½–¾ package Lipton's Onion Soup Mix

⅛ cup oil

2 tablespoons soy sauce

Mix all ingredients together in a roaster or casserole and cover. Cook according to package directions. Lift cover to mix occasionally while cooking.

TIPS & ADVICE: Can be frozen and defrosted.

NUMBER OF SERVINGS: 6

grains, pastas, matzah & kugels

did you know?
The Joshua Institute has helped to develop over 100 volunteer leaders through its innovative programming.

various daily and weekly English and Yiddish newspapers. Toronto Jews became →

couscous royale

Margie Arosh *'Couscous Royale' was a dish made in my childhood home, taught to me by my mother. She made it only for special occasions or for Yom Tov and it brings back memories of happy times for me. My mother would always give us a small bowl of cinnamon and sugar to top our couscous, which made it extra special. It is a delicious, beautifully presented Moroccan Vegetable Tagine that is made of roasted butternut squash, carrots and chickpeas dressed with almonds, apricots and prunes and served surrounding a mound of steamed couscous.*

1 large butternut squash, cut into 1–2"chunks

5 carrots, chopped into 1" thick slices (blanch for 10 minutes until slightly tender)

5 tablespoons canola oil, divided

6 tablespoons honey, divided

2 teaspoons cinnamon

½ teaspoon nutmeg, freshly ground

kosher salt and freshly ground black pepper to taste

1 cup chicken or vegetable stock

2 cups chicken stock, vegetable stock or water

¾ cup almonds, toasted

¾ cup prunes, pitted

¾ cup dried apricots

2 cinnamon sticks

1 large onion, cut into thin strips

1 can chickpeas, drained and washed

½ teaspoon turmeric, divided

½ teaspoon ground cloves

couscous (prepared according to package directions)

Preheat oven to 375°F. Combine squash, carrots, 3 tablespoons of oil, 3 tablespoons honey, ground cinnamon, nutmeg, salt and pepper to taste and 1 cup of stock in a large roasting pan. Place the pan in the centre of oven and roast approximately 30–40 minutes until vegetables are fork tender. Meanwhile, toast almonds in a dry skillet until fragrant. Place the dried fruit along with the cinnamon sticks, clove and 3 tablespoons of honey in a small saucepan and barely cover with water or stock. Simmer for 10 minutes or until the liquid has reduced and is syrupy and the fruit is plump.

In a frying pan over medium heat, place the onion with 2 tablespoons of oil and sauté until slightly golden, approximately 5 minutes. Add the chickpeas, season to taste with salt, pepper and turmeric. Add 1 cup of water or stock and cook for 15 minutes until all the water evaporates and the chickpeas are caramelized. When the vegetables and chickpeas are cooled slightly, gently combine together. Prepare couscous according to package directions, adding ¼ teaspoon of turmeric to the couscous for a beautiful golden color. This dish is traditionally served with a mound of couscous surrounded by the vegetables and topped with the dried fruit and garnished with almonds.

TIPS & ADVICE: This dish can be made vegetarian as above, but is also delicious with the addition of braised chicken.

NUMBER OF SERVINGS: 10

truffled polenta

Elisa Palter *My mother-in-law has all of her kids and grandkids for Shabbat all winter long and she has a lot of allergies/vegetarians/preferences/fussy kids etc. to deal with. Her table is likely to have about 15 different things on it, and if you've ever said something is your fave, it is sure to be there. Everything has onions; she uses every pot and pan in the house (we do the cleanup) and everything is delish! This one gets used a fair amount as it covers off the vegetarian, the lactose intolerant, the picky eater, the filled-with-onions, and the "I don't have any more room in the oven" requirements, all at once!*

1 large tube prepared polenta

8–10 mushrooms, finely chopped

2 large onions, chopped

chicken stock or vegetable stock

olive oil

truffle oil to taste

salt and pepper to taste

Slice polenta into small pieces. Mash with potato masher, leaving some texture. Put in microwave friendly dish.

Using lots of olive oil, sauté onions in large skillet until golden. Add mushrooms and sauté until crisp. Add stock to polenta to moisten, a few tablespoons at a time as you don't want it too wet. Stir in mushrooms and onions. Add a bit of truffle oil to taste—it has a strong flavour so add a few drops at a time. Add salt, pepper to taste. Heat in microwave until very hot. Enjoy!

TIPS & ADVICE: Can be made well ahead and heated in microwave to serve.

NUMBER OF SERVINGS: 4–6

grains, pastas, matzah & kugels

kasha and sea shells

Arlene Shillinger *This family recipe is traced back several generations to Fannie Slonim (nee Finkelstein) z"l. She was born in Podmina, Podolski, Russia in 1902 and lived most of her life in Winnipeg. She regularly prepared this recipe for Shabbat and High Holidays to everyone's great anticipation and delight.*

3 large onions, diced

⅔ cup canola oil

2 cups small pasta shells (De Cecco Conchigliette, ½ of 500 g box)

1 teaspoon each oil and salt for pasta shells

1 box Kasha (Wolff's Kasha, medium granulation, 369 g box)

3 large eggs

4 cups boiling water for kasha

1½ teaspoons salt, or to taste

1½ teaspoons pepper, or to taste

Fry onions in oil until golden. Set aside. Boil pasta shells according to package with a bit of oil and salt. Drain. Do not rinse. Set aside. Lightly beat eggs in bowl with fork. Add kasha to eggs and stir to coat kernels. Cook the egg-coated kasha in a large non-stick pot, or one sprayed with cooking spray, over high heat 2–3 minutes, stirring constantly until egg has dried on kasha and kernels are separate. Reduce heat to low. Quickly stir in boiling water. Cover tightly and simmer for 7–10 minutes until kasha kernels are tender and liquid is absorbed. Mix shells, onions with oil, and kasha together. Season with salt and pepper.

NUMBER OF SERVINGS: 10–12

grains, pastas, matzah & kugels

mom's famous macaroni and cheese

Ellen Moss *My mother, Sylvia (Shiffy) Wasserman made this dish for years, but I have no idea where she got it. It is quick to prepare, kids and adults love it and it never fails as long as you use great, challah-toasted breadcrumbs.*

2 tablespoons flour

2 tablespoons butter or margarine

½ cup milk

1½ cups cheddar cheese, shredded

1 cup elbow macaroni

½–1 cup toasted challah breadcrumbs for topping

1 tablespoon butter, cut into pieces, for topping (or more)

In a double boiler, mix the flour and butter and make a paste and then add the milk and cheddar cheese and mix until sauce becomes smooth. Boil the macaroni until it is tender, drain, and add to the cheese sauce; stir. Place in a greased oven proof casserole, top with toasted breadcrumbs and pieces of butter. Bake for about 15–20 minutes in 375°F preheated oven until crispy on top, and bubbly.

Breadcrumbs: Slice challah, (it can be a few days old), toast it on a low oven (200°F), until crispy, then grind in a food processor.

NUMBER OF SERVINGS: 4

(later Associated Hebrew School) in 1907. Social life was organized around the city's

pasta and feta cheese casserole

Marnie Burke *This recipe was passed down to me from my aunt, Gail Skopit. She is my mom's sister and we are very close. She usually makes it to break the fast on Yom Kippur and I have too for many years. It was definitely a favourite growing up and still always a crowd pleaser.*

½ pound penne or shell shaped pasta

2 tablespoons olive oil

1 onion, chopped

2 garlic cloves, chopped

1 green pepper, diced

¼ cup flour

2½ cups (1%) milk

3 tablespoons tomato paste

1 teaspoon each salt and pepper or to taste

¼ cup + ½ cup grated Parmesan cheese, divided

½ pound feta cheese, cubed

½ cup green olives, pitted and sliced

½ cup diced pimento, drained

2 tablespoons parsley, chopped

½ teaspoon dried oregano

Preheat oven to 350°F. Cook pasta as directed on package and drain. In another pot, sauté onion, garlic and green pepper in olive oil for 3-4 minutes. Stir in flour and sauté for another 3 minutes. Add milk, tomato paste, salt and pepper and bring to a boil. Reduce heat and simmer 5 minutes, stirring often. Combine pasta with sauce and add feta, ¼ cup of Parmesan, olives, pimento, parsley and oregano. Transfer to a greased 9 x 13" baking dish and sprinkle with remaining Parmesan. Bake for 30 minutes uncovered.

NUMBER OF SERVINGS: 8

grains, pastas, matzah & kugels

spaghetti diavolo with imitation crab

Liza Gutfrajnd *This is my go-to recipe with guests. The compliments flow whenever I make this.*

1 package spaghetti or linguine

¼ cup olive oil

1 package imitation crab sticks, shredded on the long side

4 garlic cloves, minced

⅛ teaspoon cayenne pepper or 1 teaspoon crushed red pepper flakes

1 cup white wine

1 can (540 ml) seasoned, diced tomatoes

1 can (796 ml) whole Italian tomatoes

1 tablespoon dry oregano

1 handful fresh parsley, chopped

1 bottle green olives, sliced and drained

12 fresh basil leaves, chopped

salt and pepper to taste

freshly grated Parmesan cheese (optional)

Cook pasta according to package directions and set aside, reserving cooking water in pot. In a large skillet, heat olive oil on medium heat and add garlic and cayenne pepper. Stir until garlic starts to brown. Add imitation crab and stir constantly for a few minutes. Add wine, both cans of tomatoes, oregano, parsley and basil, stirring until the whole tomatoes fall apart into big pieces. Add the olives and season with salt and pepper. Let simmer for a few minutes.

To serve: Immerse the pasta into the hot cooking water to heat, then place it in a bowl and put a generous amount of sauce on top. Some grated Parmesan cheese can be sprinkled on for added flavour.

TIPS & ADVICE: Cayenne pepper is very spicy, so use according to your own taste. I serve this dish with naan bread and melted mozzarella cheese cut into triangles.

NUMBER OF SERVINGS: 6–8

grains, pastas, matzah & kugels

sesame noodles

Randi Bass *This dish was brought to me by a dear cousin when I was hosting a dinner. It was such a hit with young and old that I asked for the recipe. It has now become "my" recipe and I am asked to bring it as a contribution to dinners. It is so easy to make with ingredients that many already have in their pantry. My boys now make my sesame noodles at university.*

1 (16 ounce) package fettuccine noodles

6 garlic cloves, minced

6 tablespoons sugar

6 tablespoons rice vinegar

6 tablespoons soy sauce

2 tablespoons sesame oil

1–2 teaspoons hot chinese chili sauce or crushed red pepper flakes

6 scallions, sliced

1 teaspoon sesame seeds, toasted

If you would like to add sautéed vegetables:

½ each red, orange and yellow peppers or 1½ cups total of any colour, sliced thinly

1 zucchini, sliced

2 cups mushrooms, sliced

oil for sautéing

Cook pasta according to package directions, drain and transfer to large serving bowl. Combine garlic, sugar, vinegar, soy sauce, sesame oil and chili flakes in a saucepan over a medium-high heat. Bring mixture to boil, stirring constantly until sugar dissolves. Pour over pasta, tossing to coat. Sprinkle with scallions and sesame seeds. Add sautéed vegetables if desired.

TIPS & ADVICE: My preference is to make the pasta and dressing earlier in the day as the pasta absorbs the dressing and it enhances the flavour.

NUMBER OF SERVINGS: 8–10

vegetable kugel

Jane Herman *This dish originated as a Passover side dish for our family Seder. The original recipe, which produces a consistently fantastic kugel for a crowd of 30+, is made with 10 cups of zucchini (4 large), 7 cups carrots (2 pounds), 8 cups potatoes (white and sweet—about 5 pounds), and 3 cups chopped onions (1 pound), 16 eggs, 2 cups matzah meal, 2 tablespoons salt and 2 teaspoons pepper. It is a popular side dish for many family dinners and is delicious reheated. This recipe has been downsized for a smaller group.*

1 large green zucchini, shredded

2 medium carrots, shredded

1 large sweet potato, peeled and shredded

1 medium white potato, shredded

1 medium onion, chopped

3 eggs

½ cup matzah meal

1½ teaspoons salt

½ teaspoon ground black pepper

Preheat oven to 350°F. Use the shredding disc of a food processor to grate the zucchini, carrots, and potatoes. Transfer the shredded vegetables to a large bowl after processing. Use the blade to chop the onions and add them to the shredded vegetables. Toss the vegetables to combine and then return the mixture to the food processor in batches, using the blade and pulsing lightly.

Beat the eggs and add to the pulsed vegetables. Add the matzah meal, salt and pepper and combine thoroughly. Spoon the vegetable mixture into a well-oiled, 9 x 13" rectangular baking dish. Bake for approximately 45 minutes until golden brown.

TIPS & ADVICE: Feel free to use all white potatoes or all sweet potatoes, depending on your family's preference. This is a great recipe because you can make it ahead and then just reheat it the day you are serving. It's so easy to serve; you just cut it into squares.

NUMBER OF SERVINGS: 10–12

grains, pastas, matzah & kugels

politics and play games of dominoes, cards and chess. *Before the war and into*

pesach apple matzah keegel

Barbara Jerome *This Pesach apple matzah keegel (I am from Winnipeg and we say Keegel, not Kugel) recipe has been in my family for years. This dish is a staple at Passover as a side dish or for breakfast, cold or hot.*

When I was about 4, my mother was almost finished making the keegel when she had to rush out to take my cousin to the hospital as it was an emergency. Her Mahjong ladies had just arrived when my mother left. They asked me if the eggs were already added and I told them no. They added 6 eggs and put it in the oven to bake. Well, I was wrong—the eggs had already been added so the keegel had 12 eggs! This is a very easy recipe and everyone loves it.

8–10 matzahs, soaked in hot water and drained

5–7 apples, peeled and cut into small chunks

1½ cups raisins

1 cup sugar

5 tablespoons oil

1 lemon, rind and juice

1 orange, rind and juice

cinnamon

6 eggs, well beaten

Preheat oven to 350°F. In a large bowl, combine all of the ingredients. Place in a well- greased 9 x 13" pan. Bake 1 hour or until brown. Serve warm or cold.

TIPS & ADVICE: Freezes well.

NUMBER OF SERVINGS: 12

grains, pastas, matzah & kugels

the 1920s, anti-Semitism in Toronto was prevalent, with Jews denied many employment →

murray house potato pudding

Lorraine and Aubie Himmel and the late Peggy Silver *This recipe was from Murray House Caterers, who operated in Toronto from 1939-75. They were one of the first independent kosher caterers in Toronto. Their "Hashkachah" came from Rabbi Ochs. Lorraine's mother and father, Dora and Jack Arons, founded the business which had its first home on Murray Street with a main dining room that seated 75. They then moved to Beverley Street with a main dining room that seated 450 people and from there they moved to Steeles Avenue where the dining room seated 1000 people. When Abba Eben came to Toronto, he spoke at The Murray House and they squeezed 1200 people into the building with people sitting in the hallways!*

1 (9 x 13") disposable tin foil container; oil for greasing pan

20 medium sized potatoes, medium diced

8 medium sized onions, medium diced

12 large eggs

1½ cups flour

½ cup matzah meal or breadcrumbs

2 teaspoons baking powder

2 tablespoons salt

1 teaspoon pepper

The night before: Peel and cut the potatoes into a medium dice. Place in large containers and cover with water. Refrigerate overnight.

Assembly: Preheat oven to 350°F. Place diced onions in a bowl. Crack the eggs into another extra large bowl. Mix the dry ingredients together in a third bowl and then add to the egg mixture, stirring to combine. Drain the raw potatoes and puree (grate) in batches in the food processor until smooth. Add each batch of pureed potatoes to the egg mixture and stir. Puree onions in batches until smooth and add to potato and egg mixture and stir to combine thoroughly. Grease the tin pan with oil and sprinkle with matzah meal or breadcrumbs. Add the pudding mixture to the pan and place pan on cookie sheet. Sprinkle with more matzah meal crumbs and bake in oven uncovered for 90 minutes. Cool completely on wire rack.

NUMBER OF SERVINGS: 8–12

grains, pastas, matzah & kugels

potato pudding

Mark Milgram *My Mom made THE BEST potato pudding. Try as I might, I could not replicate it. So, I started asking relatives and friends about their potato pudding recipes. I experimented with the best features of various recipes until I formulated this one of my own.*

3 tablespoons vegetable or canola oil

¼ cup flour

1½ teaspoons salt

pepper, to taste

3 eggs

½ Spanish onion, sliced

1 zucchini, sliced

6-7 Yukon Gold potatoes, peeled and cut into pieces

Preheat oven to 375°F. Heat oil in 9 x 13" pan in oven. Combine dry ingredients in a small dish. Set aside. Add eggs, onion, zucchini and a small amount of potatoes to a food processor and process for 30 seconds. Add dry mix and the rest of the potatoes to the food processor and blend until creamy. Put potato mixture in pan. If there are lumps, just spoon them out. If desired, put a couple of capfuls of oil on the top of the potato mixture to brown top. Put in a preheated oven for 1½ hours.

TIPS & ADVICE: Preheating oil in pan before adding potato mixture is essential. Do not freeze. Reheat leftovers uncovered in oven at 325°F for 30 minutes.

NUMBER OF SERVINGS: 8

spinach noodle pudding

Shari Silverstein *This recipe was given to me by my Aunt Pearl who prepared this dish every year for the breaking of the fast. It's easy, fast and delicious.*

2 packages frozen chopped spinach

1 cup cottage cheese

1 cup Swiss cheese, grated

1 can cream of mushroom soup

1 teaspoon dried mustard

½ cup Miracle Whip

⅛ teaspoon pepper

1 large package medium or broad egg noodles

Take 2 packages of frozen spinach from freezer the night before and allow to thaw. Preheat oven to 350°F. Drain to remove all water from defrosted spinach. In a large bowl, combine cottage cheese, Swiss cheese, mushroom soup, dried mustard, Miracle Whip and pepper. Add chopped spinach. Boil noodles according to instructions on package. Drain. Add to above mixture and combine well. Pour into a well greased 9 x 13" pyrex baking dish. Bake for 1 hour at 350°F. Allow to cool slightly and serve.

NUMBER OF SERVINGS: 16

grains, pastas, matzah & kugels

Despite anti-Semitic attitudes and incidences, there was considerable civic and media →

apple kugel

Sarena Koschitzky *I originally got this recipe from a cousin in Los Angeles. It is a favourite at the Shabbat and holiday table as a side dish or dessert.*

2 eggs

1¼ cups flour

1 cup sugar

¾ cup canola oil

1 teaspoon vanilla

1 teaspoon baking powder

5 large baking apples, peeled and sliced (or 2 quarts of blueberries if you want to make it a breakfast cake)

1 teaspoon cinnamon

Preheat oven to 350°F. Grease a 10" pie plate. Combine all ingredients except apples, mixing well with a big spoon or fork. Add apples and mix lightly to combine. Pour into prepared dish and sprinkle with cinnamon. Bake for 1 hour and serve warm.

TIPS & ADVICE: Can be frozen. Can also be prepared in muffin tins—bake for 20 minutes. I have substituted blueberries instead of the apples to make it more like a breakfast cake. Just fold in the blueberries.

NUMBER OF SERVINGS: 6–8

bubbie zelda barlin's kugel

Elly Barlin-Daniels *This is my late mother's famous recipe from my hometown of Winnipeg.*

1 package medium noodles, cooked and well drained

½ cup butter

1 (8 ounce) package Philadelphia cream cheese

6 tablespoons sugar

½ teaspoon salt

4 eggs

2 cups milk

2 handfuls crushed cornflakes

¾ teaspoon cinnamon

¼ cup sugar

Preheat oven to 350°F. With an electric mixer, cream butter and sugar until well blended. Add cream cheese, salt and eggs and mix until fluffy. Heat milk until warm; not too hot. Add to creamed mixture. Add drained noodles. Pour into 9 x 13" pan that has been sprayed with cooking spray. Mix cornflakes with cinnamon and sugar. Sprinkle on top. Bake at 350°F for one hour and 15 minutes.

NUMBER OF SERVINGS: 6–8

grains, pastas, matzah & kugels

support for the Jewish community and the Zionist movement at this time.

carrot pudding

Esta Palter *Everyone enjoys this recipe as it tastes like cake.*

½ pound or 1 small tub canola margarine

1 cup brown sugar

2 eggs

3 (398 ml) cans whole style baby carrots

3 cups flour

1 teaspoon baking powder

1 teaspoon nutmeg

1 teaspoon cinnamon

¼ teaspoon salt

Spray or grease well a 10" bundt pan. With a hand beater or mixer, cream margarine and sugar until well blended. Drain and rinse baby carrots. Cut up into small pieces. Add the cut up carrots, eggs, flour, baking powder, nutmeg, cinnamon and salt to the margarine and sugar mixture. Mix until well blended. Pour into bundt pan. Refrigerate for 3–4 hours before baking. Bring to room temperature. Bake for 1 hour 15 minutes in a preheated 350°F oven.

TIP & ADVICE: Easy to make and freezes well unbaked. I always have one waiting in the freezer.

NUMBER OF SERVINGS: 12–16

did you know?
The Joshua Institute has helped to develop over 100 volunteer leaders through its innovative programming.

 The 1920s saw another wave of immigration, mainly from Poland but also the →

hot carrot pudding

Susan Fremar *This pudding is a wonderful side dish and can be made into muffins as well!*

½ cup Crisco shortening

2 large eggs

1¾ cups carrots, grated

1 tablespoon lemon juice plus zest of half a lemon

1 cup brown sugar, packed

1 cup flour

½ teaspoon salt

½ teaspoon pepper

½ teaspoon baking soda

½ teaspoon baking powder

In a mixing bowl using a paddle attachment, cream shortening, adding eggs one at a time. Mix until light and fluffy. Add carrots, sugar, lemon juice and zest on low speed.

In a separate bowl, sift flour with salt, pepper, baking soda and baking powder. Add to wet ingredients but do not overmix. Pour into a well-greased 8 x 8" pyrex dish. Bake for 25–30 minutes in a 350°F preheated oven. Serve warm.

NUMBER OF SERVINGS: 4–6

peach noodle kugel

Elana Carr Horowitz *This is always a hit at our Shabbat meal and I usually make it for Rosh Hashanah because it is sweet.*

1 package medium sized egg noodles

6 eggs

1 cup sugar

1 tablespoon vanilla

¼ cup orange juice

4 tablespoons margarine, melted

1 large can peaches, drained and diced

sprinkle of cinnamon

Preheat oven to 350°F. Boil noodles until soft according to package directions. Drain and set aside. In a bowl, beat eggs, sugar, vanilla and orange juice with an electric mixer. Add melted margarine to mixture. Add drained noodles and peaches to mixture. Mix by hand.

Spray large ovenproof (pyrex) dish with non-stick spray and pour in mixture. Sprinkle cinnamon on top. Bake 45 minutes to an hour at 350°F and cut into squares.

TIPS & ADVICE: Freezes well.

NUMBER OF SERVINGS: 8

Ukraine and Russia. ✡ By 1921, Toronto's Jewish population had almost doubled →

shirley's noodle kugel

Corrie Gancman and Debbie Bank *Friday night dinners and Jewish holidays were always special because we knew our mom, Shirley, was going to bake her sweet delicious noodle kugel, which had been passed down from generation to generation. As soon as you walked into her house, you could smell the pineapple. As our mom cut the kugel into squares, we always waited around to scrape the crispy noodles that were stuck to the bottom and sides of the pyrex.*

Since our mom is no longer with us, it is our turn, and one day, it will be our children's turn to continue with family tradition. As we bake her kugel, we feel her with us and can still hear her giving us instruction, "the secret to a perfect kugel is warming the oil up for 5 minutes before pouring the ingredients into the pyrex". It would have been our mom's pleasure to share this recipe. Enjoy!

grains, pastas, matzah & kugels

1 package wide egg noodles

5 eggs

½ cup white sugar

1 can crushed pineapple, drained

½ cup vegetable oil

1 (19 ounce) jar apple sauce

1 teaspoon lemon juice

1 teaspoon vanilla

2 cups crushed corn flakes

½ cup brown sugar

cinnamon to taste

¼ cup raisins (optional)

Preheat oven to 350°F. Boil noodles according to directions on package. With an electric mixer, beat together eggs and white sugar until foamy. When noodles are cool (very important), mix together with egg and sugar mixture and set aside. Combine pineapple, vegetable oil, apple sauce, lemon juice, and vanilla by hand and add to cooled down egg/noodle mixture. Raisins are optional.

Grease 9 x 13" pyrex with oil. Warm pyrex in oven for 5 minutes before pouring in ingredients. Once pyrex has been warmed, pour mixture into pyrex.

Topping: Mix together corn flakes, brown sugar and cinnamon (to taste). Sprinkle on top of noodle mixture. Bake at 350°F for 1 hour.

TIPS & ADVICE: Freezes well.

NUMBER OF SERVINGS: 15 squares or more

from ten years earlier to 34,619. (*our story continues on page 128 . . . read on*)

vegetable sides & mains

Augusta Fruit Market, 1956

baked stuffed eggplant

Henza Miller and Michelle Fishman

2 medium eggplants, halved lengthwise

1 cup red quinoa (cook according to package instructions)

2 tablespoons olive oil, divided

2 garlic cloves, minced

1 large onion, chopped

1 pint cherry tomatoes, sliced lengthwise

2 portobello mushrooms, coarsely chopped

¼ cup curly parsley

3 tablespoons lemon juice

salt and pepper to taste

¼ cup goat cheese

Preheat oven to 400°F. Score cut sides of eggplant ½" deep to help cook evenly. Arrange the cut sides face down on a parchment paper lined baking sheet. Roast until soft (approximately 30 minutes). Let the eggplant cool, then scoop out the flesh to use in the stuffing. Reserve the skins to be stuffed later.

Cook quinoa according to package directions. In a skillet, heat oil, garlic, and onion. When caramelized, add cherry tomatoes and mushrooms. Cook for 5–8 minutes. Add quinoa and flesh of eggplant, parsley, lemon juice, and seasoning.

After combining all of the ingredients, spoon a generous, heaping portion of stuffing into eggplant skins. Bake for 20 minutes at 400°F. Sprinkle goat cheese on top with 5 minutes remaining in cook time.

NUMBER OF SERVINGS: 4

vegetable sides & mains

visit our website
www.JewishToronto.com/BathurstStreetKitchen

The Jewish Immigrant Aid Society of Canada (JIAS) established in 1922 was

brussels sprouts with breadcrumbs

Tiffaney Klein Goodman *These Brussels sprouts go really well with a nice steak, veal chop or with fish instead of potatoes as a side dish.*

1 bunch of small Brussels sprouts (4–5 cups) washed and trimmed and cut in half

1½ tablespoons olive oil

1 tablespoon kosher salt

¾ cup fresh or packaged breadcrumbs

1 tablespoon butter (substitute for olive oil if making pareve recipe)

1 freshly squeezed lemon

freshly ground pepper to taste

Preheat oven to 375°F. Wash and cut Brussels sprouts in half and then toss in olive oil and salt and roast on a pan lined with parchment paper. Roast Brussels sprouts for 25 minutes or a little more depending on size of Brussels sprouts—they should have a brown, caramelized look to them. While they are still hot out of the oven, have a bowl ready to toss the hot Brussels sprouts with butter/oil, breadcrumbs and lemon juice. Serve immediately or have them in warming oven for a few minutes.

NUMBER OF SERVINGS: 6

vegetable sides & mains

corn pudding

Lissie Sanders *This is a recipe that was given to me by my mother-in-law, Vera Sanders, who was one of the committee members of the Kinneret Cookbook. It is my go-to recipe for Friday night dinners and it is one of my recipes that people constantly ask for. It adds a bit of "sweetness" to a heavier meat meal or can be a main dish as part of a dairy buffet.*

½ cup sugar

½ cup margarine or butter

5 eggs

2 large tins creamed corn

1 large can corn niblets

½ cup flour

1 teaspoon baking powder

Using an electric mixer, cream margarine (or butter) and sugar. Add eggs one at a time and mix until mixture is smooth. Add all three cans of corn, flour and baking powder and stir just until flour and baking powder have been mixed through. Pour into a 9 x 13" greased baking pan. Bake for 1 hour and 15 minutes.

TIPS & ADVICE: This recipe can be doubled or tripled for larger crowds. If you would like to make it earlier in the day, you can bake it for one hour and then reheat for 15 minutes just before serving. Can be made pareve but for a dairy meal, I like to use butter.

NUMBER OF SERVINGS: 8

responsible for persuading the Canadian government to accept 3400 stranded Ukrainian Jewish →

vegan corn pudding with fresh thyme and rosemary

Marla Hertzman *When I told my husband, Gordy, I was making a pudding for dinner, he thought he was getting chocolate pudding. Was he surprised when he found out that this recipe had no milk, no butter, no flour . . . and no chocolate!*

2 tablespoons arrowroot flour

½ cup unsweetened almond milk (you could use soy milk)

6 cups fresh corn niblets, divided

2 tablespoons Earth Balance Buttery Spread, melted

2 tablespoons cornmeal

4 teaspoons baking powder

1 teaspoon salt

¼ teaspoon black pepper

⅛ teaspoon cayenne pepper

2 teaspoons fresh thyme

2 teaspoons fresh rosemary

Preheat oven to 350°F. Whisk arrowroot in ½ cup of almond milk. Put 2 cups of corn niblets and almond milk in the food processor. Puree. Add "melted butter", cornmeal, baking powder, salt, pepper and cayenne to the food processor, and process well. Add remaining corn, thyme and rosemary to the food processor and pulse 5 or 6 times, just until mixed; you should still have some of the texture of the corn. Grease a 9 or 10" round baking dish with canola oil or coconut oil. Scrape corn mixture into dish. Bake uncovered for 30–40 minutes or until slightly brown around the edges.

NUMBER OF SERVINGS: 6

did you know?
Circle of Care provides more than 30,000 rides to over 900 frail seniors each year.

lyonnaise potatoes

Lynda Weinrib *When we began dating in 1969, my late husband raved over the Lyonnaise Potatoes at Basil's restaurant. I adapted the recipe into a kosher version (both to serve with dairy and meat) and it became a family favourite for holiday dinners, with a turkey.*

2 tablespoons butter or margarine

1 tablespoon olive oil or more

1 large sweet Spanish or Vidalia onion, diced finely

1 tablespoon brown sugar

2 pounds yellow potatoes, peeled and diced

pinch salt, pepper, smoked paprika

Heat butter in large frying pan. Once it is melted, add olive oil and then add onions. Fry until onions start to brown. Add brown sugar and stir. Add potatoes to frying pan. Add a pinch of salt, pepper and smoked paprika while this cooks over low heat until browned. Add a bit more olive oil and seasonings if needed. Once browned, this can be finished in a low (200°F) oven or, as I prefer, on the stovetop for a crispier finish.

TIPS & ADVICE: You can leave this cooking over a low to medium heat for a long time.

NUMBER OF SERVINGS: 4

smashed potatoes

Carole Winberg *It's easy, it's quick and it's yummy!*

6 medium red potatoes, scrubbed, unpeeled

10 cups cold, salted water

¼ cup olive oil

¼ cup red onion, finely chopped

2 tablespoons fresh lemon juice

2 teaspoons roasted garlic

salt and freshly ground pepper to taste

Place potatoes in pot and cover with cold salted water. Bring to a boil over high heat. Turn heat to medium, and simmer under tender (around 15–20 minutes). Drain well and return potatoes to pot on turned-off burner to dry out. Place potatoes on oil-sprayed baking sheet. With a potato masher, press potatoes carefully just until the skin splits and potatoes begin to burst. Combine oil, onions, lemon juice and garlic and season with salt and pepper. Spoon on to potatoes and bake for 20 minute in a preheated 400°F oven or until potatoes are brown and crisp.

TIPS & ADVICE: This is a make-ahead recipe. Leave the smashed potatoes on the baking sheet and combine the other ingredients to make the dressing. When ready to serve, top with the dressing and bake as instructed above.

NUMBER OF SERVINGS: 6

were one of the last groups of Jewish immigrants to make it to Canada and Toronto until after

spicy and sweet potatoes

Marla Schwartz *This recipe has been a menu standard in our house for years and my son Gabe's favourite potato recipe. It is a wonderful accompaniment to anything grilled. The potatoes are also great sliced even thinner for a nibble to have with a glass of wine or champagne. They are addictive and even the pickiest eater will enjoy this flavourful recipe.*

4 large sweet potatoes (about 3 pounds), cut into ¼" rounds

¼ cup vegetable oil

Rub:

2 tablespoons sugar

2 tablespoons chili powder

1 teaspoon salt

Preheat oven to 400°F. Use a mandolin to slice thinner for an appetizer. Place potatoes in a large bowl and toss with vegetable oil. Combine sugar with chili powder and salt in a small bowl. Toss with potatoes. Arrange in a single layer on baking sheets lined with cooking oil-sprayed tin foil. Roast for 20 minutes or until brown on the bottom. Turn potatoes over and roast 10–15 minutes longer. If you are making the very thin slices, reduce baking time or they will burn.

NUMBER OF SERVINGS: 6–8

roasted sweet potatoes and pumpkin seeds

Shawna Page *This is my favourite sweet potato recipe of all time, and a 100% guaranteed crowd pleaser! It's delicious and flavourful, healthy, heart-smart, easy to prepare, and impossible to make a mistake. The ingredients can all be adjusted up or down to suit your palate, and truth be told, I never ever measure anything when I make this at home and it always comes out great! Enjoy!*

4 large sweet potatoes, peeled and cut into chunks

4 heaping tablespoons extra virgin, organic coconut oil

5 garlic cloves, crushed

2 tablespoons dried basil

2 tablespoons dried oregano

½ teaspoon sea salt

1 cup roasted unsalted, organic pumpkin seeds, chopped

Preheat oven to 400°F. Line a baking sheet with parchment paper. In an oven-safe mixing bowl, melt coconut oil just until melted. Toss in sweet potatoes. Add garlic, basil, oregano, salt and pumpkin seeds and toss well. Layer the mixture on to the parchment lined baking sheet. Bake for around 45 minutes tossing every 15 minutes until roasted and crispy.

NUMBER OF SERVINGS: 6–8

the Second World War. The Great Depression brought increased poverty and

roasted apples, carrots and parsnips

Daphna Zacks *Apples, carrots, and honey are some of the symbols of Rosh Hashanah, or Simanin as they are called. Over the centuries of Jewish history, these symbols have become a part of the holiday meal. Everyone knows that apples dipped in honey are a symbol of our wish for a sweet new year, and this is a side dish that incorporates these ingredients for your Rosh Hashanah or any autumn meal.*

1½ pounds parsnips, trimmed, cored, and cut into 1" pieces

2 Granny Smith apples, trimmed, cored, and cut into 1" pieces

2 pounds carrots, peeled trimmed and sliced on an angle

2 tablespoons olive oil

½ teaspoon smoked paprika

½ teaspoon kosher salt

1 tablespoon honey or date syrup

1 tablespoon balsamic vinegar or red wine vinegar

1 tablespoon fresh dill, chopped (optional)

Preheat oven to 425°F. Toss the parsnips, apples and carrots with the oil, paprika, and kosher salt. Roast the vegetables in the oven until tender and browned, about 25 minutes. Toss with the honey, vinegar and dill.

TIPS & ADVICE: This recipe can be easily doubled.

NUMBER OF SERVINGS: 4–6

vegetable sides & mains

visit our website
www.JewishToronto.com/BathurstStreetKitchen

anti-Semitism to Toronto. Many establishments banned Jews from entering with

roasted potato, cauliflower and edamame mash

Rose Reisman *I was so tired of plain old mashed potatoes. People think of them as hospital food, and they're often laden with butter and cream. I thought that by roasting the potatoes, I would create a better flavour. I added a few more healthy ingredients and voila! A mashed potato dish that's trendy, delicious and nutritious—anything but boring!*

1 head garlic

1½ pounds Yukon Gold potatoes cut into wedges, unpeeled

1 pound raw cauliflower, broken into pieces

2 cups onions, diced

2 teaspoons vegetable oil

1 tablespoon brown sugar

1 tablespoon olive oil

1 tablespoon sesame oil

¼ cup 2% milk

¾ cup frozen shelled edamame, blanched

pinch salt and pepper

Preheat the oven to 400°F. Line a baking sheet with foil sprayed with vegetable oil. Cut the top off the garlic head and wrap with foil and place on the baking sheet along with the potatoes and cauliflower. Spray the vegetables with vegetable oil. Roast for 30 minutes or just until tender, turning occasionally. Squeeze out the garlic cloves from the skins.

Meanwhile, add the onions to a skillet along with the vegetable oil and sauté on medium heat for 10 minutes just until tender. Add the brown sugar and sauté for another 5 minutes.

Mash the potato wedges with the skin in a large bowl. Place the cauliflower in a food processor along with the olive oil, sesame oil and milk and purée. Add to the mashed potatoes along with the onions, garlic cloves and edamame and stir to combine. Add the salt and pepper to taste.

NUMBER OF SERVINGS: 8

signs that read "Gentiles Only" or "No Dogs, No Jews". In August of 1933, local →

sweet potato and squash puree

Helaine Shiff *My family loves sweet potatoes and squash. Instead of cooking them on their own, I tried combining them into this puree. They liked it so much that they always ask me to make it this way. My daughter Melissa now makes this recipe for her family.*

4 whole sweet potatoes

2 whole butternut and/or acorn squash

2 tablespoons margarine or butter

1 tablespoon brown sugar

1 teaspoon nutmeg

additional nutmeg, brown sugar to dust top, to taste

small bits of margarine or butter to dot top

Place sweet potatoes in microwave (cut off ends and score in the middle prior) and microwave for 5–10 minutes or until soft. Take out of microwave and cut in half to cool; once cooled, scoop out flesh and place in food processor. Put whole squash (one at a time) in microwave (cut off end of squash and score in the middle prior) and microwave for 10 minutes or until soft. Once cooled, scoop out seeds and discard, scoop out the rest and place in food processor. In food processor, blend to puree both sweet potatoes and squash.

Mix puree in a bowl with the margarine, brown sugar and nutmeg. Place in an oven proof bowl and dust top with additional brown sugar, nutmeg and small bits of margarine or butter. Place tin foil lightly over top—don't seal foil over dish. Bake for 30 minutes to 1 hour, until top appears lightly browned. Enjoy!

NUMBER OF SERVINGS: 6–8

vegetable sides & mains

sweet potato mash with pecan streusel

Elly Barlin-Daniels *My husband and I have been vegetarians for 23 years, and we raised our two girls as vegetarians. I am always on the lookout for new ways to prepare vegetables and this recipe tastes more like dessert than a vegetable side dish.*

5 pounds sweet potatoes, peeled and cut into large chunks

½ cup butter, divided

¼ cup whipping cream

¼ teaspoon each salt and pepper

½ cup flour

½ cup brown sugar

¾ cup pecan pieces

In a large saucepan, cover sweet potatoes with water and bring to a boil. Cook until tender—8 minutes or so. Drain and return to pot over medium heat, shaking pan to dry potatoes. Mash potatoes with ⅓ cup of the butter, plus the cream, salt and pepper. Put into a 9 x 13" buttered casserole. Smooth out the top. In a small bowl, rub together the remaining butter, flour, and sugar. Mix in the pecans and sprinkle over potatoes. Bake in a preheated 400°F oven until golden, about 25–30 minutes.

NUMBER OF SERVINGS: 10

anti-Semites, inspired by Hitler's rise to power, adopted the swastika symbol. →

madame laracine's potato gratin

Johanna Samuel *Whenever I travel in France, I always ask cooks for tips on preparing potato gratins. In the Savoy region, many cooks mention the double-cooking method, in which you first cook the potatoes in milk and water or simply in whole milk, discard the cooking liquid and then bake the potatoes in a blend of cream and Gruyere cheese. Madame Laracine, the chef / proprietor of a small family ferme/auberge in the Village of Ordonnaz, makes stunning gratins prepared with homegrown potatoes, milk and cream from her own cows and cheese from a nearby dairy.*

3 pounds baking Russet potatoes, peeled and very thinly sliced

2 cups whole milk

2 cups water

3 garlic cloves, minced

¾ teaspoon salt

3 bay leaves

1 teaspoon nutmeg, freshly ground, divided

1 teaspoon black pepper, freshly ground, divided

1 cup heavy cream (or crème fraîche), divided

2 cups imported French or Swiss Gruyere cheese, freshly grated, divided

Preheat oven to 375°F. Place potatoes in a large saucepan and cover with the milk and water. Add the garlic, salt and bay leaves. Bring to a boil over medium-high heat, stirring occasionally so that the potatoes don't stick to the bottom of the pan. Reduce the heat to medium and cook, stirring from time to time, until the potatoes are tender but not falling apart (approximately 10 minutes).

Using a slotted spoon, transfer half of the potatoes to a large, 14 x 9 x 2" gratin dish. Sprinkle with the nutmeg, pepper, half of the cream or crème fraîche, and half of the cheese. Cover with the remaining potatoes and sprinkle again with nutmeg, pepper and the remaining crème fraîche and cheese. Bake the gratin until crisp and golden on top, about 1 hour. Serve immediately.

NUMBER OF SERVINGS: 6–8

The Balmy Beach Swastika Club attacked Jewish bathers, attempted to have

→

sicilian tomato and eggplant sauté

Eva Rosenthal *I made this dish and would send it in batches to my daughter, Hannah, who was away at university. This is a great vegetarian dish and can be used as a main dish, side dish or, as my daughter told me, it can be added to pasta. It's very tasty and easy to prepare.*

¼ cup olive oil

5 garlic cloves, chopped

1 medium or large eggplant, cubed

1 (796 ml) can crushed tomatoes

1 (398 ml) can black olives, pitted, sliced, and drained

1 (341 ml) can corn, drained

1 (85 g) package sun-dried tomatoes, chopped

salt to taste

Heat oil in a large pot over medium heat. Add garlic and sauté about 2 minutes until garlic is slightly browned. Add eggplant and stir until the eggplant is soft. Add crushed tomatoes and stir. Add olives, corn, sun-dried tomatoes and salt. Cover and simmer for 10–15 minutes, stirring occasionally. Remove from heat. Serve hot or cold.

YIELD: 4 cups

vegetable sides & mains

did you know?
$5,000 enables 8 Jewish children from low-income families to participate in Jewish Family & Child's Homework Club.

shakshuka

Lauren Wilner *Shakshuka is one of my husband's favourite dishes, in part, I think, because it reminds him of home. When we were living in Israel, I asked my mother-in-law, Sylvia Eilath, to teach me how to make it, though I still can't quite make it like her. Tunisian in its roots, Shakshuka takes many forms. Some recipes are so painfully spicy that you may need to dab your forehead every now and then, others are more subtle with spinach and cheese, and still others have bright flavours, long pepper strips, greens, and herbs. These variations reflect the meaning of the word shakshuka, "a mixture," and are a testament to how easily this dish can be adapted to suit your favourite tastes or whatever you have left over in the fridge.*

This recipe is a collaboration of my mother-in-law, Sylvia Eilath's Tunisian and Israeli roots and my own Persian background.

vegetable sides & mains

2 red bell peppers, cubed

½ green bell pepper, cubed

4–5 garlic cloves, finely chopped

1–2 tablespoons olive oil

1 (8 ounce) can diced tomatoes

½ jalapeno, diced (or red pepper flakes to taste)

4 eggs (or 1 per person)

salt and pepper to taste

Potential additions:

½ yellow onion, diced

½ cup feta cheese, crumbled

¼ cup green olives, sliced

1 cup spinach, chard, or kale, chopped

dried or fresh parsley to garnish

In advance, chop up your peppers and set them aside in a bowl. Heat the oil in a pan over medium heat. Add the garlic (and if you're using onions, add that, too). Stir so the garlic doesn't burn. After a few minutes (if you're using onions, wait until the onion has begun to caramelize), add the tomatoes, salt, and pepper (Sylvia recommends quite a bit!). Once the tomato sauce starts 'popping', lower the heat to medium low. Stir in the peppers until they are well incorporated, and if you're using leafy greens, add them now, too. Also add the jalapeno/red pepper flakes. If it looks like your sauce has become too thick, add 1–2 tablespoons of water. Let the shakshuka rest and don't stir it anymore.

Crack the eggs on top and using a fork, spread the egg white around the dish so the eggs cook evenly. Cover with the lid slightly ajar and cook until the egg whites have set. Top with parsley.

NUMBER OF SERVINGS: 4

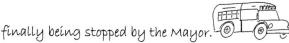

finally being stopped by the Mayor. *A few days later, with racial animosities*

white bean and beet green cassoulet

Bonny Reichert *This is a new recipe I made up because I have many vegetarians in my life and I wanted something satisfying and substantial to serve to them. This recipe never disappoints and although the ingredients are simple, the results are very sophisticated.*

½ cup olive oil, divided

4 shallots, thinly sliced, divided

1 celery root, peeled and diced

1 small turnip, peeled and diced

2 parsnips, peeled and diced

4 cups dried navy beans that have been soaked in water overnight (2 cups dry/presoak)

3 cups vegetable broth

1 cup water

1 bunch baby beets, with tops

2 or 3 Chioggia and/or golden baby beets, without tops

salt and pepper, to taste

Preheat oven to 350°F. Heat half the oil in a large ovenproof saucepan. Add half the shallots, and all of the celery, turnip and parsnips, and sauté for about 10 minutes. Drain beans well and add to pan. Sauté for a moment to coat with oil and mix with vegetables. Add broth and water, cover and cook 1½–2 hours, or until beans and vegetables are soft and most of the liquid is absorbed. (If liquid is already absorbed at this point, add an additional ½ cup water.) Stir, remove lid and cook 20 minutes longer to allow beans and vegetables to brown slightly on top.

Meanwhile, remove tops from red beets. Trim stems and discard. Wash greens very well, chop coarsely and set aside. Bring a small saucepan of salted water to a boil. Using a sharp knife, peel 3 baby beets of mixed colours. Starting with the lightest coloured beets, simmer 10–15 minutes, or until tender. Red beets should be done last. When cool enough to handle, slice beets into circles.

Heat remaining olive oil in a small saucepan. Add remaining shallot rings and fry until crispy—about 2 minutes. Remove from oil with a slotted spoon and blot on kitchen towel. Reserve shallot oil.

Remove beans from oven and season with salt and pepper. While still hot, add beet greens and mix well. Serve cassoulet topped with sliced beets in different colours, crispy shallots and a bit of shallot oil.

TIPS & ADVICE: If you're in a hurry, use canned instead of dried beans. No need to soak. Cooking time will come down to approximately 40 minutes.

NUMBER OF SERVINGS: 6

vegetable sides & mains

nona's bourekas

Dianne Cadesky *The Jewish community in Greece dates back to before the Common Era. Before the Holocaust, there were approximately 73,000 Jews living in Greece, the majority in my mother's hometown of Salonika or Thessaloniki. After their expulsion from Spain, the Ottoman Empire welcomed these Sephardic Jews who integrated their Ladino language and cuisine with those of the Jewish Greeks among whom they settled. Ninety-three percent of Greek Jewry was decimated in the Holocaust. My mother, Esther Tivoli Mucher, was fortunate to have found a safe haven to hide in and was one of 3 orphans later brought to Canada by the JIAS. My father, Eli Benyacar Mucher, also a survivor from Greece, was eager to meet someone "who could cook like his mother". They met and the rest is "delicious"!*

Dough:

10 sheets phyllo dough (½ package) defrosted

½ cup melted butter

Cheese filling:

4 eggs

1 pound feta cheese

1 pound dry cottage cheese

salt to taste if feta is not too salty

or

Spinach filling:

3-4 eggs

4-5 green onions chopped, lightly sautéed

3 packages chopped frozen spinach, squeeze out all the water

handful dill, chopped

1 pound feta cheese

½ pound cottage cheese

Salt and pepper to taste

Remove 5 sheets of phyllo dough from package and wrap the rest up in a wet towel to be used later for the top. Brush each sheet separately with butter and place in a 9 x 13" pan, which has been greased or lined with parchment paper.

Preheat oven to 350°F. Beat eggs for whichever filling you choose (cheese or spinach). Add remaining ingredients and mix well. Pour filling over phyllo dough in pan. Brush remaining phyllo sheets with melted butter and place over filling. Make sure top sheet is brushed with butter as well. Cut some slits in the phyllo sheets so that the hot air can escape. Bake for 1 hour at 350°F or until top is brown.

TIPS & ADVICE: Nona (Grandmother in Ladino) takes the time to make these into individual triangle shapes. The recipe above is easier to make because it is all in one big pan but it still tastes great!

NUMBER OF SERVINGS: 10

etica's potato knishes

Anita Robins *In Romania, my mother Etica, made her own puff pastry but was happy to find ready-made dough here in the grocery store. The knishes freeze well in ziptop freezer bags. Reheat gently and for best results, cover with foil so pastry does not burn.*

1 package frozen puff pastry

10 small red skin potatoes

1 medium onion, chopped

1–2 tablespoons oil for sautéing

1 teaspoon salt

½ teaspoon pepper

1 egg

1 egg, beaten, for egg wash

2 tablespoons sesame seeds

Thaw puff pastry in refrigerator overnight. Peel potatoes and boil in salted water until soft. While potatoes are boiling, sauté onion in oil until very golden brown. Drain potatoes and mash, adding salt, pepper and fried onion. Let cool for a short time and then add egg. Mix well.

Pastry: Cut thawed dough in half along centre crease. Roll out one section into thin rectangle on lightly floured board. Stretch dough if needed. Place half of potato mixture along long edge and roll up, then put it seam side down on parchment-covered cookie sheet. Beat the egg and brush on dough and then sprinkle with sesame seeds. Repeat with second piece. Cut each roll on an angle into 10 pieces/roll. Bake for approximately 30 minutes in 400°F preheated oven until lightly browned on top.

YIELD: about 20 knishes

potato latkes

Helaine Robins *My daughter-in-law's mother, Etica Levy, always made the latkes for my Chanukah party. They always arrived frozen in a ziplock. She finally taught me how to make them. I now make and freeze them before the party and take them out to serve, just as she did.*

4 medium red potatoes, cut in small chunks

1 onion, cut in chunks

2 eggs

¾ teaspoon salt

½ teaspoon pepper

⅓ cup flour

1 teaspoon baking powder

vegetable or canola oil for frying

Put all ingredients except oil in food processor with regular blade. Process 1 minute. Pour into bowl. Put a lot of oil in fry pan, and when hot, add a tablespoon of mixture. Cook both sides until latke turns brown and crispy. Drain on brown paper.

TIPS & ADVICE: Can freeze in single layer in ziplock. To reheat, place in 450°F oven for 5 minutes. Do not double the recipe—it becomes too wet. Work fast when frying so mixture won't become watery. Only use red potatoes as they are not as watery.

YIELD: 12–16 latkes

between thousands of spectators. The violent fight, involving baseball bats and

faux shepherd's pie

Allan Barsky *This is a recipe that I use for 'meat-atarian' friends who sometimes scoff at vegetarian cooking. Although it's a faux shepherd's pie, the results are so hearty and delicious that our guests can't believe it's meatless.*

8–10 medium-sized potatoes (Yukon Gold or red)

2 packages vegetarian ground beef (total 24 ounces)

½ cup red wine

1 cup peas, fresh or frozen

1 cup carrots, diced (fresh-parboiled or frozen)

1 onion, chopped

4 tablespoons olive oil

3 tablespoons of tomato paste or puree (ketchup will do in a pinch)

1 tablespoon thyme, dried

1 tablespoon oregano, dried

salt and black pepper (optional)

1 cup hot, rich vegetable stock

1 tablespoon potato starch (or flour)

1 cup milk or soymilk

2 garlic cloves, minced

1–2 tablespoons paprika

Preheat the oven to 350°F. Cut potatoes into small pieces (unpeeled or peeled). Place them in a pot of boiling water. Lower heat to simmer for about 30 minutes or until tender. As the potatoes are boiling, mix the following ingredients in a low rectangular casserole dish or glass baking dish (approximately 9 x 6 x 3"): veggie ground beef, wine, peas, carrots, onion, olive oil, tomato paste, thyme, and oregano. Mix vegetable stock and starch or flour in a separate bowl, and add to the vegetable mix in casserole dish. Stir thoroughly. Add salt and black pepper to suit your taste. Mash potatoes together with milk and garlic until smooth and creamy. Add potatoes to top of casserole, spreading gently to cover all the vegetables. Lightly sprinkle paprika on top of potatoes. Bake in the oven, uncovered, for 30 minutes at 350°F.

Allow to cool for 10 minutes prior to serving, so that it will cut and serve better. Also, the vegetables tend to stay very hot. Alternatively, allow to cool completely and freeze for "future use," as my mother's old cookbooks used to say. Leftovers always taste better anyway.

NUMBER OF SERVINGS: 6–8

visit our website
www.JewishToronto.com/BathurstStreetKitchen

metal pipes, broke out when supporters of the St. Peter's team raised a white bed sheet with the →

eggplant casserole

Leslie Mendelson *This recipe was discovered by my mother, Naomi Mendelson, and is loved by many in the family—even the carnivores. This is an easy recipe. Chop, mix and bake.*

1 eggplant, peeled and cubed (approximately 1" squares)

3 cups mushrooms, cut in quarters

2 cooking onions, cut in 4 and broken up

2 green or 2 red peppers, diced

1 can diced tomatoes with juice

½ pound or more old cheddar cheese cut up into pieces

Spray a 9 x 13" pyrex well. Put all ingredients into the pyrex and mix them up. Bake in a preheated 400°F oven, uncovered, for 1½– 2 hours. This casserole is best if it is baked for a long time and the vegetables caramelize.

TIPS & ADVICE: You can stir it or leave it. It is even better reheated. Serve it as a side dish or over brown rice with a side salad, as a meal. The casserole bakes right down so double it for a crowd. The quantities are not magic and can easily be varied. Does not freeze well.

NUMBER OF SERVINGS: 4

ellen's broccoli soufflé

Ellen Zabitsky *It all started with trying to get my kids to eat veggies! The original recipe comes from one of my favourite Passover cookbooks, and over the years, I've made some healthy substitutions, like trading the frozen packaged broccoli for fresh. Our kids LIVE on this during Passover.*

5 large heads of broccoli

3 eggs

2 tablespoons onion soup mix

½ cup low fat mayonnaise

1 tablespoon canola oil

salt and pepper to taste

Preheat oven to 350°F. Start by cutting the broccoli heads from the stems, leaving about 1" of stem. Steam the broccoli well in a large pot until very soft. When done, remove most of the water, leaving about ½" at the bottom. Use a hand blender to purée the broccoli well, and set aside. In a medium size bowl, mix the eggs, soup mix, mayonnaise and oil with a fork, then season with salt and pepper to taste. Add this mixture to the pot of puréed broccoli, and stir together. Taste again to adjust salt and pepper. Note, this will taste a bit saltier once cooked! Pour mixture into greased 7 x 12" rectangular pyrex, leaving a little space at the top. Bake for 45-50 minutes, until top is golden.

TIPS & ADVICE: Try sprinkling a little more oil on the top of the finished mixture in pyrex, for a little extra crispy touch.

NUMBER OF SERVINGS: 6–12

swastika symbol and a Jewish group of men, supported by Italian allies, tried to tear it down.
$\longrightarrow$

fondue (with cumin cucumbers)

Seth Mersky *It's a cold snowy night, a fire is roaring in the fireplace, and we're having fondue. Our first fondue was at the ski home of friends in Collingwood. Everyone was hungry following a day of skiing. Our friends opened two packs of "President's Choice" fondue and put it in a fondue pot. It wasn't bad, but we were all still starving after it was quickly scooped up. We resolved to do better at home and a tradition was started. Some of my fondest memories are of the three kids, mom and me around our oval dinner table, hungry and excited to feast on fondue.*

vegetable sides & mains

Fondue:

9–12 cups cheese (1½–2 pounds), shredded (see tips & advice)

⅓ cup flour

1 bottle white wine (something you would drink, but not too expensive)

1 peeled garlic clove, split in two

1 shot kirschwasser or vodka

pinch or two cayenne pepper

pinch or two nutmeg, grated

1 baguette, cut into cubes

vegetables (can be broccoli, cauliflower, baby potatoes or cut up potatoes, mushrooms, snow peas, asparagus spears, anything else you want to dip in cheese)

Cumin cucumbers:

1 English cucumber

2 teaspoons cumin seeds, whole, not ground

juice of one half lemon

Salt to taste

1 healthy pinch cayenne pepper (or to taste)

Fondue: Put the shredded cheese in a plastic bag, add the flour and shake to mix. The amount of cheese is determined by how many you're feeding. A pound and a half will feed four, two pounds will feed six or seven; beyond that, start doubling the recipe. Note, the amount of flour stays the same whether it's a pound and a half or two pounds of cheese. If you're not eating for awhile, the cheese can come to room temperature.

Pour the wine in an enamelled cast iron pot (not the glass pot that fondue sets come with) and add the split garlic. Bring to boil and let boil one minute. Turn the heat to low and remove the garlic and discard. Begin adding the cheese by the handful and between each handful, whisk the mixture until smooth with a wire whisk. Keep repeating until all of the cheese has been added. At this point, add the kirschwasser and gently whisk to incorporate. Add the cayenne and nutmeg. Continue whisking for a minute or two and the mixture should become quite smooth. Grab one of your children and with an air of conspiracy, let him/her taste it with you before bringing the pot to the table. This step won't do anything, but it will make your child feel special.

Cucumbers: Peel the cucumber and slice it lengthwise into quarters or eighths. Cut across into 4" spears. Place the cucumbers and the rest of the ingredients in a plastic bag or non-metal bowl and let marinate for at least an hour. Arrange on a plate and serve.

TIPS & ADVICE: We generally serve fondue with cubed baguettes, new potatoes that have been steamed 10 minutes and any of the following vegetables steamed for 4 minutes: pea pods, broccoli or cauliflower florets, green onions, mushrooms and asparagus. We also like to

The Christie Pits Riot spread to nearby neighbourhoods and lasted for over six hours.

serve cucumbers marinated with lemon and cumin, olives, jalapeno pepper strips, pickled onions or pickles. The cucumbers are an East Indian addition to our fondue routine. When we went skiing in Klosters, the fondue place in town served pickled vegetables with the fondue and we all thought that was great. Cumin cucumbers is our effort at keeping up with the Swiss.

One of the several traditional aspects of family fondue is that everyone gets to complain about it after or during the meal. Typical complaints are "too sour", "too runny", "too thick". As long as everyone is fed, don't take the complaints too seriously as no one is offering to do a better job. In any event, the cheese that seemed to be the least controversial is Gruyere and its more expensive French cousin, Comte. Over the years, we've also used half Gruyere with some combination of Appenzeller, Raclette, Vacherone and others. Try Gruyere the first time and then experiment.

NUMBER OF SERVINGS: 4–6

black bean sun burger

Karen Gilman *These black bean burgers are quick and easy to make. They are a good source of protein and iron and a great alternative for a meatless meal. I love serving them with avocado, tomatoes and some chipotle mayonnaise.*

½ cup sunflower seeds, toasted

¼ cup white onion, chopped

1½ cups canned black beans, drained and rinsed

⅓ cup chickpea flour

2 tablespoons low sodium, tamari soy sauce (similar to soy sauce but gluten free)

½ teaspoon smoked paprika

salt and pepper to taste

⅛ cup coconut oil or other oil for frying

In a food processor, pulse the sunflower seeds until coarsely ground. Add the onion, black beans, chickpea flour, tamari sauce, paprika and salt and pepper. Process until well combined but with some texture. Shape into patties. Heat oil in a frying pan and cook patties 4–6 minutes each side or until browned.

TIPS & ADVICE: Feel free to use other flours if you don't have chickpea flour on hand. I suggest cooking the burgers in coconut oil but any oil will do.

NUMBER OF SERVINGS: 4–6 burgers

 Even though certain local media blamed it on the Jews, Toronto's Jewish →

indonesian tofu

Ellen Grossman *I was giving a cooking class for young adults who wanted to learn how to cook at the Prosserman Culinary School. I knew many of the participants were vegetarian so I searched for an easy recipe that would contain protein as well as interesting flavours. The class learned how to follow a recipe and carry out cooking skills all by themselves! Aside from the fun they all had, they cooked a great dish and gained kitchen confidence along the way.*

1 small serrano pepper or jalapeno, chopped

3 tablespoons fresh ginger

½ medium onion, finely chopped

5 garlic cloves

1 tablespoon sesame oil

2 tablespoons olive oil

¼ cup honey

3 tablespoons molasses

½ cup brown sugar

1½ cups soy sauce

1 block extra firm tofu

2 tablespoons vegetable oil

You can use a food processor or do everything by hand, which is good for your cutting skills. Chop the peppers (discard the seeds as that's the part that is HOT) and remember not to touch any part of your face. Wash hands well. Peel and zest ginger and garlic. Chop onions to a very fine chop. Add sesame oil to a saucepan over medium heat and add the onions, garlic, ginger and peppers until they begin to sweat (no colour); 2–3 minutes. Turn the heat down to low and mix in brown sugar, honey, molasses and olive oil. Stir until the sugar is almost completely dissolved, then add soy sauce. Bring to a boil then reduce heat and let simmer for about 30 minutes. Allow to cool before using.

Cut tofu into 1" thick slices and place in shallow dish. Pour the marinade over the tofu, cover, and refrigerate for maximum 3 hours. Heat 2 tablespoons vegetable oil in a frying pan over medium heat. Add tofu to hot pan, cook to caramelize (one to two minutes on each side). If the pan is not hot enough, it will stick. Serve with rice or noodles.

NUMBERS OF SERVINGS: 4

community became more unified by the incident and fear of further violence led city council →

lentil walnut loaf with dijon maple glaze

Marla Hertzman *Vegan meatloaf may sound like a bit of an odd concept, but I can assure you that it is a tasty one. There is even ketchup in the glaze. It is high in fiber and protein and low in fat. This may not be your Mother's meatloaf recipe, but it is now mine!*

Meatloaf:

1 cup uncooked green lentils (chickpeas work well too)

3 cups water

1 cup walnuts, finely chopped

3 tablespoons ground flax + ½ cup water

1 teaspoon extra virgin olive oil

1½ cups onion, diced

3 garlic cloves, minced

1 cup celery, diced

1 cup carrot, grated

⅓ cup apple, peeled and grated

¾ cup breadcrumbs

½ cup rolled oats

2 teaspoons fresh thyme (or ¾ teaspoons dried thyme)

¾ teaspoon salt

¼ teaspoon dried mustard

¼ teaspoon black pepper

¼ teaspoon red pepper flakes

Balsamic Dijon glaze:

2 tablespoons ketchup

2 tablespoons Dijon mustard

2 tablespoons balsamic vinegar

1 tablespoon pure maple syrup

Rinse lentils well. Place into pot along with water. Bring to a boil and season with salt. Reduce heat to medium/low and simmer, uncovered, for 40-45 minutes. Stir frequently and add more water, if needed. You want to overcook the lentils so it will be easy to mash them. Mash lentils slightly when ready. Toast walnuts at 325°F in preheated oven for about 8-10 minutes. Set aside. Increase oven temperature to 350°F.

Mix ground flax with water in a small bowl and set aside. Heat a teaspoon of olive oil in a skillet over medium heat. Sauté the onion and garlic for about 5 minutes. Season with salt. Add in the celery, carrot and apples. Sauté for about 5 minutes more. Remove from heat. In a large mixing bowl, mix all of the above ingredients and breadcrumbs, rolled oats and spices together. Grease 2 loaf pans and line with parchment paper. Press mixture firmly into pan.

Mix glaze ingredients and then spread on top of loaf. Bake at 350°F for 40-50 minutes, uncovered, until edges are light brown. Cool in pan for at least 10 minutes before transferring to a cooling rack. Do not slice while the loaf is hot. Wait about 10 minutes.

YIELD: 2 loaves

vegetable sides & mains

to ban the Swastika symbol from Toronto streets. By 1924 until after the Second

asparagus tart

Wendy Kay *This recipe is one of my favourites, especially in May and June when Ontario asparagus are the freshest. Our family enjoys it for brunch on the weekends.*

¾ cup flour

¼ teaspoon salt

⅓ cup cold butter

1 egg

2 cups asparagus, cut into 6" pieces

1 tablespoon butter

1 tablespoon fresh lemon juice

¾ cup crème fraîche

⅛ cup parsley, chopped

2 eggs

4 cherry tomatoes

¼ cup grated cheese (your choice)

salt and pepper to taste

Mix the flour and salt and cut the butter into the mixture to form a dough. Add 1 egg and knead. Put in the freezer for 10 minutes. Transfer the dough to a tart pan and press it on the bottom and up the sides about 2 inches high. Put in the freezer for another ten minutes. Remove from freezer and bake in preheated oven at 400°F for 10 minutes and then let cool.

In a large pan, melt 1 tablespoon butter and cook asparagus for five minutes. Season with lemon juice, salt and pepper. Mix crème fraîche with chopped parsley, then add eggs and stir well. Season with salt and pepper, arrange the asparagus on the tart shell, cut tomatoes in three slices each and put on the asparagus. Pour the egg mixture over it and bake at 350°F for 15 minutes. Remove from oven and sprinkle with grated cheese and bake for another 10–15 minutes.

YIELD: 1 tart

did you know?
In 1969, the first UJA Walk for Israel was established. It is now the world's largest Israel Solidarity Walk. The 2014 Walk had over 20,000 participants.

hot asparagus crisp

Maureen Zieper *As a young bride in South Africa, I began making this easy and delicious recipe which always seemed to impress my guests. Over all the years, it has remained a hit and family favourite. I have passed this recipe on to my children who regularly make it for their own families. Over the years, I have compiled recipe books of all my favourite recipes for my 7 grandchildren and this recipe is most definitely included.*

3 tins of asparagus cuts, reserving liquid

3 tablespoons butter (plus extra for greasing baking dish)

3 tablespoons flour

½ cup of asparagus liquid from tins

½ cup cream

1 cup grated cheddar cheese

salt and pepper to taste

plain potato chips

Preheat oven to 400°F. Drain asparagus and reserve the liquid. Place the asparagus into a 9 x 13" buttered dish. Melt the butter in a small pot over medium heat, add the flour and mix. Remove from the heat and gradually add in the ½ cup of asparagus liquid while stirring. Place back onto the heat and stir until thickened. Add the cream, salt and pepper to taste. Pour the mixture over the asparagus and sprinkle with the grated cheese. Sprinkle some hand crushed potato chips on top to cover the asparagus crisp in a thin layer. Bake at 400°F for about 15 minutes.

NUMBER OF SERVINGS: 8

zucchini quiche

Linda Friedlich *When my daughter got engaged, her wonderful mother-in-law made a delicious quiche to bring to a brunch we were having. The quiche was the most incredible tasting and easy-to-make recipe I have ever been given; every morsel was gone. I have made this recipe many times since that day and I get the same reaction. The recipe was handed down from her mother.*

3 cups zucchini, shredded

1 small onion, shredded

1 cup Bisquick biscuit mix

4 eggs

½ cup canola oil

¼ teaspoon each salt & pepper

8 ounce Swiss emmenthal cheese, grated

Mix all ingredients together. Pour into a 9" quiche pan sprayed with cooking spray. Bake in 350°F preheated oven for 45–50 minutes until lightly browned on top.

TIPS & ADVICE: Great to double in a 11" or 12" quiche pan. I doubt there will be any leftovers, but if there are, you can re-warm to serve. Should be made the day you are serving.

NUMBER OF SERVINGS: 8

impossible for Jews to come to Canada. Between 1933 and 1939, Canada accepted →

zucchini mushroom bake

Suzanna-Lee Engels *Several years ago, my garden's fall harvest was overwhelming. I was giving things away because we just couldn't eat our abundant yield. By late November, a small portion of my garden had ended up at the very back of my fridge. During one of my "Clean-up" modes, I found a few lonely zucchinis and wondered what to do with them. So, with a little pondering and some quick kitchen gymnastics, I put together this wonderful dish. So wonderful that my 7 year old and my 4 year old said to me, "Please Mom, can I have more?" This dish gets the "Kid's approval" gold star. This recipe is easily adapted for those who are gluten-free, vegan and/or vegetarian.*

3 large zucchini (cut on a diagonal in 2.5 mm medium sizes wedges)

1 can mushroom soup (do not add water)

3 teaspoons butter

2 teaspoons butter for garnish

¾ cup unseasoned breadcrumbs (or gluten-free breadcrumbs)

1 medium cooking onion, chopped

1 cup grated brick cheese or mozzarella type of cheese (you can use vegetarian and/or vegan cheese substitution)

pepper to taste (this dish really does not need salt, due to the cheese and the soup)

Preheat oven to 350°F. Prepare a shallow quiche dish with your favourite cooking spray. Dot bottom of the dish with the 3 teaspoons butter. Spiral the zucchini wedges starting on the outside working into the centre of the dish. Sprinkle the chopped onion on top. Pour the can of mushroom soup on top, coating the zucchini and the chopped onion. Sprinkle the cheese on top. Dot with the garnish butter. Add fresh pepper to taste. Cover the mixture with the breadcrumbs.

Bake for 1 hour at 350°F or until the cheese gets bubbly. Ovens can vary, so please check at around the 50 minute mark.

TIPS & ADVICE: This dish works well as a very hearty side dish.

NUMBER OF SERVINGS: 6–8

vegetable sides & mains

fish

grilled fish tacos

Carolyn Tanner-Cohen *Grilled fish tacos are something that almost everybody loves and they have become a staple in my home. In the winter, I broil the fish and in the summer, I grill it.*

2 teaspoons ground ancho chili powder

2 garlic cloves, minced

½ teaspoon ground cumin

1 chipotle chili in adobo from the can (with a little sauce), minced

½ teaspoon kosher salt

freshly ground pepper, to taste

2 tablespoons extra virgin olive oil

2–3 pounds firm while fish, haddock, halibut, snapper, cod, or tilapia

3–4 limes cut in wedges

1–2 dozen fresh corn tortillas, can be purchased at any store specializing in Mexican products

Fixings: shredded cabbage, sour cream, salsa, and guacamole

In a small bowl, mix together chili powder, garlic and cumin. Add chili in adobo with a little adobo sauce, mix again, and then add salt, pepper and olive oil. Mix again until a loose paste is formed. Rub the mixture all over the fish. Let stand at room temperature for 30 minutes marinating or up to 4 hours in the refrigerator. If in the fridge, bring to room temperature while you are preheating the grill (30 minutes) to medium-high. When the grill is hot, turn one part of the grill on low, leaving the other parts on med-high. The fish will go on the "low" part. Oil the grill grates well using spray or a damp paper towel dipped in vegetable oil. Place the fish on the cooler oiled part of the grill and cook each side until golden grill marks are formed, about 3–4 minutes per side. Remove to a cutting board and roughly chop. Place shredded cabbage on a platter to form a bed; place fish on top. Decorate with lime wedges.

Divide the tortillas into two stacks, wrap in foil and heat on grill for about five minutes. Each person should top their tacos with a scoop of fish, some cabbage, a drizzle of sour cream, a squeeze of lime, salsa, and guacamole on the side or in the taco.

TIPS & ADVICE: Chili in adobo comes in a small can found in the ethnic grocery section of the grocery store. Use what you need and freeze the rest. I put one chili with some sauce in a little ziplock bag, repeat until the can is used up.

Sometimes I make a very large batch of the Taco paste and freeze the paste in portions.

This fish recipe is so versatile, it can be served taco style or simply as a whole piece of Mexican flavoured grilled fish with salsa, guacamole, and a little sour cream on the side.

NUMBER OF SERVINGS: 6–8

fish

max's seared sesame tuna

Max Daviau *I learned how to make this tuna dish working as a pantry chef one summer at a high end Toronto restaurant. I have adapted the final touches and the presentation with my own unique twist. My parents, my sisters and brothers all beg me to make it up at our cottage or for Friday night dinner. I like to serve it with Asian style vegetables (eg. green beans with garlic and soy sauce) and rice. The dish is meant to be shared with several people. One tuna steak serves two or three as part of a main course.*

1 large (8 ounce) tuna steak, sushi grade

1 teaspoon coarse kosher salt

¼ cup sesame seeds (or enough to coat tuna steak completely) —any colour

1 tablespoon vegetable oil for frying

2 tablespoons soy sauce

1 tablespoon toasted sesame oil

½ lemon, sliced

squeezed lemon juice to taste

fresh salad greens

Sprinkle tuna liberally on all sides with kosher salt and allow to sit for 15 minutes until the sides and edges of tuna turn sticky. Cover all surfaces of tuna steak with sesame seeds so that no meat is showing. Cover the sesame-coated tuna steak tightly with plastic wrap and place in the fridge for 1 hour. Heat oil in heavy frying pan until hot, but not so hot that sesame seeds burn or you see black smoke. Sear tuna on both sides for approximately 1–2 minutes (depending on thickness). Outer edges on each side should be fully cooked but dark red on inside. This dish is meant to be served rare. (If pink, then cooked too long.) Remove from pan and let sit until room temp. Slice tuna into 1–1.5 centimeter slices or thinner, against the grain with sharp knife. Set up serving dish with greens and sliced lemons. Place tuna on greens—fan the tuna for best display. Sprinkle tuna with soy sauce, toasted sesame oil, and lemon juice. Enjoy!

TIPS & ADVICE: To ensure that tuna is completely coated with sesame seeds, it is best to spread sesame seeds on a baking sheet and put sides and then edges of tuna steak down on seeds until covered.

NUMBER OF SERVINGS: 2–3 as main, more as appetizer

fish

roasted halibut with basil

Paula Zivot *I cook with a lot of fresh herbs and we eat a lot of fish. My kids love halibut so I played around with different herbs and flavours and this recipe became one of our family's fish favourites! You can substitute other white fish as well, but I like halibut the best.*

1 pound fish, cut into desired portion sizes or as a larger single piece

3 tablespoons olive oil

3 tablespoons lemon juice

2 garlic cloves, minced (optional)

1 teaspoon fresh basil, chopped

1 green onion, chopped into small pieces

salt and pepper

Preheat oven to 450°F. Sprinkle the fish with salt and pepper. Mix the oil, lemon juice, garlic, basil and green onion in a bowl. Pour the mixture over the fish in a pyrex dish. Bake for 12–15 minutes.

Delicious served with rice.

NUMBER OF SERVINGS: 4

orange juice spiced halibut

Shari Silverstein *This is an amazingly delicious and easy-to-prepare recipe for halibut. Even people who think they don't like halibut (like my kids) love it when it's marinated this way. It's a terrific summer BBQ dish.*

½ cup olive oil

½ cup fresh orange juice

½ cup water

1 tablespoon fresh oregano, minced or 2 teaspoons dried oregano (you can adjust to taste)

1½ teaspoons coriander, chopped

2 teaspoons salt

½ teaspoon pepper

6 (8 ounce) halibut fillets

Mix together olive oil, orange juice, water, oregano, coriander, salt and pepper, and then place fish in a ziplock bag with the marinade. Marinate from 2 hours up to a day.

Drain the fish from the marinade (discard the remaining liquid) and then grill the halibut for a few minutes per side. Serve with some coriander sprigs as garnish.

TIPS & ADVICE: You can replace the halibut with any other thick white-fleshed fish.

NUMBER OF SERVINGS: 6

fish

a less than 10% increase from the 45,305 in 1931. The government of Mackenzie

white balsamic glazed mediterranean sea bass with fennel, leek and blood orange

Carolyn Tanner-Cohen *This recipe is wonderful hot and also at room temperature. It's a tried and true recipe in my home because it is easy enough to make for two or four people but perfect for doing ahead when you are cooking for a crowd. When I make it for 10 or more people, I serve it at room temperature and it is a hit!*

6 Mediterranean sea bass fillets; branzino, orata and arctic char also work well

3 tablespoons extra virgin olive oil

½ cup white balsamic vinegar

2 tablespoons honey

1 fennel bulb

2 leeks, white and light green parts only

2 blood oranges (or regular medium size oranges)

1 jalapeno pepper, sliced in rounds, optional

extra virgin olive oil for drizzling

kosher salt

freshly ground pepper

coarse sea salt for sprinkling at the end

Line 2 cookie sheets with foil. Preheat the oven to 425°F or 400°F convection. Make the white balsamic glaze by heating the olive oil (for the reduction) in a small pot. Add the balsamic vinegar and honey, simmer until it thickens and reduces, about 5 minutes; reserve. This step can be done well in advance (hours or a day or two).

Slice the top part of the fennel off and discard. Slice the fennel in half. Then, slice the fennel in ¼" wedges, cutting through the core so that the fennel wedges stay intact. Using only the white and light green part of the leek, slice the root end off, discard and then slice the leek in half lengthwise. Slice the leek again lengthwise into ¼" slices (julienne). Slice the two ends off both the oranges and discard, then slice the rest in ¼" rounds. Distribute the jalapeno rounds, fennel, leeks and oranges evenly over the two cookie sheets, drizzle with olive oil, toss to coat. Bake in the oven for 20 minutes.

Remove from the oven, change the oven temp to BROIL and adjust the rack to the highest position. Place 3 fish fillets on each sheet in between and around the veggies; you will need to move things around. Sprinkle the fish with salt and pepper and evenly drizzle the white balsamic glaze over the six fish fillets. Doing one sheet at a time, place the sheet in the oven on the highest position, broil for 3–4 minutes, repeat with the second sheet. Place one or two fish fillets on each plate and distribute some fennel, leek and orange around. Spoon some of the pan drippings over each piece of fish. Serve hot.

TIPS & ADVICE: You can make the balsamic glaze up to 5 days in advance. Bring the fish to room temperature for about 30 minutes before cooking.

NUMBER OF SERVINGS: 3–6

fish

fish "gremolata"

Eran Marom *I am a Sorbonne-trained culinary artist originally from Israel who settled in Toronto 10 years ago. Although I have travelled around the world, I love our great city and call it home! This is a fish gremolata that is a bit different from the norm.*

1 cup cilantro, chopped

⅓ cup extra virgin olive oil

1 teaspoon coriander seed

1 teaspoon thyme, chopped

2 garlic cloves, chopped

8 pitted green olives (not from a can)

½ cup panko (Japanese breadcrumbs)

1 lime, zest and juice

4 (4 ounce) fish fillets, skin off (any fish will work)

This recipe is better if you make the gremolata the day before and let it sit before using. Rinse the fish and pat dry with a paper towel. Sprinkle with good salt (Himalayan) and let sit for 1–2 hours in the fridge. Rinse the salt and pat dry.

Gremolata: Preheat oven to 250°F. Place all the ingredients except the fish, lime juice and panko in a small, ovenproof dish, making sure everything is covered in the oil. Bake at 250°F for 3 hours; take out and let cool. Strain out the oil and reserve; place remaining ingredients in a food processor and blend until they become a paste. Refrigerate paste and oil overnight.

On the day of use, add ½ cup of panko to the paste, mix well and set aside. Place the fish in a roasting tray lined with parchment paper, brush the paper with some of the reserved oil from the day before, then place the fish in the tray and put a full spoonful of the panko and paste mix on top of the fish. Pat it down, ensuring that the whole top of the fish is covered. Refrigerate for 10 minutes to let the crust firm up.

Preheat oven to 400°F and bake the fish for 10–15 minutes or until the crust turns crispy on top and the fish is cooked through (depending on the thickness of the fish, this can take more or less time). Mix any of the remaining reserved oil with the lime juice and serve with the fish.

NUMBER OF SERVINGS: 2–4

one of the tragic outcomes of a restrictive (and racist) immigration policy that resulted in only

leek and cherry tomato salmon

Lesley Sas *This fish presents beautifully! I went to a dinner party a few years ago and this mixture was served on halibut. The whole thing was wrapped in foil and cooked on the BBQ. My version is done in the oven but can be done on the BBQ as well.*

4 tablespoons olive oil

2 tablespoons fish spice (any brand will do)

3 leeks, white part only, sliced

3 tablespoons olive oil for sautéing leeks

2 cups different coloured cherry tomatoes

1 (4 pound) side of salmon

½ cup fresh herbs of your choice

Preheat oven to 400°F. Mix olive oil with fish spice. Brush on salmon. In a frying pan, sauté leeks until cooked through. Spread leeks on salmon and then put cherry tomatoes on top of leeks, then put fresh herbs on top of it all. Put salmon on cookie sheet uncovered and bake for 15–20 minutes or until cooked through.

TIPS & ADVICE: This recipe is also good with different coloured peppers and onions. Instead of onions, you can use shallots or scallions. A lot of times, I just use what is in my fridge. This can also be served at room temperature.

NUMBER OF SERVINGS: 8

ruby's moroccan fish recipe

Perlita Stroh *This very traditional Sephardic Moroccan recipe was passed down from my grandmother and her mother before her. My mom, Ruby Ettedgui, serves it every Friday night as it was at her mom's house when she was growing up. You know it's Shabbat or Chag when this fish makes an appearance and you smell its comforting aroma.*

2 tablespoons olive oil

1 red pepper, sliced

½ bunch cilantro, chopped

½ pint cherry tomatoes or one full tomato, chopped

6 garlic cloves, minced

1 tablespoon paprika

salt to taste

4 fillets grouper or halibut

Warm up olive oil in a pan and sauté the red pepper, cilantro, tomatoes, garlic, paprika and salt on medium heat. When sauce is nicely cooking, add the fish fillets and cook them on medium too. No need to turn them over. Cook the fish for 10–15 minutes or until it flakes. Serve fish with sauce spooned over.

NUMBER OF SERVINGS: 4

fish

5,000 Jewish refugees admitted to Canada during the Holocaust and until 1948; the lowest →

maple and soy salmon

Shari Wilson *This is actually my father, Rudy Bloom's recipe. It's so easy, it's embarrassing!!*

2 (8 ounce) pieces fresh salmon

2 tablespoons soy sauce

1 tablespoon maple syrup

freshly ground pepper

Preheat oven to 350°F. Mix soy sauce and maple syrup together and drizzle on pieces of salmon. Let marinate in fridge, preferably overnight. Place marinated pieces of salmon on a parchment-lined cookie sheet and sprinkle freshly ground pepper on top—practically covering the entire top surface of the salmon. Bake for 18–23 minutes at 350°F. Then, place it under the broiler for up to 5 minutes. Watch carefully. Serve at room temperature.

NUMBER OF SERVINGS: 2

sesame ginger salmon

Aviva Gottlieb *I borrowed this recipe from my friend Lisa and it is always a hit. Everyone loves it, and it is so easy.*

1½ cups mirin

½ cup tamari sauce

⅓ cup toasted black and white sesame seeds

¼ cup toasted sesame oil

6 green onions, sliced

3 tablespoons ginger, grated

3 garlic cloves, minced

2 (8 ounce) salmon fillets

Rinse and pat dry salmon. Combine all ingredients other than salmon in a bowl. Place salmon flesh side down, pour marinade over, making sure marinade gets under fish. Marinate for 3-4 hours or overnight. Preheat oven to 375°F. Bring marinated salmon to room temperature before cooking. Place fish on a foil-lined cookie sheet or baking dish and cook, skin side down (or bottom, if using a skinless side of salmon), putting all the good stuff on top of the fish. Bake for 20 minutes. Baste fish and then broil on high for 3-5 minutes until crispy.

TIPS & ADVICE: I often cook the fish before guests arrive and then broil it just before serving.

NUMBER OF SERVINGS: 2

roasted salmon with horseradish crust and crème fraîche

Rona Cappell *This incredible recipe came from a Food and Wine Expo my husband Rob and I fell upon in San Francisco about 10 years ago. I tasted this salmon and begged the Chef to share . . . and she did not disappoint me.*

1¼ tablespoons butter

1 cup panko (Japanese breadcrumbs)

⅓ cup prepared white horseradish

3 tablespoons fresh parsley, chopped

1 tablespoon shallots, chopped

Salt and pepper to taste

4 (4-6 ounce) salmon fillets

2 tablespoons extra virgin olive oil

¼ cup dry white wine

½ cup crème fraîche

Preheat oven to 350°F. In a small frying pan, melt butter over medium heat. Add panko crumbs and stir until golden. Remove from heat and place in a small mixing bowl. Add horseradish, parsley, and shallots and stir to combine. Season with salt and pepper.

Brush each fillet with extra virgin olive oil. Press top side of salmon into panko mixture and place in lightly greased baking dish. Bake for 10-12 minutes or until centre is slightly pink. Place each fillet on a serving dish, reserving liquid in baking dish.

Place same baking dish on stovetop over medium heat. Add wine and boil for 2 minutes or until reduced by about half. Add crème fraîche and simmer until it is thick enough to coat the back of a spoon. Remove from heat and drizzle on or around each fillet.

NUMBER OF SERVINGS: 4

fish

did you know?
220 Jewish immigrants were served by JIAS Toronto's JumpStart employment program in 2014.

that asked Canadians who they didn't want allowed into Canada indicated that their first choice →

roasted teriyaki-hoisin salmon

Rose Reisman *We've all had salmon teriyaki over the years, but try my twist using a combination of the teriyaki flavour and hoisin sauce. Garlic is an incredibly healthy vegetable. It contains allicin, which gives garlic its odour and protects us from cancer and heart disease. To activate this compound, chop the garlic and let it sit for 10 minutes before using.*

3 tablespoons packed brown sugar

2 tablespoons low-sodium soy sauce

1 tablespoon rice vinegar

1 tablespoon hoisin sauce

1 tablespoon water

2 teaspoons sesame oil

2 teaspoons cornstarch

1 teaspoon garlic, finely chopped

1 teaspoon ginger, finely chopped

1½ pounds salmon fillet

3 tablespoons cilantro or parsley, chopped

1 teaspoon sesame seeds

Preheat the oven to 425°F. Line a rimmed baking sheet with foil and lightly coat it with cooking spray. To make the sauce, combine the brown sugar, soy sauce, rice vinegar, hoisin sauce, water, sesame oil, cornstarch, garlic and ginger in a small saucepan. Bring to a boil, reduce the heat and simmer for 2 minutes or just until the mixture thickens. Place the salmon on the prepared baking sheet and pour half the sauce over it. Bake for 10 minutes per inch of thickness or until the fish just flakes when tested with a fork. Gently reheat the remaining sauce and serve over the baked salmon. Garnish with the cilantro and sesame seeds before serving.

TIPS & ADVICE: You can easily use this sauce over any other fish, chicken or tofu. Serve it over cooked vegetables but add a little water to loosen so it's pourable. I multiply the sauce recipe and freeze it in small containers for later use.

NUMBER OF SERVINGS: 4

fish

was the Japanese, their second was the Jews. Despite these racist sentiments, the

sweet and sour salmon

Patti Rotman *I have shared this recipe with many friends. The feedback is always positive. This recipe is enjoyed by all; even those that normally don't love fish!*

6 (4 ounce) wild salmon fillets

1 tablespoon sesame oil

1 teaspoon garlic, chopped

1 green pepper, sliced

1 yellow pepper, sliced

10 tablespoons vinegar

10 tablespoons sugar

6 tablespoons ketchup

8 tablespoons water

1 tablespoon cornstarch

To make the sauce, sauté chopped garlic in sesame oil until soft and fragrant. Add sliced peppers and sauté until soft. In a separate bowl, combine vinegar, sugar and ketchup. Add to peppers and simmer for 5–10 minutes. Combine water and cornstarch in a small bowl. Add to above and allow to thicken. Let simmer on low.

Preheat oven to 400°F. Place salmon fillets in a pyrex sprayed with cooking spray. Sprinkle lightly with salt and pepper. Bake for 14 minutes. When done, immediately cover with sauce and enjoy.

TIPS & ADVICE: For Passover, swap vegetable oil for sesame oil and potato starch for cornstarch. Freezes well, and can be doubled and tripled.

NUMBER OF SERVINGS: 6

roasted salmon with kumquats and ginger

Ashley Farnell *Using small kumquats gives the salmon a zing (sweet skinned but sour on the inside) and a sweet and sour effect. I got the idea for this dish when I was travelling in Corfu where the kumquat is bountiful and they make it into a liqueur.*

20 kumquats

2 teaspoons unsalted butter

2 teaspoons fresh ginger, peeled and minced

1 medium red onion, sliced very thin

4 (4 ounce) salmon fillets

2 tablespoons fresh lemon juice

½ teaspoon kosher salt

½ teaspoon fresh ground pepper

Preheat oven to 450°F. Spray a 9" square baking pan with non stick spray. Thinly slice the kumquats horizontally, removing the seeds as you go. Melt the butter in a large, non-stick pan over medium high heat. Add the kumquats and ginger and cook, stirring, until the kumquats are just starting to brighten in colour, about 2 minutes. Scatter the onion slices over the bottom of the baking pan, then top with the salmon. Scatter the kumquat pieces and ginger and their juices on the salmon and sprinkle with the lemon juice, salt and pepper. Bake until the fish is barely pink in the centre and the kumquats are tender, 15–20 minutes, depending on the thickness of the fish.

NUMBER OF SERVINGS: 4

fish

postwar economy was booming, and business needed labour to expand and it is this that finally

moroccan fish

Annette Cohen *Great served warm or cold as a starter at Friday night dinners.*

1 (1 pound) white fish fillet

½ bunch parsley, separated

1 bulb garlic, separated into cloves (unpeeled)

2 red peppers, sliced

1 teaspoon paprika

dash cayenne pepper

½ teaspoon salt

½ teaspoon pepper

½ teaspoon turmeric

2 tablespoons olive oil

¼ cup water

Cut the fish into 6 pieces. Reserve 3 sprigs of parsley and spread the rest on the bottom of a skillet. Top evenly with cloves and peppers. Chop the reserved parsley and mix with paprika, cayenne, salt, pepper, turmeric and olive oil, creating more of a liquid than a paste (add a bit of water if too thick). Dip fillets into the paprika/spice mixture to coat and place on top of the peppers in a single layer in the skillet. If there is any of the paprika mixture left, pour evenly into the skillet. Add a ¼ cup of water and set onto high heat until it starts to boil. Reduce heat to medium low and let simmer slowly until the liquid evaporates and fish is cooked.

TIPS & ADVICE: Try adding tomato slices to the pan with peppers and replace the parsley with coriander. Any kind of fish may be used.

NUMBER OF SERVINGS: 4–6

tuna pastel

Sally Berman *This makes a hearty winter brunch or dinner. Our kids love it!*

12 potatoes, peeled

6 eggs, hard-boiled and peeled

2 cans flaked tuna, drained

1 can olives, sliced

1 cup hot pepper rings

1 teaspoon canola oil

1 teaspoon nutmeg

1 teaspoon cinnamon

1 teaspoon salt

½ teaspoon pepper

⅓ cup sugar

additional oil for drizzling

Preheat oven to 350°F. Boil potatoes in salted water. Drain most of water out, leaving some behind. Add oil, nutmeg, cinnamon, salt, pepper and sugar to potatoes. Mash the potatoes well. Grease a deep 9 x 13" foil pan. Take half of the potato mixture and make a bottom layer of potatoes in the pan. Then, add a layer of tuna (both cans), sprinkle the olives and add hot pepper rings. Slice the hard-boiled eggs evenly. Layer the eggs on top of the tuna, olives and hot peppers. Cover all of it in a top layer of potatoes. Drizzle some of oil on top. Bake uncovered for 1 hour and 15 minutes or until golden brown.

TIPS & ADVICE: We use albacore tuna for a lighter meal. Ground beef can be substituted for tuna for a heartier meal.

NUMBER OF SERVINGS: 6–8 small servings

fish balls in tomato sauce

Michelle Factor/Esther Sachs *This is the fish we grew up on. We ate this every Friday night on Shabbat. This is easy, tasty and comes out perfectly every time. You can make it a couple of hours before dinner and it tastes great at room temperature.*

Sauce:

¼ cup olive oil

6 garlic cloves, minced

1 teaspoon paprika

1 teaspoon salt

1 teaspoon pepper

1 handful each fresh parsley and cilantro, chopped

1 large can tomato sauce

2 pounds white fish, chopped

½ teaspoon black pepper

½ teaspoon salt

2 eggs

2 tablespoons breadcrumbs

1 tablespoon fresh ginger, grated

1 handful each fresh cilantro and parsley, chopped

Sauce: Sauté garlic in olive oil with paprika, salt, pepper, parsley and cilantro. Add tomato sauce. Simmer for 20-30 minutes.

Fish: Mix pepper, salt, eggs, breadcrumbs, ginger, cilantro and parsley into fish. Make small balls and add to sauce. Simmer on low for another 30–40 minutes.

TIPS & ADVICE: You can use a bit of cayenne pepper in the sauce to kick it up.

NUMBER OF SERVINGS: 4–5

did you know?
Each year, approximately 900 young Torontonians take part in a Birthright Israel trip, & another 8,000 alumni are served through post-program activities.

to post-War immigrants, thousands of Holocaust survivors settled in Canada; approximately

exotic stuffed fish pinwheels

Gloria Clamen *This recipe is terrific with any firm fleshed fish. Fresh herbs elevate the taste of the stuffing.*

6 fish fillets

3 tablespoons canola oil, divided

5 green onions, thinly sliced

2 large garlic cloves, minced

½ cup flat-leaf parsley, chopped

¼ cup mint, chopped

2 tablespoons tarragon, chopped

1 tablespoon cilantro, chopped

1 cup walnut pieces

¼ cup dried cranberries

¼ cup raisins

¼ cup lime juice

1 teaspoon kosher salt

¼ teaspoon ground pepper

Wash and dry fish fillets and place each fillet on flat surface. Prepare stuffing by heating 2 tablespoons oil in a skillet over medium heat. Add onions, garlic, parsley, mint, tarragon and cilantro. Stir and cook for about 10 minutes. Stir in walnuts, cranberries, raisins, lime juice, salt and pepper. Set aside. Place a couple of generous tablespoons of stuffing at widest end of fillet and roll up in pinwheel fashion. Secure with skewer or toothpick (don't forget to leave a couple of inches of the skewer sticking out so it can be removed after baking). Place pinwheels in a baking dishing that has been lightly seasoned with oil, seam side down. Brush fillets lightly with oil. Bake in preheated oven at 425°F for 15–20 minutes.

TIPS & ADVICE: Any leftover stuffing can be used as a side dish to the fish.

NUMBER OF SERVINGS: 6 + leftover stuffing

fish

visit our website
www.JewishToronto.com/BathurstStreetKitchen

8,000 in Toronto alone. (our story continues on page 166 . . . read on)

Irving Ungerman, aged 18, in front of Royce Avenue Poultry Market, 216 Royce Avenue, Toronto, 1941

poultry

baba sarah's oven fried chicken

Adell Shneer *My Baba Sarah was a fabulous cook. She made this chicken, which she called "Chelzelah Chicken", as the coating resembled the flour mixture used to stuff kishka. In our family, we affectionately renamed this "Baba's Chicken" in her honour. This recipe is simple, foolproof and a crowd favourite. I always find someone in the kitchen nibbling on the crispy bits that have stuck to the baking sheet; usually it's my husband, Michael.*

½ cup all-purpose flour

1½ teaspoons kosher salt

1½ teaspoons garlic powder

1 teaspoon paprika

¼ teaspoon pepper

¼ teaspoon dry mustard

¼ cup vegetable oil

8 chicken breasts, thighs, or legs

Preheat oven to 375°F. In a bag, shake together flour, salt, garlic powder, paprika, pepper and mustard powder and set aside.

In small saucepan, warm oil. Coat each chicken piece in oil, then shake in flour mixture. Place in single layer on well-greased baking sheet. Bake until golden, crisp and juices run clear when chicken is pierced, about 1 hour.

TIPS & ADVICE: This is just as good the next day straight out of the fridge so plan to make enough for leftovers.

NUMBER OF SERVINGS: 8

debonayr mayo chicken breasts

Debbie Myers *I enjoy coming up with new and yummy ways to prepare my chicken each week. When my friend said she had seen a chicken coated with potato chips on the Food Network, I was inspired. I had used mayonnaise before to cook salmon, and it was very moist. Combining these ideas together, I ended up with a new family favourite that takes less than ten minutes to prepare and less than 30 minutes to bake.*

½ cup mayonnaise

2 teaspoons paprika

1 teaspoon black pepper

1 teaspoon hot sauce

½ teaspoon celery seeds

zest of one small lemon

4 boneless chicken breasts

1 large bag potato chips, crushed

Line a small, rimmed baking sheet with parchment paper. In a small bowl, whisk together mayonnaise, paprika, pepper, hot sauce, celery seeds and lemon zest. Slather the chicken with this mixture. Marinate in the fridge up to two hours. Preheat oven to 400°F. Dip slathered chicken into crushed potato chips and coat both sides. Place on baking sheet and bake until done, 20–30 minutes.

NUMBER OF SERVINGS: 4

 ✿ The result was, that by 1951, the Jewish population of greater Toronto had grown

balsamic braised chicken

Adam Palter *When my mom told me I should submit a recipe, this was my first choice. When I come home from university, this is almost always on the list of meals I want to have. This is a great recipe because you can do most of it ahead of time.*

6 boneless or bone-in chicken thighs

¼ teaspoon salt

¼ teaspoon ground pepper

2 teaspoons olive oil

⅓ cup shallots, finely chopped

2 tablespoons fresh thyme, minced

¼ cup red wine

¾ cup balsamic vinegar

¼ cup chicken broth

¼ cup honey

1 bay leaf

Season chicken with salt and pepper. Heat olive oil in a braising pan and sear chicken on all sides until brown. Remove to a plate. Add shallots and thyme to the pan and sauté until golden. Add wine and scrape up any bits left from the chicken. Cook one to two minutes until nearly all liquid has evaporated. Add balsamic vinegar, broth, honey, bay leaf and chicken and bring to a simmer. Cover and cook until chicken is deep brown and cooked through, turning once.

Remove chicken to a plate and discard bay leaf. Boil remaining sauce until reduced to about half.

Add chicken back to pan to warm and serve.

TIPS & ADVICE: We like to brown the chicken and put it in the fridge covered, and make the sauce early in the day. That way, all you have to do at the last minute is put the chicken in the sauce to cook through and reduce the sauce. Take the chicken out 30 minutes before if making ahead so it isn't so cold. Because of this, our family often makes it for company, as it leaves the oven free for other things. We usually double the chicken and triple the sauce as the sauce is the best part. I like it best with rice or orzo to soak up all the extra sauce.

NUMBER OF SERVINGS: 4–6

poultry

bubie rae's chicken fricassee

Sharon Appleby Hussman *My mother's fricassee was always something we got excited about. She made it on the High Holidays as an appetizer, but we all loved it so much that we had two or three helpings. This is why I started to make it as an entree. Dipping fresh challah or matzah into the gravy completed this incredible meal and family favourite. I make it as a treat in between holidays. When I make it with my sister, she rolls the turkey balls while I watch the wings. This quickens the preparation time, but once you've made it a few times, it doesn't take long. I hope you enjoy and treasure this fricassee as much as all of the Applebys, Pustils, Hussmans, Ansells, and Millers do!*

Turkey balls:

2 pounds ground turkey

1 egg

4 tablespoons breadcrumbs

1 teaspoon garlic powder

1 teaspoon kosher salt

4-6 tablespoons canola oil, divided (use lesser amount if your pan is nonstick)

1 small onion, finely chopped

15 chicken wings, tips removed and split in half

2 tablespoons paprika

1 teaspoon garlic powder

1 teaspoon kosher salt

3 heaping tablespoons white flour

boiling water

Preheat oven to 350°F. To make turkey balls, combine ground turkey, egg, breadcrumbs, garlic powder, and salt in a bowl. Mix well. Roll small balls, approximately 1" in diameter in your hands. Lay them side by side on a 11 x 17" nonstick cookie sheet. Bake 15 minutes. In large pot (preferably nonstick), heat 2 tablespoons oil on medium heat. Add chopped onion and cook until softened. Remove onion from pot and set aside.

Sprinkle chicken wing pieces with paprika, garlic powder, and salt until evenly coated. Add 2-4 tablespoons of oil into pot and heat to medium high. Lay wings flat on bottom and brown well on both sides. Sprinkle wings with flour and mix well along with the scrapings at the bottom of the pot. Add the cooked onions and boiling water, just enough to cover the wings; mix until all scrapings have dissolved and gravy has formed. Add the cooked meatballs and juice and stir all together. Simmer on low for 20 minutes.

Skim off the fat and thin the gravy with a little water if it is too thick.

TIPS & ADVICE: You can make this the day before to lessen your workload for dinner. It also makes it easier to skim the fat. For Passover, substitute matzah meal for breadcrumbs in the ground turkey and cake meal for white flour for the gravy.

NUMBER OF SERVINGS: 6 as an entree or 12 as an appetizer

Toronto was said to require higher entrance grades from Jews than other applicants and until

chicken fire poppers

Hinda Silber *This is a recipe that everyone loves. I make it only for special occasions to keep it feeling special. I recreated it from a dish that I tasted at someone's house at Sukkot. It's very spicy so you have to adapt to your taste.*

½ cup flour

2 tablespoons cornstarch

2 tablespoons sugar

1 teaspoon baking powder

½ cup water

4 boneless chicken breasts, cut into cubes

oil for frying

½ cup packed brown sugar

½ cup Frank's hot sauce

¼ cup honey

Preheat oven to 350°F. Combine flour, cornstarch, sugar, baking powder, and water. Coat chicken with this mixture. Heat a small amount of oil in a pan and fry the chicken until cooked through. Grease a 9 x 13" baking dish with non-stick spray. Add chicken. Combine brown sugar, hot sauce and honey and pour over chicken. Bake uncovered for 20 minutes.

TIPS & ADVICE: I find ½ cup of hot sauce too spicy for me so I use ⅓ cup of hot sauce and add honey to fill to ½ cup for the sauce instead. Very yummy. Kids love it.

NUMBER OF SERVINGS: 4

chili chicken

Dianna Vaturri *My husband and I spent two years living in Japan and I brought this recipe back to Edmonton. It's become a family favourite and is also a favourite of my friends in Toronto.*

8 limes, juiced

5 garlic cloves, crushed

2 tablespoons chili powder

salt to taste

1 whole chicken cut into 8 pieces

Mix all ingredients (except the chicken) in a bowl to make marinade. Add chicken and marinate for at least 3 hours. Bake uncovered for one hour at 375°F.

TIPS & ADVICE: The longer you marinate, the better the results!

NUMBER OF SERVINGS: 6

poultry

1962, Mount Sinai Hospital was denied status as a University of Toronto teaching hospital.

chicken and rice

Michele Frankel *The tastiness is in this dish's simplicity. Even my mom, Ruth Henry, who's never loved to cook, made this dish often when I was growing up because there's no easier dinner. I still remember the warm smells of rice and roasted chicken that filled my home on cold, winter evenings. This recipe is adapted from the Jewish food bible Second Helpings Please! I've swapped out Lipton's Onion Soup Mix for ras el hanout, a Middle Eastern spice. Different flavours—but no love lost.*

grapeseed oil for frying

kosher salt and freshly ground black pepper

4–5 pound chicken, cut in 8 pieces

3 garlic cloves, finely chopped

2 shallots, finely diced

1 cup (250 mL) jasmine rice

1 teaspoon (5 mL) ground ras el hanout

1 cup (250 mL) chicken broth

1 cup (250 mL) white wine

4 sprigs fresh thyme

Preheat oven to 350°F. In a large oven proof pot with tight fitting lid, heat 1" of oil over medium high heat. Sprinkle chicken with salt and pepper. Working in batches, fry chicken until golden, about 3–5 minutes per side, transferring pieces to plate or wire rack to drain.

Pour off all but one tablespoon oil from pot. Add garlic and shallots to pot and sauté until lightly browned, about 30 seconds to one minute. Using a wooden spoon, stir in rice and ras el hanout. Add chicken, broth, wine and thyme. Bake covered in for 1 hour.

TIPS & ADVICE: Ras el hanout is a popular Moroccan spice mix that can be purchased at gourmet or specialty food stores. Ras el hanout usually includes cardamom, nutmeg, anise, mace, cinnamon, ginger, various peppers, and turmeric. If you can't find it ready made, you can research recipes online and make it yourself.

NUMBER OF SERVINGS: 4–6

poultry

Jews were not admitted as members of Toronto's Granite Club or the Royal Canadian →

chicken machmoosa and fried chickpeas

Rochelle Chester and Melanie Zeldman *Our father is from Poland and our mother was born in India, but her family was originally from Iraq and lived there for many generations. We grew up in an Ashkenazi household in every way ritually, except for the food that our mother cooked. When we were little, we didn't always love our mother's unusual cooking! As we got older and especially after our mother passed away, we started to long for those familiar smells and tastes of our childhood. These two dishes may be served together or separately. Enjoy!*

Chicken machmoosa:

1 pound ground chicken

1 large onion, chopped

1 tablespoon fresh ginger, chopped

1 garlic clove, minced

1 tablespoon turmeric

salt and pepper to taste

2 tablespoons oil for frying

Fried chickpeas:

1 can chickpeas, drained and rinsed

½ cup green onions, chopped

½ tablespoon ground cumin

salt and pepper to taste

2 tablespoons oil for frying

Combine ground chicken with other ingredients and fry in oil until chicken is cooked. Add additional spices to taste.

Combine chickpeas, onions and seasonings. Fry in oil until chickpeas soften. Add additional spices to taste. Serve with basmati or plain rice.

NUMBER OF SERVINGS: 4–6

did you know?
Over 1,000 women and children are served by Jewish Family & Child's Women Abuse/Children Witnessing Violence program.

poultry

chicken with za'atar and fattoush salad

Nira Rittenberg *I fell in love with za'atar in Jaffa on one of my trips to Israel. This spice blend (which usually includes sumac, sesame seeds and herbs and is available in Middle Eastern stores) is now a staple in my house and I use it on eggs, fish, pitas, yogourt, and in soups. I am Israeli-born and feel this meal brings the best of Israel to my table.*

Chicken:

8 bone-in or boneless chicken thighs

about ½ cup olive oil, divided

4 teaspoons za'atar, divided

1 teaspoon each salt and pepper

4 tomatoes, chopped

3–4 garlic cloves, finely chopped

1 cup pitted olives, Kalamata, Spanish or green

1 onion, thinly sliced

1½ pounds baby red or golden potatoes

Fattoush salad:

3 tomatoes, chopped

1 cucumber, chopped

½ cup mint, chopped

½ cup parsley, chopped

3 green onions, chopped

juice of 1 lemon

olive oil equal to lemon juice

1 garlic clove, minced

salt and pepper to taste

1 teaspoon sumac, optional

2 pitas, opened, toasted and cut into triangles, optional

Preheat oven to 375°F. Drizzle chicken with a small amount of olive oil and sprinkle with za'atar, salt and pepper. Rub to cover well, adding more seasonings if needed. Heat about 3 tablespoons of oil in a large, oven-proof skillet until hot. Add the chicken. Cook both sides until brown. Remove chicken and set aside on paper towel. Add a little more oil to the skillet and sauté tomatoes, onion, garlic and olives. Add potatoes and sprinkle with 1 teaspoon za'atar. Bake 20 minutes. Remove skillet from the oven and add the chicken pieces. Bake an additional 45 minutes.

Just before chicken is ready, combine all the salad ingredients in a bowl. Taste and adjust the seasonings. Serve alongside chicken.

TIPS & ADVICE: This dish can be made with other chicken parts, such as breasts, but you need to ensure the breasts don't dry out. It can also be adjusted to suit the size of any family event. The dish reheats well and is great over rice. Serve this dish with hummus and/or babaganoush and you have a lovely Israeli feast.

NUMBER OF SERVINGS: 6

chutney chicken with mango

Lorraine Neumann *We love the flavour of the chutney, curry and mango; it's delicious!*

2 pounds chicken thighs or legs (dark meat works better in this recipe)

½ cup chutney (ingredients below)

2 tablespoons Dijon mustard

juice of ½ lemon

1 teaspoon cinnamon

2 teaspoons curry powder

1 teaspoon kosher salt

Chutney:

2 mangos, diced small

1 small red onion, diced small

¼ cup lime or lemon juice

2 tablespoons sugar

¼ teaspoon salt

Preheat the oven to 350°F and arrange the chicken pieces in a 9 x 13" baking dish—either use glass or line the pan with foil because the sauce is sticky. To make the chutney, in a small pot, combine the mango, red onions, lime or lemon juice, sugar and salt. Bring to a boil and cook over high heat for about 8 minutes, until the mango is tender.

In a small bowl, combine the chutney, mustard, lemon juice, cinnamon, curry and salt. Mix to combine, then pour it over the chicken, and toss it so the pieces are coated. Cover the dish with foil and bake the chicken for 30 minutes, covered. Then remove the foil and bake for another 15–20 minutes. The skin doesn't necessarily get crispy. The chicken is good hot or cold.

NUMBER OF SERVINGS: 8

poultry

cornish game hens with orange-rosemary glaze

Bonny Reichert *Although this is my own recipe, it was really inspired by my mom, Toby Reichert, who often serves Cornish hens instead of chicken at the holidays. What a great discovery she made! They're sophisticated looking and very tasty, but still easy to source and prepare. Cornish hens have a more interesting flavour than chicken, and they look much fancier, so consider this recipe for a special meal. The orange and rosemary pair beautifully and the honey ensures a nice brown skin. And simple? You bet.*

4 oranges (Sevilles are nice in season, but navels are fine too)

1 tablespoon honey

2 Cornish game hens, about 1½ pounds each

2 teaspoons salt

freshly ground pepper, to taste

3 sprigs fresh rosemary, 2 whole and 1 with needles reserved and stem discarded

3 small onions, peeled and quartered

Preheat oven to 375°F. Cut two of the oranges in half and squeeze their juice into a small bowl. Discard spent halves. Combine juice with honey and mix until honey dissolves. Set aside. Season hens on all sides with salt and pepper. Cut a third orange in half and place a piece in the cavity of each bird, along with a sprig of rosemary.

Line the bottom of a large roasting pan with onions. Cut remaining orange into wedges and scatter among onion pieces. Place hens over onions and oranges, and drizzle generously with honey orange sauce, reserving a couple of spoonfuls for later. Scatter hens with rosemary needles. Roast breast side up on bottom rack of oven. After about 50 minutes, brush hens again with sauce and, if breasts are getting too brown, cover loosely with a piece of foil. Continue roasting 10–15 minutes longer, or until juices run clear and leg joints feel loose. Serve hens with a few onions and roasting orange pieces.

TIPS & ADVICE: Seville oranges have a distinctive floral flavour, but they aren't sweet. They are in season only in wintertime. If you can't get them, use regular navel oranges but add a squeeze of lemon juice to increase the acidity, which really brings out the flavour of poultry.

NUMBER OF SERVINGS: 4

poultry

 In response to the municipal migration of Jews northwards especially in the Manor

judi's friday night special chicken

Judi Urowitz *I have been making this recipe for over 20 years. It always comes out perfectly. It's a great, fast meal when I'm short on time. I was making this last week with my 15 year old granddaughter and we were laughing; I picked up a bottle of white wine vinegar instead of white wine. Within minutes, I smelled my mistake, tasted the sauce and realized my error: it was far more sour than usual. I quickly added two tablespoons honey to mellow the sour taste. Everyone raved about it anyways. This is so fast, colourful, healthy, and a real crowd pleaser. It can be doubled without changing the flavours.*

1 cup flour

1 teaspoon oregano

½ teaspoon Montreal steak pepper

4 boneless, skinless chicken breasts

4 boneless, skinless chicken thighs

2 tablespoons olive oil

1 cup chicken soup, canned or homemade

½ cup white wine

2 cans artichokes, drained and cut up

2 small zucchini, sliced

1 red pepper, cut into strips

1 pint cherry tomatoes

½ red onion, sliced

salt to taste

Combine flour, oregano, and Montreal steak pepper. Dredge chicken in mixture. Heat oil in electric frying pan at 375°F and cook chicken pieces until brown on both sides. Add chicken soup and wine. Reduce heat to 350°F. Add the vegetables and salt to taste. Cover and cook 45 minutes.

TIPS & ADVICE: This recipe can also be made on top of stove but I have always used an electric fry pan. Makes great leftovers.

NUMBER OF SERVINGS: 6–8

poultry

sara goldman's shabbat chicken

Genevieve Korman *This Shabbat chicken dinner recipe has been handed down over the years. My grandmother first made it; then my mother and now I make it. It is delicious and easy to make and a real crowd pleaser. This recipe is perfect on Shabbat with Matzah ball soup. You can also make chicken salad with the leftover chicken the next day.*

1 chicken cut into eighths

4–6 Yukon gold potatoes, peeled and cut into medium chunks

3–5 tablespoons garlic powder

3–5 tablespoons kosher salt

3–5 tablespoons paprika

Preheat oven to 350°F. Rinse chicken with cool water. Add ½" of cool water into aluminum pan. Arrange chicken, skin side down, and potatoes in pan. Cover generously with garlic powder, kosher salt and paprika. Cover pan with tin foil. Cook for 1 hour. Uncover pan and flip chicken so skin is up and sprinkle again with garlic, salt and paprika. Cook uncovered for 2 hours, basting every ½ hour. Can be broiled at the end for extra crispiness but watch it carefully. Serve with gravy from the bottom of the pan. Enjoy!

NUMBER OF SERVINGS: 4

chicken sofrito

Renee Gozlan *Also known in our house as Yellow Chicken, this recipe has been passed down in our family for generations.*

1 whole chicken

4–5 tablespoons oil

5–6 carrots, diced

1 tablespoon paprika

1 tablespoon parsley

1 tablespoon turmeric

1 teaspoon whole peppercorns

1–2 cups water

Heat oil in a large pot on medium heat. Place the whole chicken in the pot and cover. Lightly brown each side of the chicken, then remove from heat. Add the carrots and sprinkle the whole chicken with paprika, parsley, turmeric and peppercorns so it is covered with the spices. Then, add 1½–2 cups of water until the chicken is covered and bring to a boil. Place the lid back on the pot and let the chicken simmer on medium heat, watching to make sure it doesn't burn.

Boil out the water until only the oil is left. This is a dish that has to be watched. Baste chicken with sauce as it is cooking. It needs to cook for at least a couple of hours. After the chicken is cooked, sprinkle with salt to taste. Serve with rice or couscous.

NUMBER OF SERVINGS: 4

poultry

between Sheppard and Finch in 1958. Both the 'Y's provided a greater sense

shnitzel with mushroom wine sauce

AJ Schur *This dish is based on a recipe of my late aunt, Barbra Gluck, who was a wonderful person. I have tweaked this recipe to enhance some of the flavours and it is a favourite item on our catering menu at the Kosher Gourmet.*

6 boneless chicken breasts

½ teaspoon granulated garlic

½ teaspoon granulated onion

¼ cup flour

3 eggs, beaten

½ cup cornflake crumbs

1 cup breadcrumbs

2 tablespoons oil

Sauce:

1 cup chicken broth

½ cup dry white wine

1 teaspoon chicken soup mix

10 button mushrooms, sliced

Preheat oven to 350°F. Sprinkle chicken breasts with granulated garlic and onion, then coat with flour. Dip in eggs and then coat with crumb mixture. Heat oil in a frying pan and cook the chicken until lightly brown on both sides. Place in a baking dish.

Heat broth, wine, and chicken soup mix until boiling. Add sliced mushrooms and simmer for 10–12 minutes. Pour the sauce over the chicken and bake covered for one hour.

NUMBER OF SERVINGS: 6

poultry

visit our website
www.JewishToronto.com/BathurstStreetKitchen

of Jewish community and identity in Toronto. In 1955, Nathan Phillips, a child

kibbeh bamya

Leanne Hazon *Kibbeh Bamya is a traditional Iraqi Jewish version of the popular Middle Eastern dish kibbeh, and is a favourite in our family. My aunt used to watch her mother make it in Baghdad and this superb meal came with them when they emigrated to Israel in 1951, and eventually to Canada. My cousins and I remember our grandmother making it for the family and now my aunt, Nirah Mayer, often makes it for us for Shabbat and special occasions, including for her grandson's Bar Mitzvah. Her kibbeh is even better than her mother's—in fact, it's kind of legendary in the Iraqi community in Toronto! The whole family gets excited when we hear Safta Nirah is making kibbeh. She jokes that it takes her three hours to make enough for everyone and only 20 minutes for us to demolish it!*

2½ medium onions, chopped, divided

2 pounds ground chicken or beef

¾ cup parsley, finely chopped

salt and pepper

pinch turmeric

Dough:

4 cups Cream of Wheat

½ pound bulgur

1 cup water

salt

Kibbeh: Chop the onions and salt them. Leave them for a couple of minutes and then rinse off the salt. Combine chicken or beef, 2 chopped onions and parsley together in a bowl and mix with your hands. Add black pepper, salt, and turmeric to taste.

Dough: Mix the Cream of Wheat and bulgur together with water and a little salt until you have a sticky and malleable dough mixture. You may use a little more or less water for the desired consistency of the dough. Take a small amount of the dough and flatten it into a circle on the palm of your hand. Make sure it is thin. In the middle, put a dollop of the meat mixture and close the ball around it.

Sauce: See ingredients list on following page. Cut the tops off of the fresh okra and soak them in water with a bit of salt for a couple of minutes. Sauté the chicken bones and the remaining chopped onion in a large pot until the onions are soft. Safta Nirah doesn't use anything to sauté the chicken bones and onion, but feel free to add a little oil, if you want. Add crushed tomatoes and a little salt. Fill the empty crushed tomato bottle with water—add 2½ bottles of water, salt and pepper to taste and a pinch of turmeric to the pot.

Bring to a boil and let simmer on low heat for 15 minutes. Add the okra and cook until softened (but not mushy). Take okra out and set aside. Discard the bones. Bring the sauce to a boil and add the kibbeh balls. Bring to a boil again and reduce to medium heat. Add the lemon juice and brown sugar. Simmer for approximately 20 minutes. Serve over basmati rice.

poultry

Sauce:

2 pounds fresh or frozen okra

½ pound chicken bones to flavour the sauce

1 (22 ounce) bottle crushed tomatoes

water

salt and pepper, to taste

pinch turmeric

2 lemons, juiced

1–2 tablespoons brown sugar

TIPS & ADVICE: If you are using frozen okra, it does not need to be defrosted. The kibbeh balls can be frozen before cooking; just take them out and make some sauce when you want to eat them.

NUMBER OF SERVINGS: 60 kibbeh balls

roast chicken breasts with lemon juice and olives

Susan Segal *This is a delicious and easy recipe that utilizes fresh and simple ingredients. It is original and a family favourite.*

6 bone-in chicken breasts

¼ cup of olive oil

3 tablespoons fresh thyme

½ teaspoon hot red pepper flakes

salt and pepper to taste

1 shallot, sliced not too thin

½ lemon, juice and zest

1 cup dry white wine

handful oil-cured black olives

Preheat the oven to 450°F. Combine chicken with oil, thyme, red pepper flakes, salt and pepper. Rub mixture into chicken. Arrange chicken, skin side up, in an oven-proof pan. (Not too shallow, because you will be adding liquid later.) Roast chicken for about 20 minutes, until it begins to brown. If chicken is looking too brown, turn oven down to 425°F. Add the shallot and drizzle lemon juice and wine over the chicken and roast for about 5–10 minutes more. If the liquid is drying up, add more wine and lemon juice. Scatter olives and lemon zest over and around the chicken.

Roast until the skin is golden brown and chicken is cooked through about 10–15 minutes more. Let stand for 10 minutes prior to serving. Best served with rice or pasta.

NUMBER OF SERVINGS: 6

poultry

staying in office until 1962. Phillips was a very visible symbol of the idea that Jews

lichee garden's sweet and sour chicken

Ellen Cole For years our family congregated at Lichee Gardens on Sunday nights. Whoever was hungry and available would meet us there. My husband, Tubby, knew exactly what to order for the assembled crowd and this dish was always a crowd pleaser. The owner, Ken, gave us the recipe and we made it healthier by omitting the batter and deep-frying; we stir fry the chicken instead.

Sauce:

1 cup water

4 teaspoons cornstarch

½ cup sugar

½ cup white vinegar

¼ cup tomato paste

Marinade:

2 tablespoons cornstarch

2 tablespoons vegetable oil

½ teaspoon salt

1 egg

2 chicken breasts cut into 1" strips (across the grain)

assorted vegetables (sliced red and green pepper, onion chopped in chunky pieces, snow peas, baby corn)

oil for frying

For the sauce, dissolve cornstarch in water, mix in the sugar, vinegar, and tomato paste. Cook on medium heat until thick. Cool and set aside. Mix the four marinade ingredients and marinate the chicken strips for about two hours. Stir-fry the chicken in small batches in hot oil until just cooked; do not overcook. Set chicken aside. Stir-fry the vegetables in hot oil and set aside. When you are ready to serve, heat the sauce, add the chicken and vegetables and heat but do not overcook it. Serve with steamed or fried rice.

TIPS & ADVICE: The dish can all be prepared a few hours in advance and put together at the last minute.

NUMBER OF SERVINGS: 4

and, immigrants in general, could be included and play leadership roles in mainstream life.

simple roast chicken with root vegetables

Mark McEwan *This is a sentimental recipe to me as it is a family favourite, perfect for any occasion; something that everyone can agree upon and never disappoints!*

Chicken:

1 tablespoon each of freshly minced sage, rosemary and parsley, combined

1 tablespoon margarine

1 top-quality chicken, 2½–3 pounds

½ teaspoon sweet paprika

Root vegetables:

2 garlic cloves, crushed

4 medium sunchokes, scrubbed and halved

4 medium variegated beets, peeled and quartered

4 small turnips, scrubbed and quartered

12 baby carrots, scrubbed and trimmed

12 fingerling potatoes, scrubbed

2 tablespoons olive oil

salt and pepper

salt

3 tablespoons olive oil

1 sprig thyme

½ lemon, grilled until lightly charred

2 garlic cloves, smashed

½ cup chicken jus from the bottom of the pan

Preferably 24 hours in advance, combine herbs and margarine and massage into the skin of the chicken on all sides. Sprinkle with paprika. Place on a rack and set aside in the refrigerator. Set one rack in the lower third of the oven and another in the middle and preheat the oven to 425°F.

Root vegetables: Combine the garlic and vegetables in a roasting pan large enough to accommodate them in a single layer. Add the oil, season and toss well and place on the lower rack of the oven.

Salt the chicken generously inside and out. In a skillet just large enough to accommodate the bird, heat the oil over medium high heat. Brown the bird lightly on all sides. Place it breast side up on a roasting rack and carefully stuff the thyme, lemon and garlic into the cavity. Set the rack in a roasting pan, add to it the oil from the skillet, and place in the centre of the oven.

After 15 minutes, turn the vegetables and baste the bird and lower the heat to 350°F. After another 20 minutes, baste again. After a total time of 45 minutes, test the bird for doneness—check if the juices run clear from a pieced thigh or if the internal temperature of the breast has reach 160F. Allow to rest 15 minutes before carving. Serve accompanied with the near-caramelized root vegetables and if you choose, the chicken jus.

NUMBER OF SERVINGS: 2–4

The 1960s were the turning point of this integration of Jews into Toronto society

lissie's marinated turkey roast

Wendy Kay *My children's favourite Auntie Lissie is known for her delicious turkey roast and my kids love it! She was kind enough to share the recipe with me.*

3 pound rolled turkey breast roast

3 tablespoons olive oil

2 garlic cloves, crushed

1 tablespoon paprika

salt and pepper to taste

Glaze:

¾ jar apricot jam

½ cup orange juice

¼ cup honey

Make a paste with the olive oil, garlic, paprika and salt and pepper. Rub all over the turkey breast and marinate overnight.

Preheat oven to 350°F. Mix the apricot jam, orange juice and honey in a bowl. Place marinated turkey in a roasting pan and add a little water to cover the bottom of the pan. Pour half the glaze over the turkey breast. Save the remainder for later. Cover the turkey with foil and cook ½ hour per pound until internal temperature is about 165°F. Remove foil and drizzle the remaining glaze over the turkey for the last half hour of cooking time. Remove from oven, cool a little, and remove netting before slicing. Lay slices onto a serving platter and cover with juice from the pan to keep moist.

NUMBER OF SERVINGS: 6–8

poultry

did you know?
The Jewish Hospice Program serves over 130 clients with compassionate, home-centered programs.

joyce's famous crispy duck

Lissie Sanders *My mother, Joyce Strauss, has many specialties but one of her extra special ones is her crispy duck, which we eat on Rosh Hashanah. I have taken over her duties of duck maker and it's become almost as good as hers. The key to delicious duck is to rub it all over with sugar and cook it and cook it and cook it and cook it. The crispier the better!*

2 (4 pound) ducks (most kosher ducks can only be bought frozen)

2 apples, halved

1 orange, halved

2 teaspoons salt

2 teaspoons pepper

2 handfuls white sugar

non-stick cooking spray

Wash ducks well, drain and dry very well using paper towels inside and out. Use non-stick cooking spray to grease two chicken stands that are used to roast chickens in the oven or on the barbeque. Place each stand into its own drip pan. (I like to use foil pans that can be thrown out after cooking because of all the grease.) Place the half pieces of each fruit inside the cavity of the duck. Carefully place each duck on its own roasting stand and into the drip pan, making sure that the fruit pieces don't drop out of the duck. Rub the salt and pepper mixture onto each duck. Prick each duck well with a fork all over the duck skin. Take two handfuls of sugar in your hands and rub it all over the ducks to cover as well as possible.

Roast the ducks in a very hot oven at 450°F for 20 minutes. Keep pricking the ducks often, allowing the fat to drip out of the ducks. Reduce the oven heat to 375°F and allow the ducks to cook for at least 2.5 hours (maybe even 3 hours) until crispy. You may have to pour out fat as you roast the duck if it comes up too high in the roasting pan.

When the duck is nice and crispy, cut into quarters and place an orange slice on top of each quarter as decoration.

TIPS & ADVICE: Because duck is so fatty, you have to keep an eye on it in the oven so you won't have any fire issues. I once tried to cook my ducks on the BBQ. Flames flew up to my second story window. Oy! Duck is delicious and totally worth the effort to roast it.

NUMBER OF SERVINGS: 8

poultry

when they were finally offered membership to two of the most powerful private clubs in Ontario, the →

passover chicken pie

Etica Levy *This is a favourite family recipe from Romania that I modified to be used for Passover. This is a nice main course to serve as an alternative to brisket or roast chicken.*

5 regular sheets of matzah

5 eggs, divided

1 teaspoon salt (or to taste)

½ teaspoon pepper (or to taste)

1 medium onion, chopped

1 pound ground chicken

1 bunch parsley, cleaned and coarsely chopped

½ teaspoon salt

½ teaspoon pepper

1–2 tablespoons oil for sautéing

Soak matzah pieces in enough water to cover, then squeeze out excess moisture and break up matzah with a fork or with hands. Add 4 eggs, one at a time, mixing well after each addition. Add salt and pepper and set aside until ready to assemble the pie.

Sauté onion in oil until softened and beginning to brown. Add chicken, pressing down with fork/spatula to brown and incorporate the onion well. Cook until thoroughly done.

Let cool and then place in food processor with parsley, salt and pepper. Pulse food processor approximately 8 times until well mixed. Grease an 8 x 8" pyrex pan well and spread bottom with half of matzah mixture. Add the chicken and cover with rest of matzah mixture. Beat the 5th egg and brush top of matzah. Bake for 30 minutes until nicely browned.

TIPS & ADVICE: Two chopped leeks (white part only) can be added to the meat mixture when cooking, as can a small amount of spinach. Ground beef can be used instead of ground chicken following same procedure.

NUMBER OF SERVINGS: 8

did you know?
The Jewish Agency's Youth Futures program mentors 200 at-risk children and teens in Eilat.

poultry

Rideau Club in Ottawa and the Granite Club in Toronto. (our story continues on page 186 . . . read on)

B. GOLDSTEIN

GLATT KOSHER (COR 105) MEATS · POULTRY · DE

RETAIL · WHOLESALE

TAKE/OUT · FREE DELIVERY

B. GOLDSTEIN · MEATS · FREE DEL

Tzivie Hirschman
B. Goldstein Meats,
Wilson at Bathurst,
Toronto, circa 1965

meat

chulent or cholent

Linda Waks *Chulent is a traditional Shabbat dish. In Hungary, it is called Cholent and my mother would make it for the High Holidays. The addition of dill at the end is typically Hungarian. My father-in-law always looked forward to my cholent. This is an 'old school' traditional dish. I do not make it very often, but when I do, it brings back happy memories of my mother's kitchen and of my four young daughters 'helping' me prepare it in my kitchen.*

2 cups dried beans (either kidney or a combination of navy and lima beans)

¼ cup flour

2 teaspoons kosher salt

½ teaspoon paprika

¼ teaspoon fresh ground pepper

1½ pounds flanken (beef short ribs) or stewing beef cut into chunks

2 tablespoons canola oil

2 onions, large dice

2–3 garlic cloves, finely diced

6 cups boiling water

1–2 bay leaves

½ cup barley

3 large potatoes, peeled and cut in chunks

¼ cup Italian parsley, chopped

¼ cup fresh dill, chopped

Wash and rinse the dried beans. Soak beans in cold water overnight in the fridge or cover with boiling water and let sit for one hour at room temperature. Drain the beans and set aside. Place flour, salt, paprika, and pepper into a plastic bag and shake well. Add chunks of beef to the bag, several pieces at a time to coat with flour mixture and set aside. In a large stockpot, heat oil on medium heat. Add the onions, stirring until lightly browned. Add the garlic and cook for one more minute. Add the chunks of meat to the pot and sauté until browned on all sides. Add drained beans to the pot, and stir to combine with meat. Add the boiling water to cover the meat/bean mix by about 2". Add bay leaves. Bring the mixture to boil, skim any foam that forms on top and discard, and then reduce to simmer. Simmer gently for 1½ hours, stirring occasionally. Check to see if additional water is needed to keep contents covered. Add the barley and continue to simmer for another ½ hour.

Add potatoes to the pot and stir. Continue to simmer, stirring occasionally. The stirring may break up the potatoes and meat. The beans will soften and yield a creamy texture. After 2½–3 hours, the beans will have released their starchy interiors and combine with the meat and potatoes to create a thick soupy stew. Discard bay leaf and mix in parsley and dill just before serving. Add more salt and pepper to taste.

TIPS & ADVICE: Cholent is wholesome and hearty, but cooks slowly. This recipe can be made in a slow cooker or prepped on the stove in a Dutch oven and left in a 200°F oven overnight. Just make sure there is adequate water to cover, so that the stew does not dry out. If thinned out with water or broth, this recipe can be served as a hearty soup rather than a stew. I prefer to use Yukon gold potatoes, however any potato will work well.

NUMBER OF SERVINGS: 8–10

 Louis Rasminsky may have been the Jewish governor of the Bank of Canada,

dafina (also known as scheena, the moroccan version of cholent)

Michelle Factor *Both my parents are Moroccan. Scheena is an all-in-one meal that was cooked all night until noon on Shabbat. My mother remembers bringing her family's pot to the non-Jews (Arabs) who used their outside ovens to cook these meals for the Jews. They would bring the pots back to each family on Shabbat in time for lunch. I love all the different flavours and how they blend together. The smell is very distinct! This is a heavy meal but welcomed all winter in my house. It feeds a lot of people, which is fantastic.*

2 (16 ounce) cans chickpeas, rinsed and drained

1 large onion, sliced

2 large onions, sliced—sautéed until caramelized in paprika, salt, and olive oil, divided

3 pounds London broil, cut into chunks

2 marrow bones

3 pounds red or white potatoes

salt, divided

fresh ground pepper

1 teaspoon turmeric

4–6 large eggs

½ cup wheatberries

3 cups beef broth, divided

head of garlic

1 cup uncooked rice

Cover the bottom of a large Dutch oven pan with the chickpeas. Add onions, meat, marrow, and potatoes. Sprinkle with salt, pepper, and turmeric. Place uncooked eggs carefully throughout the pan Add enough water to cover these ingredients. Using a plastic baking bag, add wheatberries, 1 cup beef broth, a head of garlic and sautéed onion. Seal the bag and place on one side of pan. Using another plastic baking bag, add rice, remaining sautéed onion, salt, and 2 cups of beef broth. Seal the bag, and place on another side of the pan. Bring to a boil, cover and reduce to low and cook for one hour. Place in preheated 225°F oven overnight for Shabbat lunch. To serve, place the arisa (wheatberries) and rice in their own separate bowls.

TIPS & ADVICE: Remove air from the baking bags or they will inflate and lift the lid off the pan.

NUMBER OF SERVINGS: 8–10

meat

and his signature was on all the money used at the Rideau (and everywhere else) but until this

harissa

Ruthy Tanenbaum *My mother, who is Tunisian, has been making this for our Shabbat lunch for as long as I remember. When I have company, this dish is a real conversation piece!*

1–2 cups wheat or spelt berries

1 cup boiling water

½ teaspoon baking soda

6 onions, diced

olive oil to sauté onions

1 strip flanken

1 piece cheek meat

1 teaspoon salt, divided

1 teaspoon pepper, divided

1 teaspoon paprika, divided

½ teaspoon hot paprika

3 potatoes or 1 sweet potato

2 whole heads garlic, washed, skin on

1 whole nutmeg, grated

Rinse wheat or spelt berries and soak in boiling water with baking soda to soften the grains. Sauté the onions in olive oil, until they are caramelized. Add the meat, ½ teaspoon each of salt and pepper and paprika(s), and mix well. When the meat is brown, layer the meat and onions on the bottom of the crockpot and then add the wheatberries, potatoes and whole garlic. Sprinkle grated nutmeg on top and add another ½ teaspoon each of salt and paprika. Set crockpot on high for 3 hours and turn to low overnight. Check to make sure it doesn't dry out. If necessary, add more water.

TIPS & ADVICE: I prepare this Thursday and put it in my crock pot in the fridge. I use the Bob's Red Mill brand of wheat or spelt berries. Use less paprika if you don't like it spicy. I add the potatoes, water, and whole garlic on Friday before Shabbat.

NUMBER OF SERVINGS: 6

meat

visit our website
www.JewishToronto.com/BathurstStreetKitchen

time, he wasn't allowed in the doors of those hallowed institutions where all of the business and

arisa

Michelle Factor *My husband is Ashkenazi but requests this every Shabbat, even in the summer. I add about ½ teaspoon of cayenne pepper when my youngest is not with us for lunch.*

¼ cup olive oil

1–2 tablespoons paprika

1 small onion, chopped

1 teaspoon salt

dash white sugar

1½ cups soft wheatberries

3 cups water

1 head fresh garlic, papery husks removed

10 small potatoes

2 large strips beef flanken

In pan, sauté olive oil, paprika and onion. Cook slowly until onion caramelizes. Add more paprika, salt and sugar. Mix in wheatberries and water. Stir. Add the head of garlic and potatoes. Put everything in crockpot/slow cooker and set to low for 1–2 hours, add meat once the 1–2 hours is up, then set to warm overnight.

TIPS & ADVICE: My crock pot is an older model. The timing and settings may differ on newer models. This can be made in the oven overnight. I would suggest bringing it to a boil before placing it in the oven on a low temperature.

NUMBER OF SERVINGS: 6–8

eric's red wine risotto with short ribs

Rona Cappell *Our family was dining at a favourite Italian restaurant in San Diego. My son Eric and I shared this dish and we both went nuts! I replicated the recipe to the best of my ability as the chef wouldn't share. Eric says it's even better than the original.*

1 pound boneless beef short ribs, cut into ½" cubes

¼ cup extra virgin olive oil

½ cup Vidalia onion, chopped

1 medium carrot, chopped

2½ cups arborio rice

3 cups Chianti wine

4 cups beef stock

Salt and pepper to taste

Heat oil in a large saucepan. Season the short ribs with salt and pepper and add them to the pan. Brown the meat over medium high heat on all sides, about five minutes. Remove from the pan and set aside in a bowl, reserving pan juices in the pan. Add onion and carrots to the saucepan and sauté until onions are translucent, 2–3 minutes. Add rice to the pan and just enough wine to cover the rice. Bring to a boil. Repeat the process, alternating the beef broth and the wine until approximately only 1 cup of broth remains. Add the short ribs back into the pan and again cover with enough stock to cover the rice and the meat. Allow the liquid to fully absorb one final time. Remove from heat. Season with salt and pepper to taste.

NUMBER OF SERVINGS: 3–4 as a main, 6 as an appetizer or side

meat

political elite gathered. *Club membership may seem trivial but it was a reflection*

ouma's simple madras curry

Laura Orzy *Indian food is a staple in South Africa. Sunday night was take-out Indian food night in our family. We loved to try the various Indian dishes and learned so much by doing so. My family's business was in the spice world and so my Grandmother (Ouma) always made interesting Indian foods. The rule of thumb was "add spice not fire". Don't spice it up so high that you burn your mouth and taste buds! This recipe reminds me of my Grandmother's cooking.*

2 tablespoons oil

3 pounds lamb or beef, cubed

1 large onion, sliced

1 large apple, preferably Granny Smith, peeled and diced

1 cup celery, diced

2 tomatoes, skinned and diced

1 chicken bouillon cube, crushed

1 carrot, diced

2 teaspoons salt

½ teaspoon pepper

1 tablespoon vinegar

1 tablespoon apricot preserve or chutney

1 tablespoon flour

1 tablespoon curry powder

2 or 3 potatoes, halved and parboiled

Heat oil in a large saucepan and brown meat, half at a time. Remove and set aside. Using the same saucepan, sauté onions lightly. Return meat to the saucepan and add remaining ingredients, with the exception of the flour, curry powder and potatoes. Simmer for 1½ hours. Mix flour and curry powder with a little cold water to form a paste and stir into the stew. Add parboiled potatoes and simmer over low heat for an additional 30 minutes.

TIPS & ADVICE: I add 2–3 tablespoons of curry and 1 teaspoon chili powder to the ingredients to make it stronger.

NUMBER OF SERVINGS: 6

meat

miriam's chilean empanadas

Sharon Bizouati *My friend, Miriam Grunwald, made Aliya to Israel from Toronto several years ago and we have been missing her amazing cooking ever since. This is one of our favourite dishes. As her best friend, I would like to share it with the community.*

Filling:

3 onions

3 garlic cloves

2 tablespoons oil

1 pound lean ground beef

dash each of salt, pepper, Tabasco sauce and paprika

1 teaspoon cumin

2 hard-boiled eggs, sliced

1 can black olives, sliced and drained

Dough:

3 cups all-purpose flour

1 teaspoon baking powder

pinch of salt

¾ cup warm water mixed with 1 egg yolk

½ cup oil, warmed

1 egg beaten for egg wash

Filling: Chop the onions and garlic in a food processor. Transfer onions and garlic to a frying pan with oil and cook until translucent (about 5 minutes). Add the meat and brown. Add salt, pepper, Tabasco, paprika and cumin and to taste. Mix well and refrigerate. This should be prepared the day before if possible. The meat mixture must be cold before putting it on the dough.

Dough: Put the flour in a bowl, add the baking powder and salt and mix. Make a well in the centre and add the warm water and warm oil mixed with the egg yolk. Mix well to make a soft dough.

Turnovers: Cover the dough with a towel to keep moist as you are working with each turnover. Divide the dough into 6 or 7 pieces. Roll each piece into a thin circle. Cut out 3–4 circles using a glass or round cutter. Put 1 tablespoon of meat mixture in the centre of the circle and top with 1 piece of hard boiled egg and a few slices of olives. Fold the dough over and seal into a semi-circle. Use egg wash to seal the edges. Brush the egg wash over the top of the turnover and place them on cookie sheet that has been sprayed with cooking spray. Bake in preheated oven at 400°F for 30 minutes. Serve hot.

TIPS & ADVICE: These turnovers freeze very well. Before freezing, bake for ten minutes, then cool and wrap in foil or put in plastic container for up to two months. After defrosting, bake on a cookie sheet sprayed with cooking spray at 350°F for 15–20 minutes. Put a pan with water in the lower shelf of oven when heating so empanadas don't dry out.

NUMBER OF SERVINGS: approximately 2 dozen

meat

cabbage rolls

Marilyn Gotfrid *For decades, I always made my grandmother's cabbage rolls. One day, I decided to check the internet to see what variations I could come up with. I combined two recipes and replaced some of the sugar with agave. I found that combining the raisins and apples allowed me to make a traditional Eastern European specialty with a slightly healthier twist. The cider vinegar gives the recipe a bit of zip. I've converted the skeptics in my family and I think my Grandma would have loved the changes too!*

2 whole cabbages (green or savoy)

Sauce:

2 (28 ounce) cans whole tomatoes, broken into large pieces plus juice

1 onion, finely chopped

1 Granny Smith apple, peeled, cored and grated

1 cup Thompson raisins

¼ cup each agave syrup and brown sugar, firmly packed

¼ cup lemon juice, freshly squeezed

1 tablespoon kosher salt

1 teaspoon apple cider vinegar

¼ teaspoon freshly ground pepper

Filling:

2 pounds ground chuck

6 tablespoons long grain rice

6 tablespoons water

½ cup onion, grated

2 teaspoons salt

Preheat oven to 350°F. Remove the core of the cabbage and place the cabbage in a colander in a deep pot with boiling water. Steam until the leaves are tender enough to peel off one at a time. Set the leaves aside. To make the sauce, place the tomatoes and their liquid in a saucepan, bring to a boil and simmer uncovered for 15 minutes. Then, add the onion, apple, raisins, agave syrup, brown sugar, lemon juice, salt, vinegar and pepper. Bring the sauce back to a boil and simmer covered for approximately 15 minutes.

Combine the rice, water, onion and salt into the ground meat. Place a generous amount of meat at the core end of the leaf. Fold the 2 sides over and roll. Place the cabbage roll, seam side down in 2 (9 x 13") casserole dishes, leaving a little room between each one for the sauce. Chop any extra cabbage and sprinkle on top. Pour the sauce over top to coat, making sure that some sauce falls between the rolls. Cover tightly with heavy tin foil and bake 1½–2 hours.

TIPS & ADVICE: This recipe is easy to prepare the day ahead or for freezing. Just under-cook it by ½ hour or so to allow for the reheating. Make sure to keep the dish tightly covered while cooking to prevent the top of the cabbage rolls from drying out or burning.

YIELD: Approximately 2 dozen cabbage rolls

meat

Trudeau was elected, he appointed the first ever Jewish Cabinet Minister (and the 2nd, 3rd and →

cabbage roll casserole

Wendy Klein *This is a family favourite. It is a custom in our family to serve this on Sukkot. It is a very hearty meal but much easier than making cabbage rolls!*

1 onion, diced

2 tablespoons oil

3 cups tomato sauce

4 ounces wine sauerkraut (Strub's) drained of most liquid

½ cup brown sugar

2 (16 ounce) bags shredded cabbage (you won't use it all)

2 pounds ground meat (I use veal)

4 tablespoons ketchup

3 handfuls rice

1 onion, diced

1 egg

1 teaspoon salt

1 teaspoon garlic powder

pepper to taste

Preheat oven to 350°F. Sauté the onion in oil and add in the tomato sauce, wine sauerkraut and brown sugar to warm. Place ¾ bag of shredded cabbage at the bottom of 9 x 12" pan. Mix ground meat, ketchup, rice, onion, egg, salt, garlic powder and pepper. Place on the cabbage. Place another ¾ of a package of cabbage on top of the meat layer. Pour the tomato sauce mixture over top. Cover and bake for 2½ hours.

NUMBER OF SERVINGS: 10–12

meat

4th) and in 1970 he made Bora Laskin the first Jew on the Supreme Court and later named →

stuffed eggplant

Shinshinim from 2014/15 *These 18-year-old Israeli emissaries (shinshinim in Hebrew) have been coming to Toronto for the past several years to educate our Jewish community, especially our children and teenagers, about Israel and Israeli culture through an initiative of Makom and the UJA Federation of GTA. They have become treasured members of our community during their year of service, living with our families, and befriending and teaching our kids at school, camp and synagogue. This year, they came up with the idea of making a cookbook of their favourite foods from Israel, and sharing it with our GTA community, as a way of letting us get to know them better. In doing so, they realized that there were not a lot of distinctly Israeli dishes and that Israeli cuisine is a combination of so many different cultures, much like the Toronto Jewish community cuisine represented in this cookbook. This is one of their recipes.*

2 medium eggplants

2 onions, diced

3 garlic cloves, chopped

⅔ pound minced beef

1 large can crushed tomatoes

1 teaspoon each paprika, salt, pepper

½ cup water

Cut each eggplant lengthwise, so you have 4 pieces. Scoop out the contents of the eggplant and cut it into cubes. Place the onion, garlic, eggplant cubes and the minced beef in a large pan on medium-high heat and fry for about 5 minutes. Add the crushed tomatoes, paprika, salt, pepper and ½ cup water. Cover the pan and cook at low heat for about 15 minutes. Preheat the oven to 350°F. Divide the meat mixture among the four halves of eggplant. Put the eggplants in the oven and bake them until the beef mixture is browned and the eggplants are soft, 40–50 minutes.

NUMBER OF SERVINGS: 4

meat

did you know?
More than 8,000 families have turned to JACS Toronto (Jewish Addiction Community Services) for help.

him Chief Justice. As the community was integrating, the population was changing

sweet pepper halishkes

We received this recipe from 2 people and have included both of their stories below:

Joyce Strauss *My late mother, Ida Goldfarb was born in Kiev but cooked with a Romanian flair. She was famous for her sweet and sour peppers and came to Kitchener to make them every Rosh Hashanah.*

Sandra Hausman *This recipe is from two Montreal grandmothers: my grandmother's cabbage rolls and my daughter-in-law's grandmother's version with red peppers. A taste test showed the peppers to be the hands-down favourite. This recipe is easy to make and easily expandable to feed a crowd. It is also low in fat and uses healthy ingredients.*

1 (28 ounce) can tomatoes, preferably San Marzano type

1 Spanish onion, diced

½ cup white sugar

1 lemon, juiced

1 scant teaspoon salt or to taste

freshly ground black pepper

4 large sweet red, orange and yellow peppers

1½ pounds lean ground beef

¼ cup uncooked white rice

1 small onion, grated

salt and pepper

Combine tomatoes, onion, sugar, lemon juice, salt and pepper and simmer for at least half an hour. Cut the peppers lengthwise and remove the seeds and ribs. Place the peppers in a shallow baking dish or pyrex. Combine the beef, rice, grated onion, salt and pepper and fill each pepper half way. Cover the peppers with the tomato mixture and seal with foil. Preheat the oven to 350°F. Bake for 1 to 1½ hours, until peppers are very soft and meat and rice mixture is fully cooked.

TIPS & ADVICE: These should be made at least a day ahead for full flavour to develop. They freeze to perfection.

NUMBER OF SERVINGS: 8

as well. Between 1951 and 1961, the Jewish population in the Kensington area →

meat

beef short ribs—bbq style

Brenlee Gurvey Gales *This recipe has been in my family for years. It was passed along from my late Auntie Dora in Winnipeg to all of her sisters. It is rich and delicious.*

2½–3 pounds beef short ribs

1 onion, chopped

½ cup ketchup

½ cup water

¼ cup cider vinegar

1 tablespoon sugar

1 tablespoon Worcestershire sauce*

2 teaspoons salt

1 garlic clove

1 teaspoon Hungarian paprika

1 teaspoon Keen's dry mustard

¼ teaspoon pepper

Preheat oven to 350°F. Brown beef ribs in nonstick skillet for 5 minutes and drain away the fat. Arrange ribs in a rectangular baking dish. Mix together all other ingredients and pour over ribs. Bake for 2 hours, covered tightly with foil. Remove foil and bake for another ½ hour.

*EDITOR'S NOTE: It is some people's custom to not mix meat and fish in the same recipe. As Worcestershire sauce has anchovies, it can be replaced with tamari sauce or liquid smoke.

NUMBER OF SERVINGS: 4

braised minute steaks

Terri Levy *My husband's cousin in Los Angeles gave me this recipe 25 years ago. It's a great "do ahead" recipe for the holidays, and even for Pesach. It is a real crowd pleaser! This recipe is easy, quick, and freezes well. It makes great leftovers and looks elegant when served. The ingredients are easy to find and are staples in most households. The gravy is outstanding.*

6–8 large onions, sliced

4 garlic cloves, sliced

2 cups duck sauce

½ envelope Goodman's onion soup mix

½ cup dry red wine

10 minute steaks

Place the onions and garlic in a deep 9 x 13" roasting pan. Mix together the duck sauce, onion soup mix, and wine. Pour half of the mixture over the onions and garlic. Place the minute steaks on top. Pour remaining sauce over the steaks. Cover tightly with foil. Bake in a preheated 350°F oven for 1½ hours. The onions, garlic, wine and duck sauce will make a wonderful gravy. Enjoy!

NUMBER OF SERVINGS: 4–6

meat

daddy's lamb chops

Seth Mersky *We started making these lamb chops for Chanukah a long time ago when our kids were little. They absolutely loved them. The problem is that they are very expensive so we saved them for holiday and birthday dinners only. Funnily enough, I recently read the original Marcella Hazen recipe that this was based on and realized my method has strayed quite a bit. The altered recipe below is the way I make them now and the family loves them— sorry Marcella!*

3 racks of lamb

1 cup flour

6 eggs, beaten

1 cup unseasoned breadcrumbs

1 cup vegan non-dairy grated Parmesan cheese (optional)

salt and pepper to taste

olive oil for frying

Trim the lamb chops of virtually all fat, including between the bones, so that the result has long naked bones with a cylinder of meat at one end. Slice between the rib bones into individual chops (after confirming that your butcher took the chine bone off; otherwise, you'll never be able to slice between the rib bones). Lightly pound each lamb chop such that they are each about 1 cm thick. Sprinkle salt and pepper over the prepared chops.

You'll need a reasonably sized work area. Lay out three squares of waxed paper, like an assembly line. On the first one, place the cup of flour. On the second one, the eggs—lightly beaten—in a shallow bowl. On the third, the breadcrumbs and (vegan) cheese combined in one pile. Have a drying rack of some sort nearby. Take each chop, dredge first in flour. Shake off excess. Dip in egg to coat both sides. Coat both sides with breadcrumb mixture and place on drying rack. Repeat with each chop until you're sick of doing it. These can be made an hour or two in advance and left to dry on the counter or even longer in the refrigerator.

Preheat oven to 200°F. In a large skillet, heat olive oil over medium high heat until hot but not smoking. Add a few lamb chops at time, but don't crowd the pan. Fry about two minutes per side or until just golden. Place on heat-proof platter in oven to keep warm. Repeat until all the chops are done.

TIPS & ADVICE: One rack of lamb will feed two people. I am assuming six people for the recipe because these are usually made for celebrations. I should add that unless you have a heroic butcher willing to do the work for you, this takes a bit of time.

NUMBER OF SERVINGS: 6

meat

bigger spaces. In 1956, the Hungarian uprising brought a new influx of Jewish →

peanut butter shish-kebab

Ahuva Krieger *I received the original recipe fifty years ago when we were living in Syracuse, New York from a friend who had been living in Indonesia. My major alteration to the recipe was to switch the original ingredient of Brazil nuts to chunky peanut butter. Raising our children in Ottawa, we entertained a great deal. This was and still is one of my 'star' recipes for entertaining as well as a family favourite; everyone goes crazy for it. The mix of flavours is interesting, a bit exotic and absolutely delicious. Although somewhat time consuming to prepare, it freezes well. And it seems like a lot of onion, but don't worry, this recipe is correct!*

8 red onions (minced or pulsed lightly in food processor)

6 heaping tablespoons crunchy peanut butter

4 tablespoons soy sauce

3-5 tablespoons lemon juice

2 tablespoons ground coriander seeds

2 heaping tablespoons soft brown sugar

2 garlic cloves (minced or pulsed with onions in food processor)

1 tablespoon salt

1 teaspoon ground black pepper

1 small hot red pepper seeded and finely minced (optional— or dried pepper flakes to taste)

2 pounds lamb cut into 1½" cubes

vegetables such as onions, red or green peppers, cut into pieces (optional, for skewering between lamb)

Mix all ingredients together in a bowl except lamb and optional skewering vegetables. Taste mixture and adjust seasonings to your taste. Add lamb and mix well to cover. Cover bowl and allow to marinate in the fridge for a minimum of one day and up to three days.

When ready to make, separate the lamb from the marinade, scraping it off individual pieces as you skewer the pieces onto metal or wooden skewers. The lamb can either be placed so that it is touching or it may be separated with slices of pepper and/or onion in between. (Don't squish pieces together but don't leave spaces between.) Put marinade in pot on stove and cook on high, stirring constantly until mixture comes to a boil. Lower to simmer and stir occasionally. Taste the marinade. Add additional soy sauce, lemon and/or sugar as needed and to your taste. Keep an eye on the marinade as it can easily burn. Brush the lamb (and onions/peppers if using) with a little vegetable oil and place on bbq or broil, regular to high flame, turning as meat browns until done as desired. Drizzle the hot sauce over the lamb. Serve with rice, preferably basmati.

TIPS & ADVICE: After marinating the lamb in the fridge for a day, you can freeze in uncooked portions for up to a couple of weeks and defrost in the fridge two days before you plan to use it. Instead of lamb, feel free to use dark turkey meat. It is also delicious.

NUMBER OF SERVINGS: 4-6

meat

peppers and steak medley

Karla Schaus *This recipe was passed down to me from my aunt. A passionate cook, she has introduced me to many new and unique ways of preparing meals. This dish is healthy and flavourful. It is great for a weeknight dinner and leftovers can be reheated for lunch. It is included in my own personal cookbook!*

1 pound steak of your choice

2 tablespoons vegetable oil, divided

salt and pepper to taste

2 green bell peppers, diced

½ medium onion, diced finely

1 garlic clove, finely chopped or pressed

1 cup beef broth

¼ cup water

1½ tablespoons cornstarch

1 tablespoon soy sauce

1 can tomatoes, with juice

2 cups cooked rice

Cut the steak in half and then crosswise into small strips. In a large skillet or wok, heat 1 tablespoon of the oil over medium heat. Add the beef strips to the pan, stirring for 5-6 minutes until browned and almost cooked through. Remove beef from the skillet with a slotted spoon, season with salt and pepper; set aside. In the same skillet, heat the remaining tablespoon of oil over medium heat. Add in the bell peppers, onion and garlic, stirring for 4-5 minutes.

In a large bowl, combine broth, water, cornstarch and soy sauce. Add soy sauce mixture and the tomatoes to the pan. Cook, stirring constantly until sauce boils and thickens, about 15 minutes. Return beef to the skillet and cook for about 35 minutes until the beef is fully cooked. Serve hot over cooked rice.

TIPS & ADVICE: Let the dish cook for 45-60 minutes to enhance the flavours.

NUMBER OF SERVINGS: 4

meat

 Jews fleeing the Spanish Inquisition at the end of the 15th century had gone to →

smokey roast with chimichurri sauce

Tamara Fine *Everyone enjoys this recipe and I never have leftovers!*

Roast:

4 pound roast beef

4 teaspoons peppercorns

4 teaspoons smoked sweet paprika

4 teaspoons cumin seeds

2 sticks cinnamon, crushed

4 teaspoons mustard seeds

3 teaspoons ancho chili powder

6 cardamon seeds

1 tablespoon salt

Sauce:

1 cup olive oil

4 cups parsley

1 cup fresh mint or basil

4 tablespoons red wine vinegar

4 garlic cloves, roasted

2 tablespoons sweet onion, chopped

1 lemon, juiced

salt and pepper to taste

Preheat oven to 425°F. Mix all spices together and place in a small frying pan. Toast the spices for about 5 minutes on low heat. Cool. Grind spices in a blender and gently rub on roast. Sear roast on the BBQ (on high, searing each side for a total of 8 minutes) or in the oven at 425°F. Place in the oven for 1 hour and 20 minutes for medium rare or until thermometer reads 125°F. Combine all sauce ingredients in a blender, using the pulse option until it reaches the desired consistency. Use sauce on the side to add wonderful flavour to the beef.

NUMBER OF SERVINGS: 8

meat

did you know?
In Eilat/Eilot, educational programs have helped raise the matriculation rate of high school students from 25% in 2001 to 72% today.

brisket from montreal

Eleanor Levine *I received this recipe from an old friend who I sat beside in Grade 8 in Montreal in 1953. I remember that she was constantly sketching, and today she is an artist. She remembers that I giggled a lot, and I am a therapist today. We both moved to Toronto and she gave me this recipe in 1986. Over the years, I made some changes, such as adding more garlic and onion. The recipe is very easy to make; it feeds a lot of people and is a favourite at Seders and Shabbat dinners. During the recent ice storm in December 2013, I had bought 4 briskets and my friend Beth, who sought shelter with my husband Paul and me, was amused to see me seasoning and marinating the briskets at 11 p.m. I can also say that Beth, who never eats red meat, enjoyed this brisket at a Shabbat dinner a few weeks later.*

5 pound brisket

3 onions, sliced

1 cup celery leaves, chopped

1 cup chili sauce

½ cup vinegar

4 garlic cloves, pressed

3 tablespoons brown sugar

2 teaspoons basil

2 teaspoons garlic powder

2 teaspoons oregano

2 teaspoons salt

2 teaspoons pepper

4 carrots, sliced lengthwise

Mix all the ingredients, except carrots, and pour over the brisket. Marinate overnight in refrigerator, covered. Preheat the oven to 350°F. Roast one hour per pound, covered, fat side up, for approximately 5 hours. Add the carrots around the brisket for the last hour and remove the cover. Allow to cool before slicing. After cooling and before slicing, use a spatula to remove fat from the top of the gravy. Slice against the grain.

TIPS & ADVICE: Brisket freezes well. After slicing, cool in refrigerator until cold. You want the meat to be cold right through so that it freezes evenly and thoroughly. You can divide the sliced brisket into smaller containers for different size groups.

NUMBER OF SERVINGS: 10–12

meat

many of these Jews fled to Canada. *over the course of the 20th century, approximately*

delicious (double) brisket

Lorraine Schacht *This brisket is a Shabbat and Rosh Hashanah favourite in our family, and is especially popular with our grandsons. It is great as a sandwich the next day on fresh challah.*

5 pound brisket

1 teaspoon garlic powder

1 teaspoon pepper

½ teaspoon paprika

kosher salt to taste

1 package onion soup mix

1 bottle plain barbecue sauce

1 can ginger ale

½ cup orange juice

Preheat the oven to 350°F. Season brisket well with garlic, pepper, paprika and kosher salt. Place in a roasting pan. Mix together the rest of the ingredients and pour over brisket. Cover with tin foil and cook for 3 hours.

Uncover the roast, and continue cooking for 30 minutes, continually basting. Remove from oven, slice, and place back in juice. It may need more cooking time. Delicious served with roasted potatoes, which can be pre-cooked and placed around the roast for the last ½ hour.

NUMBER OF SERVINGS: 10–12

donna's glazed corned beef

Wendy Klein *My friend Donna Glassman gave me this recipe. It is a crowd pleaser. It's easy to prepare and makes for great leftovers.*

3 pound pickled brisket

1 orange, sliced

1 bay leaf

1 onion, quartered

2 stalks celery, cut in large chunks

water

1 cup apricot jam

1 cup Dijon mustard

1 cup brown sugar

Put the brisket, orange, bay leaf, onion, and celery in a pot, cover with water and boil for 3 hours. Take brisket out of the water, discarding water, and cool. Preheat the oven to 350°F. Mix together jam, mustard and brown sugar to form a glaze. Bake corned beef for 30 minutes basting with glaze. After it cools, slice and reheat in sauce.

NUMBER OF SERVINGS: 8

meat

25,000 Sephardic Jews from Morocco, Tunisia, Algeria, Egypt, and Lebanon fled oppressive →

linda's brisket

Genevieve Korman *My mother, Linda, makes this brisket for many special occasion dinners. It is a family favourite at Passover and Rosh Hashanah and everyone is excited to take home any leftovers! This recipe is easy to make.*

5 pound single brisket

salt

1 teaspoon onion powder

1 teaspoon garlic powder

1 teaspoon paprika

1 package onion soup mix (approximately ¼ cup)

1 (6 ounce) can tomato paste

1 cup Heinz chili sauce

1 cup Hunt's crushed tomatoes

1 cup diced tomatoes

½ cup brown sugar

Preheat the oven to 350°F. Place brisket in large disposable roasting pan. Season generously with salt, onion powder, garlic powder and paprika on both sides. Place the brisket fat side up. Sprinkle onion soup mix all over the top of the brisket. Pour tomato paste, chili sauce, crushed and diced tomatoes over the meat, making sure that the spices and sauce mix together and cover the entire brisket. Cover tightly with 2 layers of aluminum foil and cook for 5½ hours. Sprinkle brown sugar over top and cover again. Cook for another ½ hour. Slice into 1" pieces using an electric knife.

TIPS & ADVICE: You can add in sliced onions. You cannot overcook this and it freezes well too!

NUMBER OF SERVINGS: 4–6

meat

and dangerous regimes and came to Montreal and Toronto. *While the majority*

marlowe's sweet and saucy brisket

Marlowe Ain *When my mother-in-law asked me to make the brisket for Rosh Hashanah, I was nervous! She told me to look up the recipe in the Kinnereth Cookbook, so I did. I also had memories of my Bubbie Ida always worrying about whether the brisket would be too dry. I decided to take the Kinnereth recipe, triple the sauce and add some of my Bubbie's touches of extra garlic powder, dried cranberries and a lot of of basting. It's a simple recipe, but I'm now the official Brisket Queen of every family feast. I feel like my Bubbie Ida would be proud of how moist my brisket turns out every single time.*

It looks and tastes impressive but is super easy to make. It's my own tradition to save a few slices to eat cold the morning after the holiday gathering. The tender meat spends an extra night in the delicious sauce and the scrumptious leftovers serve as a reminder of special family times the night before. Yum!

7 pound double brisket

6 onions, sliced and divided

ground pepper to taste

garlic powder to taste

1½ cups ketchup

1½ cups brown sugar

6 teaspoons dry mustard

1 small bag baby carrots

1 cup dried cranberries and dried apricots, mixed

Place 3 sliced onions on the bottom of large roasting pan. Season the onions with pepper and garlic, to your taste. Place the brisket on top of onions with the fat side up. Top the brisket with the 3 remaining, sliced onions. Sprinkle more pepper and garlic powder on top of the brisket. In a small bowl, mix together the ketchup, brown sugar and dry mustard. Pour the mixture over the entire top of the brisket and spread it around evenly with the back of a spoon. Cover the roasting pan and put in the refrigerator overnight for best results.

The next day, preheat oven to 350°F degrees. Add the carrots, dried cranberries and apricots around the sides of the brisket. Cranberries will burn if you have them on top of the brisket. Bake the brisket, with roasting pan lid on, for 4 hours and baste well every 30 minutes. After 3½ hours, start to check for your desired doneness. When done, remove from oven, cool, and then carve into thick slices. When serving, make sure everyone gets some extra sauce on each slice.

TIPS & ADVICE: Leftovers freeze very well. Freeze in the extra sauce.

NUMBER OF SERVINGS: 10

went to Montreal, a significant number came to Toronto and strengthened and changed the

sweet veal brisket

Esta Palter *All children love this because it is sweet. I like to have one of these briskets cooked and sliced in my freezer at all times. Just thaw, reheat and serve. What could be easier?*

3-4 pound veal brisket

1 teaspoon each Dijon mustard, onion powder, garlic powder, paprika, basil, tarragon, thyme

3 tablespoons each water and canola oil

2 or 3 onions, chopped

1-2 jars apricot jam

¼ cup white wine vinegar

1½ tablespoons soy sauce

½ teaspoon ginger

1 teaspoon Dijon mustard

Season brisket on both sides with mustard, onion powder, garlic powder, paprika, basil, tarragon and thyme. Line roasting pan with foil or parchment paper. Add water and canola oil to roasting pan. Place brisket on top. Cover tightly. Bake 350°F for 1½ hours. While brisket is cooking, sauté onions until golden. When golden, add jam, vinegar, soy sauce, ginger and Dijon. Stir until well blended. After 1½ hours, uncover brisket. Pour off about ½ of the liquid. Pour apricot and onion sauce over top of brisket. Bake uncovered 325°F for 1 hour.

TIPS & ADVICE: Cool brisket, then refrigerate until cold. After it is chilled, slice it and put back in roasting pan with sauce. It freezes very well at this stage. Thaw and reheat, covered for about 1 hour.

NUMBER OF SERVINGS: 6-8

rack of lamb

Susan Fremar *This is a wonderful dish!*

2 racks of lamb (about 4–5 ribs per person depending on size of rack)

1 cup olive oil

2 lemons, both juice and zest

3 garlic cloves, minced

1 tablespoon lemon pepper

1 tablespoon dried rosemary

½ teaspoon kosher salt

½ teaspoon black pepper

Put racks of lamb in a ziplock bag. Add remaining ingredients and marinate 2-3 hours in the refrigerator. Bring meat to room temperature before roasting or grilling. They can also be cooked on the BBQ. I usually roast the lamb at 425°F for 40 minutes. After cooking, cover in foil for 10 minutes before slicing.

NUMBER OF SERVINGS: 4

meat

existing Toronto Sephardic Jewish community. In 1958, the Sephardic Jews

chunky meat sauce

Linda Waks *This is my daughter Whitney's favourite dish. She is the one who dubbed it 'Chunky Meat Sauce' because she loved that it wasn't uniformly grainy like some other sauces made with ground meat. This recipe is easy and quick to prepare with basic pantry staples that are usually on hand. Can be made ahead and reheated. Can also be frozen.*

2 tablespoons olive oil

1 medium sized onion, diced

2 garlic cloves, crushed or finely diced

1 pound lean ground beef

1 tablespoon tomato paste

1 (28 ounce) can San Marzano tomatoes

1 teaspoon dried italian seasoning

1 dried bay leaf

1 teaspoon kosher salt

few grinds fresh ground pepper

¼ teaspoon dried chili flakes

2 or 3 leaves fresh basil

1 or 2 sprigs fresh oregano

Remove meat from the fridge one half hour before starting to cook. Heat olive oil in a medium to large size sauce or sauté pan on medium heat. Sauté onions, stirring with a wooden spoon 3–4 minutes until softened and they begin to colour. Add garlic and cook for 1–2 more minutes, stirring occasionally, watching that the garlic doesn't burn. Increase heat to medium high.

Add ground beef to the pan by placing small mounds, roughly the size of tablespoons, and distribute evenly in the pan. The pan will sizzle with the increased heat but do NOT stir. Allow the meat to cook for a few minutes until it starts to brown on the bottom. You may push the onions and garlic around to prevent them from burning. After the meat has browned on one side, gently stir to brown the other sides of the mounds.

When the meat is almost cooked through (slight pink remains), reduce the heat to medium and add the tomato paste, stirring gently to combine with the meat without breaking up all the mounds. Cook for two minutes, then add the can of tomatoes. Gently break up the tomatoes with the wooden spoon. Bring the sauce to a boil and then reduce heat to a simmer. Add seasonings and simmer for 15–20 minutes, stirring occasionally. Taste to correct seasoning. Just before serving, remove bay leaf and add freshly chopped herbs (chiffonade). Serve over pasta or rice.

TIPS & ADVICE: Allowing the beef to caramelize and brown before stirring increases the flavour of the meat and yields a 'chunky' texture to the sauce. Use good quality ingredients for best results.

NUMBER OF SERVINGS: 4

meat

meatloaf

Peter Graben *The reason meatloaf has stayed with us through so many generations? It's a master of evolution. It's lived through ancient times, the Industrial Revolution, world wars, heart breaking depressions, nasty processed foods, and fancy gourmet versions, all because it is so adaptable.*

1 cup cornflake crumbs

1 jar tomato sauce

1½ pounds ground beef

½ pound each ground chicken and veal

2 medium onions, grated

2 large eggs

½ cup ketchup

2 garlic cloves, minced

salt and pepper to taste

Mix cornflake crumbs with tomato sauce in a bowl to moisten the crumbs. Add the rest of the ingredients to the bowl and combine until blended. Do not over mix. Spray inside of loaf pan with nonstick spray. Pack mixture in loaf pan and bake at 350°F for 55–60 minutes. Let meatloaf rest 10 minutes before slicing and serving.

TIPS & ADVICE: For different flavour, add 1 stalk celery, finely chopped, 4 sliced mushrooms, sun dried tomatoes, cilantro, jalapeno peppers, chopped parsley and 1 cup corn kernels.

NUMBER OF SERVINGS 6–8

sweet and sour meatballs

Fran Sonshine *This is a family favourite. I prepare the meat first so that the flavours of the various spices can get a chance to absorb into the meat. It is easy, tastes great the next day, freezes really well, and you can make many batches.*

Per pound of lean ground meat, add the following:

½ cup ketchup

½ cup water

1 onion, diced

1 or 2 bay leaves

1 tablespoon sugar

2 tablespoons lemon juice

paprika, salt, pinch of ginger

Boil ingredients, except meat, together. Season meat to taste. Make 1–2" balls and drop into sauce. Simmer 1 hour.

TIPS & ADVICE: I use seasoned salt, pepper, garlic salt, dehydrated onions, eggs, breadcrumbs, some water to soften breadcrumbs, a touch of mustard . . . but season the way you like it. I often make several pounds as they freeze well. I use a combination of beef and chicken, and sweetener to equal the amount of sugar.

NUMBER OF SERVINGS: 4–6 meatballs per pound of meat

meat

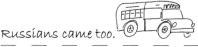 Russians came too. ✡ By 1961, the Toronto population had grown to 88,648. →

jakoya — beef stew

Brenda Cooper *This is a comfort stew that originated from my late paternal grandmother. My father shared the recipe as best as he could with my mother. She made it over and over until my father finally said it tasted like his grandmother's! My mum, Bertha Rosen, the best cook in the whole world, then adapted the recipe so that it could be made with either stewing beef or small meatballs. It became a real favourite in our household growing up and it is one that I still make today.*

2 tablespoons oil

1 large onion, sliced

1 pound stewing beef, cut up in small pieces

granulated garlic to taste

seasoned salt

6–8 potatoes, cubed

4 carrots, thickly sliced

1 can corn niblets and juice

water

Heat oil in large Dutch oven pot. Add the onion and cook over medium heat. Season the meat with garlic and seasoned salt and add to the onions. Continue to cook over medium heat, mixing well. Add a little bit of water to ensure that it doesn't stick. Add the potatoes and carrots and cook until everything is soft, mixing occasionally and adding water if it gets dry. Add corn niblets with the juice. Mix well and cook until everything is heated through.

TIPS & ADVICE: This recipe is equally delicious made with meatballs instead of stewing beef. If making with meatballs, prepare the ground beef meatballs as you would normally and add them after the potatoes and carrots. This is wonderful comfort food on a winter's night.

YIELD: one big pot

meat

visit our website
www.JewishToronto.com/BathurstStreetKitchen

Since the early 1970s, the electoral district of York Centre has the largest

italian veal meatballs with cannellini beans

Loren Lieberman *I am of Italian heritage and learned to make my meatballs in Grandma's kitchen. She was usually preparing for an army, so we would roll the meatballs and line them up on a cookie sheet to be browned in shifts. The tradition of scraping up the pan juices with a little water to enhance the flavour of the dish is one of her secrets. This recipe is healthy, warming and everyone loves it. I serve it with a crusty loaf of bread and a simple salad. I have a little video of it simmering to help lure kids home to dinner!*

1 teaspoon garlic, chopped

1 teaspoon each dried oregano, basil and salt

½ teaspoon black pepper

½ teaspoon red pepper flakes

1½ pounds lean ground veal

1 cup unseasoned breadcrumbs

1 egg, beaten

3 tablespoons olive oil

1 small onion, chopped

½ jalapeno pepper, chopped

⅔ cup water

1 (16 ounce) can cannellini beans, rinsed

28 ounce can crushed tomatoes

Divide garlic, oregano, basil, salt, and pepper. You will add half of spices to the meatballs and half to the tomato sauce. All the red pepper flakes get mixed into the meat.

Combine the ground veal, breadcrumbs, egg, and half of the spices in a medium bowl. Mix with hands and form meatballs about the size of a walnut. Heat oil in a large skillet. Brown the meatballs all around, on a medium flame.

While the meatballs are browning, add the onion and ½ jalapeno pepper to the pan and continue cooking until the onion is translucent. Add the remaining chopped garlic, cooking for one minute to release fragrance. Add ⅔ cup of water to skillet, raise heat and scrape up the pan juices (it will form a small amount of flavourful dark brown liquid). Reduce the heat. Add the crushed tomatoes and cannellini beans. Add the remainder of the spices and simmer, covered, on a low flame, stirring occasionally for 60 minutes.

TIPS & ADVICE: Jalapeno pepper can be omitted for those who like a milder dish. It tastes even better the second day!

NUMBER OF SERVINGS: 4

meat

easiest meat sauce

Naomi Oelbaum *This is a recipe that everyone in my house loves (a rare thing indeed)! The recipe can be made quickly and easily with very little mess. I usually double this recipe and it all gets eaten over a few days.*

1 tablespoon olive oil

1½ pounds lean ground beef

1 cup bottled, medium-hot salsa

¼ cup beef broth

2 tablespoons garlic, minced

2 tablespoons brown sugar, packed

1 tablespoon soy sauce

Heat oil in large pot over medium to high heat. Sauté beef until brown. Add salsa, broth, garlic, sugar and soy sauce, and bring to a boil. Cover and lower heat to medium-low, stir often; about 1 hour and ten minutes. Uncover the pot and let the sauce thicken, five to ten minutes. Season with salt and pepper, as desired.

TIPS & ADVICE: This recipe can be used as a meat sauce with medium shell pasta or rotini. It can be served over rice or as a sloppy Joe or wrapped in a soft tortilla or taco shell. Serve with extra salsa, cilantro, lime juice, avocado, tomatoes and lettuce.

NUMBER OF SERVINGS: 5

veal hamburgers

Kathy Alpert *This is an old recipe passed on from my mother-in-law from Winnipeg. She always liked using veal as she said it made the hamburger taste a little lighter. These are so juicy and delicious, you just don't want to overcook them when barbequing.*

2¼ pounds ground veal

5 tablespoons water

4 tablespoons matzah meal

2 eggs

2 garlic cloves, crushed (or more, to taste)

2 tablespoons bbq sauce (optional)

1 teaspoon salt

¼ teaspoon white pepper

Mix together all the ingredients and make patties. Wrap them individually and freeze.

Place frozen patties on barbeque and grill for 5 minutes on each side.

TIPS & ADVICE: Add about 3–4 cloves of garlic, since 2 small cloves just doesn't do it.

NUMBER OF SERVINGS: 6–8

meat

 ✡ In 1971, Toronto's Jewish population numbered 97,000. Israelis also continued

potato pastela

Sharon Bizouati *This potato pastela can be served hot or cold. It is a great dish for Passover lunches.*

1½ pounds lean, minced hamburger meat

1 onion, minced

1 small bunch fresh parsley

½ teaspoon saffron

2 cups water

½ teaspoon salt

½ teaspoon pepper

¼ teaspoon cinnamon

2 tablespoons vinegar

3 pounds potatoes (preferably yellow flesh)

6 uncooked eggs + 1 egg yolk

1 teaspoon salt

2 hardboiled eggs, sliced

4 tablespoons cooking oil

Preheat oven to 350°F. This pastela requires two preparations, the meat part and the potato part. First, mince together the meat, onion and parsley and simmer in a pan with 2 cups of water and saffron until the liquid has evaporated. Mince the meat again and add spices and vinegar. Place the meat back over a gentle heat and stir with a wooden spoon until the meat is dry.

Now prepare the potato puree. Peel, wash and cut up the potatoes and boil in salted water. When cooked, drain them and then continue to dry them out over a gentle heat, stirring with a spoon to prevent them from sticking. Mash the potatoes and beat in 4 of the eggs, one at a time, to obtain a smooth paste.

Oil an oven-proof 9 x 10" pyrex dish and spread a layer of potato puree on the bottom. Mix the meat mixture with 2 additional uncooked eggs. Cover the bottom layer of potatoes with this mixture. Place the hardboiled egg slices over the minced meat and then cover completely with the remaining potato puree. Brush over the top with egg yolk and decorate with a fork by pricking the surface. Pour the oil over the top of the pastela and cook in a preheated oven for about 45 minutes. Remove when it is a golden colour.

NUMBER OF SERVINGS: 8

meat

to come to Canada—by 1975, over 25,000 have come, split between Toronto and Montreal. →

sweet and sour meatballs

Adele Freeman *I have been making these meatballs for over 40 years. My children love them and now, my 12 grandchildren love them.*

Meatballs:

2 pounds ground beef or combination of chicken and turkey

½ cup breadcrumbs

2 eggs

salt and pepper

¼ cup sugar

Sauce:

1 (10 ounce) can tomato juice

1 (6 ounce) can tomato paste

1 (20 ounce) can tomatoes

¼ cup ketchup

1 teaspoon oregano (optional)

½ cup sugar

Combine all ingredients for the meatballs and mix well. Make small balls. Combine all the ingredients for the sauce and bring to a boil in a large pot. Drop meatballs into boiling sauce. Cook on low heat for 1½-2 hours. Serve with rice.

TIPS & ADVICE: I like to use a potato masher to mash up the tomatoes in the pot.

NUMBER OF SERVINGS: 6–8

meat

did you know?
More than 1,925 vulnerable members of Toronto's Jewish community benefit from the Jewish Family and Child 's Supplemental Financial Assistance Program every month.

When the Parti Quebecois won the provincial election in 1976, 20-30,000 Jews

meatballs

Karen Jesin *This meatball recipe is a staple in my house. It can also be used for Passover.*

3 pounds lean ground beef

½ cup matzah meal

2 eggs

2 onions, finely chopped

2 carrots, finely chopped

2 tablespoons sugar

1 teaspoon salt

¼ teaspoon ground pepper

Sauce:

2 cans tomato sauce

¼ cup ketchup

¼ cup or less sugar, to taste

1 teaspoon oregano

salt and pepper to taste

Combine ingredients for meatballs and mix well. Make little balls using wet hands. Combine ingredients for sauce and bring to a boil. Drop meatballs into boiling sauce and cook on low for 2–2½ hours. Enjoy! Delicious with pasta or rice.

NUMBER OF SERVINGS: 10

meat

fled to Toronto, fearing an independent Quebec would divide and weaken the national Jewish →

bbq pulled beef

Risa Goldenberg Wexler *This is a delicious recipe that my kids just love. It can be prepared a day or two in advance as it reheats well.*

2½ pound short rib roast or brisket

2 tablespoons olive oil

1 cup ketchup

1 large onion, chopped

½ cup celery, diced

½ cup water

3 tablespoons Worcestershire sauce*

2 tablespoons brown sugar

2 tablespoons lemon juice

2 tablespoons red wine vinegar

1 tablespoon Dijon mustard

2 teaspoons chili powder

1 teaspoon salt

In a Dutch oven, brown the meat on all sides in a little oil for 5–6 minutes until nicely browned.

Combine all of the rest of the ingredients in a bowl and then add to the browned meat. Place covered casserole in the oven and bake at 325°F for 4 hours. Remove from oven, keep covered and let cool. When meat is cool enough to touch, use two forks to pull the meat apart along the grain of the meat. Serve warm in fresh buns.

TIPS & ADVICE: I freeze it in single serving sizes in small bags that my kids take to school to make sandwiches.

*EDITOR'S NOTE: It is some people's custom to not mix meat and fish in the same recipe. As Worcestershire sauce has anchovies in it, it can be easily replaced by tamari sauce or liquid smoke.

NUMBER OF SERVINGS: 8

meat

community. (our story continues on page 216 . . . read on)

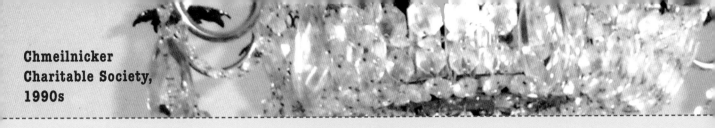

sweets

alfajores (shortbread cookie sandwiches)

Edith Rosemberg

1 cup flour

½ cup cornstarch

1 cup icing sugar, divided

¾ cup unsalted butter at room temperature, cut into chunks

1 cup dulce de leche

2 cups shredded coconut

Preheat oven to 300°F. Sift together the flour, cornstarch and ½ cup icing sugar into a bowl. Add butter and mix by hand until a soft, smooth dough forms. Cover and refrigerate for 1 hour. Form dough into a 2" thick log, place in a freezer bag and freeze until firm.

Slice log into ¼" thick slices and place slices on cookie sheet. Bake for 12 minutes. Cookies will not brown. Transfer cookies to a rack and cool. Spread 1 tablespoon of dulce de leche on a cookie. Cover with another cookie. Spread some dulce de leche on the sides of the cookie sandwich and roll sides of cookie in coconut. Dust with remaining icing sugar. Note: dulce de leche is a caramel-type sauce that can be found in many grocery/specialty stores or can be made by slowly heating sweetened condensed milk until thick and gooey (directions can be found online).

YIELD: 12 sandwiches

badner chocolate chip cookies

Nancy Gangbar *My mom started making these cookies when we were little. They were famous in the neighbourhood. People still ask about them 45 years later! Easy to make and great tasting, they are a family tradition that always brings smiles from brothers, cousins and friends. They are amazing.*

1 cup vegetable shortening

1 cup brown sugar

½ cup sugar

2 large eggs

2 teaspoons vanilla

2 cups flour

1 teaspoon baking soda

1 cup chocolate chips

Preheat oven to 365°F. Mix shortening and both sugars in the bowl of an electric mixer. Blend well. Add eggs and vanilla and mix for 3 to 5 minutes at a high speed. Add flour and baking soda on low speed. Add chocolate and mix by hand. Using a small spoon, scoop dough onto a baking sheet. Leave room between cookies as they expand when cooking. Cook each batch for 8–10 minutes.

TIPS & ADVICE: Any type of chocolate works well.

YIELD: 24 cookies

sweets

South African Jews, who began coming to Canada in the 1960s, came in large

betty's baklava

Linda Friedlich *As a little girl, I remember my mom and dad, Betty and Maurice, having parties. We had so much fun sneaking in to see what was going on and making sure we enjoyed all the wonderful food that my mom always made from scratch. One of the desserts that often found its way onto her table was baklava. Always gooey and delicious! I would help her bake it and wouldn't leave the kitchen until I could have the corner pieces she would cut and not serve because they were imperfect. I have continued the tradition and love making this to this day.*

2 cups sugar

1 cup water

1 scant tablespoon lemon juice

1½ tablespoons rose water

3 cups shelled almonds

¾ pound unsalted butter

1 pound prepared phyllo pastry

¼ cup sugar

¼ teaspoon ground cardamom

pinch salt

Begin by making the syrup, which should be cool before being added on top of baklava. Combine sugar, water and lemon juice in a small saucepan and cook over high heat for 7–8 minutes. Add rosewater and boil for 1 minute. Remove from heat and cool.

Blanch and grind almonds and set aside. Melt butter in a double boiler over simmering water. Place pastry flat on a board and put an 8 x 12" pan on top. With a sharp knife, cut pastry 1" larger than the pan. Brush pan with butter and set pastry in the pan, one sheet at a time, brushing the top of each sheet with approximately 1 teaspoon of melted butter before adding the next sheet. Continue until you have used half the pastry.

Preheat oven to 350°F. Mix together almonds, sugar, cardamom and salt. Sprinkle mixture on top of pastry in the pan and then continue layering the remaining pastry sheets, brushing each sheet with butter. Tuck the dough around the edges of the pan to even it out. With a sharp knife, cut the Baklava into diamond shapes 3–4" long. Make sure to cut through to the bottom. Spread remaining butter evenly and generously on top. Bake on lower rack of oven for about 20 minutes, then reduce heat to 300°F and bake on top shelf for about 25 minutes. When lightly golden, remove from oven, let cool 2–3 minutes, then spread the syrup evenly over the top with a spoon. Adjust the amount of syrup to your taste—you might not need it all.

YIELD: 60 pieces

sweets

waves in the late 1970s and mid 1980s fleeing South Africa's apartheid policies, its political →

alison's extra something brownies

Alison Himel *I love this recipe because it's easy and fun to make. I used to make them because I didn't love brownies and managed to not eat them. I'm not so lucky now—I eat them right out of the oven when they taste a bit like chocolate soufflés.*

4 ounces unsweetened chocolate

½ cup butter

4 large eggs, at room temperature

½ teaspoon salt

2 cups sugar

1 teaspoon vanilla extract

1 cup flour

4 Skor bars, broken into little pieces (or M&Ms, Smarties, and/or chocolate chips)

Preheat oven to 350°F. Butter and lightly flour a 9 x 13" baking pan (or line bottom and sides with parchment paper). Melt chocolate and butter in a double boiler over simmering water. Let cool to room temperature.

Using a whisk, beat eggs and salt in a bowl until very fluffy. Gradually mix in sugar and vanilla. Fold in cooled chocolate mixture. Gently fold in flour just until blended, keeping batter as fluffy as possible.

Gently fold in broken Skor Bars or other candy and pour batter into prepared pan. Smooth the top, making sure there is batter in each corner. Bake 25–30 minutes. Cool before cutting.

YIELD: 18 brownies

sweets

did you know?
Hillel of Greater Toronto benefits 15,000 Jewish students studying at Toronto universities and colleges annually.

oma's bublanina

Ruth Ekstein *This recipe was a stalwart of my dad's mom, Anna Ekstein, and the other women in her family who came from Czechoslovakia in the late 1930s, fleeing Hitler. Among the 5000 Jews who were accepted under the "None is Too Many" immigration policy, they came to Canada with absolutely nothing except their lives and their knowledge. While the men created new lives, the women attempted to maintain normalcy by cooking and baking their favourite foods. My mother is a child survivor and was taught to cook and bake by her mother-in-law, Anna Ekstein. This dessert became a weekly family favourite and I now bake it at every family gathering and frequently for friends. It is a perennial hit and makes me feel that I am keeping my grandmother's tradition alive.*

4 eggs

1 cup sugar

1 cup vegetable shortening

¾ cup flour

3 tablespoons cocoa

1 teaspoon baking powder

1 can pitted Bing cherries in syrup

icing sugar for garnish (optional)

Preheat oven to 350°F. Separate eggs into mixing bowls: whites into a small bowl, yolks into a large bowl. Beat whites to stiff peaks and set aside. Beat yolks on low speed and slowly add sugar, shortening, flour, cocoa and baking powder, one at a time. Mix thoroughly, scraping down sides of bowl as needed. If the mixture is too dry, add a few teaspoons of the cherry syrup.

Add egg whites and mix in very gently, either on lowest speed or by hand. (It is ok for the whites to not be totally mixed in.) Pour mixture into a greased 9 x 13" pan, using spatula to smooth top. Place cherries evenly in mixture. Bake 40–45 minutes or until a toothpick come out clean. Allow to cool in pan. Sprinkle with icing sugar. Cut into 4 x 6" pieces to get 24 pieces.

TIPS & ADVICE: You can substitute fresh raspberries for the pitted cherries. My aunt uses the cherries and adds chocolate chips. A cousin uses fresh plums. My mom occasionally makes a vanilla version, which simply means leaving out the cocoa but adding more flour instead.

YIELD: 24 pieces

They weren't the last big influx—in the early '90s, another 10,000 South African →

baba blanche's moon cookies

Devra Wasser *This recipe is from my fabulous Grandmother Blanche Posen, and her wonderful sister, my Aunt Harriet. Think Betty White in "Golden Girls" and the mother from "Everybody Loves Raymond" all rolled into one. Baba's favourite expression was "My Lands!" I loved spending my March Break in Scottsdale with her. She had a particular way of showing she cared for me. When I would ask to use her bicycle to go for a bike ride or a walk or to play tennis, she would always reply with, "Are you sure you want to do that? You know my cousin Gert's husband's brother's aunt's daughter had a terrible accident doing that, and now she is lame in one leg." Or has cancer (ssshhhh), or developed a limp, or, well . . . you get the picture.*

1¾ cups flour

1 cup sugar

½ cup butter

2 tablespoons milk or cream

1–2 tablespoons poppy seeds

1 egg

½ teaspoon salt

½ teaspoon vanilla

Preheat oven to 450°F. Mix all ingredients together. When adding the last cup or so of flour, start kneading into a ball and refrigerate until chilled. Roll out on floured surface until very thin. With a round cookie cutter or any round object, cup or drinking glass, cut into cookies, re-rolling scraps as you go. Bake until light brown, about 8–10 minutes.

YIELD: 2 dozen cookies

chocolate meringue cookies

Vera Sanders *These light chewy cookies are nice with tea and can be used for Passover.*

4 egg whites

pinch salt

½ teaspoon pure vanilla extract

1 cup sugar

2 cups chocolate chips, melted

½ cup chocolate chips

Preheat oven to 325°F. Line two baking sheets with parchment paper. Using an electric mixer, beat egg whites with salt and vanilla until foamy. Slowly add sugar until mixture has stiff peaks. Fold in melted chocolate with a spatula. Once mixed (trying to keep peaks stiff), add regular chocolate chips just until mixed in. Drop by tablespoon onto prepared baking sheets so that cookies are about 1½" in diameter. Bake for 8 minutes. Cool for 15 minutes on baking pans.

YIELD: 2½ dozen cookies

chocolate baklava (nut free)

Shelley Sefton *My family and I went to the "Taste of the Danforth" festival and had traditional Greek baklava. The next night, we had friends coming for dinner. We really wanted to make a baklava ourselves, but their son has a nut allergy. We thought about what we could use instead of nuts, and chocolate came to mind. We made it and all of my kids took turns brushing the phyllo. It was a real family effort and turned out delicious!*

1 package phyllo dough, thawed

1¼ cups butter, melted

3 cups semi-sweet chocolate chips

¾ cup brown sugar

2 tablespoons cocoa powder

2 teaspoons ground cinnamon

Syrup:

½ cup apple or orange juice

½ cup sugar

½ cup water

½ cup honey

4 tablespoons lemon juice

Preheat oven to 325°F. Place phyllo between 2 damp dishcloths to prevent drying out. Grease a 10 x 15" baking pan. Brush a sheet of phyllo dough with melted butter and place it in the pan. Repeat 7 more times adding each of the next 7 sheets to the existing layers.

In a bowl, combine chocolate chips, brown sugar, cocoa and cinnamon. Sprinkle ⅓ of the mixture over the top layer of phyllo. Layer and brush 4 more sheets of dough with butter. Top with another ⅓ of the chocolate chip mixture. Layer and brush four more sheets of dough with butter; top with remaining chocolate chip mixture. Top with the remaining dough, brushing each sheet with butter. Drizzle any remaining butter over the top. Cut baklava into 1½" diamonds using a sharp knife. Bake 50–60 minutes or until golden brown.

Meanwhile, combine syrup ingredients in a saucepan and bring to a boil over medium heat, stirring occasionally. Reduce heat to low; simmer, uncovered, for 20 minutes. Pour over warm baklava. Cool completely in pan set over a wire rack.

TIPS & ADVICE: Can be made with pareve margarine. This is an amazing nut-free version that both kids and adults adore!

YIELD: 12 pieces

sweets

162,605. By 2010, roughly half of Canada's Jews—about 180,000—called the →

222

chocolate caramel oatmeal bars

Syd Palter *My mom was invited to a neighbour's Christmas cookie exchange dinner party. Guests were asked to bring a cookie recipe with a taste for everyone and copies of the recipe to hand out. She brought Mandelbrot, which no one had heard of before. This recipe was contributed by a neighbour and it has become a family favourite. It's a really good bar that everyone likes, it freezes well and because it's nut-free, I can bring it to any of my friends' houses or even to school.*

1½ cups flour

½ teaspoon baking soda

½ teaspoon salt

1 cup butter or margarine, at room temperature

1 cup brown sugar

2 teaspoons vanilla extract

1¼ cups quick cooking oatmeal

1 cup miniature chocolate covered soft caramels, divided

1 (300 ml) can sweetened condensed milk (low fat is fine)

1 cup chocolate chips

Preheat oven to 350°F. Line a 9 x 13" pyrex with parchment paper. In a medium bowl, whisk together flour, baking soda and salt until mixed. In another bowl, using an electric or hand mixer, beat together butter, brown sugar, and vanilla until creamy. Scrape down sides and beat in flour mixture; mix in oatmeal. Using floured hands, press about ⅔ of the mixture evenly into pyrex. Bake until deep golden brown in colour around edges, about 25 minutes. Add ½ of the chocolate candies into remaining oatmeal mixture; mix well with your hands.

When baked, remove base from oven. Evenly drizzle condensed milk over the hot base. Sprinkle with remaining candies and chocolate chips. Crumble remaining batter over top (it will not cover completely). Bake until topping is deep golden brown and edges are bubbling, about 25 to 27 minutes. Cool in pyrex on rack; cut into bars. Serve warm or at room temperature. Store bars in an airtight container.

YIELD: 30 bars

fabulous cookie dough

Fern Orzech *This dough tastes great, is easy to work with, is excellent for hamentashen and regular cookies, and is one of my family's favourites. My mother always baked cookies with my children and now I bake with my grandchildren and my daughter bakes with her children. My grandchildren love this recipe especially when I use the dough for hamentashen and use a brownie recipe as the filling.*

1½ cups vegetable shortening

1 cup sugar

2 eggs, lightly beaten

½ cup orange juice

2 teaspoons vanilla

4 cups flour

1½ teaspoons baking powder

Preheat oven to 350°F. Cream together shortening and sugar with an electric mixer. Add eggs and blend until smooth. Add orange juice and vanilla. Add flour and baking powder and mix together to form the dough. Divide into 3 balls, wrap in plastic and refrigerate for 1 hour to make the dough easier to roll out. Roll dough on a floured surface to ¼" thick. Cut out shapes with cookie cutters or with a glass for hamentashen. Bake for 10 minutes.

TIPS & ADVICE: You can make the dough and freeze it, or freeze the cookies after they're baked. If making hamentashen, fill circles with a teaspoon of your favourite filling (poppy seed, prune, jam or nutella) and fold to form a triangle shape. Bake as directed. You can also use this dough for jam strudel. Spread jam (nuts and coconut are optional) on rolled out dough and roll up into a log. Place on a cookie sheet. Bake for 30 minutes. Remove from oven and cut into slices.

YIELD: 4 dozen hamentashen or cookies

ginger cookies

Rena Buckstein *This is a much-loved ginger cookie recipe given to me by the wife of a beloved patient who passed away.*

2¼ cups flour

2 teaspoons ground ginger

1 teaspoon baking soda

¾ teaspoon ground cinnamon

½ teaspoon ground cloves

¼ teaspoon salt

¾ cup margarine, softened

1 cup + 2 tablespoons white sugar, divided

1 egg

¼ cup molasses

1 tablespoon water

Preheat oven to 350°F. Sift together flour, ginger, baking soda, cinnamon, cloves and salt. Set aside. In a large bowl, cream together margarine and 1 cup sugar until light and fluffy. Beat in egg, then molasses and water. Gradually stir the sifted ingredients into the molasses mixture.

Shape dough into walnut sized balls and roll them in remaining 2 tablespoons sugar. Place cookies 2" apart on an ungreased cookie sheet and flatten slightly. Bake for 8–10 minutes. Cool on baking sheet for 5 minutes before removing to a wire rack to cool completely. Store in airtight container.

YIELD: 24 cookies

lemon squares

Wendy Kay *A woman at my school gave me this recipe that was handed down from her grandmother. The squares come out perfectly every time! The filling can also be used in a tart or pie shell.*

1 cup flour

½ cup butter

¼ cup icing sugar

1 cup white sugar

4 tablespoons fresh lemon juice

3 tablespoons flour

2 eggs

¼ teaspoon baking powder

Preheat oven to 350°F. Mix the first 3 ingredients and press into pan. Bake for 20 minutes. Mix the next 5 ingredients with a whisk and let stand while bottom bakes. Mix again and pour over bottom. Bake another 25 minutes. Cool. Cut into squares.

YIELD: 16 squares

sweets

ALONE counts 38,940 Jews as members of its community, Vaughan 33,090 and Toronto →

ginger white chocolate macadamia biscotti

Adell Shneer *I developed these biscotti after falling in love with Starbuck's biscotti one holiday season. I gifted them to friends and family, and even sold them for a while at Pusateri's. They keep well for weeks in an airtight container at room temperature. They are for spice lovers, with lots of ground ginger to give them heat. Those who want more can add crystallized ginger for a bigger ginger hit.*

3 eggs

½ cup sugar

½ cup light brown sugar, packed

¼ cup vegetable oil

¼ cup fancy molasses

1 teaspoon vanilla

3 cups flour

2 tablespoons ground ginger

1 teaspoon baking soda

1 teaspoon cinnamon

½ teaspoon salt

¼ teaspoon ground cloves

8 ounces good-quality white chocolate, chopped

½ cup macadamia nuts, chopped

¼ cup crystallized ginger, chopped (optional)

In bowl, beat eggs with granulated sugar until light and fluffy. Add brown sugar and continue beating. Add oil in a thin stream, then molasses, and vanilla. In another bowl, whisk together flour, ginger, baking soda, cinnamon, salt and cloves. Add to egg mixture, stirring just until combined. Stir in chocolate, macadamia nuts and crystallized ginger, if using. Refrigerate dough for 30 minutes.

Preheat oven to 325°F. On a sheet of floured waxed paper, form dough into 4 equal rolls, about 12" long. Place 4" apart on parchment or Silpat lined baking sheets (2 per sheet). Flatten each roll to make it about 3" wide. Bake in oven, switching top and bottom pans halfway through baking, until firm to touch and golden, 30 minutes. Let cool in pan for 10 minutes. Transfer to cutting board and turn oven down to 300°F. With serrated knife, slice into ¾" thick slices. Place cut-side down on baking sheets and bake biscotti, turning once, 15 minutes per side. Let cool on rack. Store in airtight container.

TIPS & ADVICE: You can substitute almonds, pecans or walnuts for the macadamia nuts or omit for a nut-free version. If desired, substitute dried cranberries, sour cherries or chopped dried apricots for the nuts.

YIELD: 44 pieces

sweets

nanny mollie's mandelbroit

Shelley Allen *My Nanny, Mollie Gold, loved to bake for her family and friends. She passed on her recipes to her daughters, Marilyn and Judy, who gave them to their daughters, who now share them with their children. We all remember her as a perfectionist who lined up her ingredients on the counter, wore her flowered apron, hair in place, listening to classical music as she prepared her favourite dishes. This recipe is wonderful as an addition to dessert or served anytime with a cup of tea or coffee; that's how Nanny Mollie offered hers.*

3 eggs, at room temperature

¾ cup white sugar

⅔ cup oil

⅛ cup shredded coconut and/
or raisins, cranberries, chocolate
chips

1 tablespoon cinnamon

juice from ¾ lemon

1 teaspoon baking powder

1 teaspoon vanilla

pinch salt

2½ cups sifted flour

1 cup almonds, slivered and
chopped

¼ cup pecans, chopped

Preheat oven to 375°F. Beat eggs and add all ingredients one at a time. Add flour and nuts last and mix well. Wet hands slightly and form long and thin (approximately 2 x 4") rolls of dough. Place on oiled cookie sheet and bake 35–40 minutes. Remove from oven when medium brown and cool slightly. Increase oven to 400°F. Cut rolls with sharp serrated knife into narrow pieces. Separate pieces on cookie sheet and put back in oven. Watch closely until toasted. Turn over as needed. Remove and place on stone counter or large platter to cool.

TIPS & ADVICE: Stores well in airtight container and freezes well too.

YIELD: approximately 2 dozen mandelbroit

did you know?
The Ayalim and Young Communities program has brought 2,200 Israeli students to study and work in peripheral communities throughout Israel to help transform the lives of over 36,000 Israelis.

had been for decades and moving back south into some of the neighbourhoods inhabited by the

marshmallow brownies

Pearl Gropper Berman *These are easy to prepare, go with everything and can be stored for more than a week in your refrigerator.*

3 squares bittersweet chocolate

½ cup butter

2 large eggs

1 cup white sugar

½ cup flour

1–2 cups kosher marshmallows

1 cup icing sugar

⅓ cup butter

3 tablespoons cocoa

3 tablespoons table cream

Preheat oven to 350°F. Combine chocolate and butter in a double boiler until melted. Remove from stove, cool slightly and gradually add sugar, eggs and flour. Pour mixture into greased 9 x 9" pan and cook on the middle oven rack for 20 minutes. Allow to cool. Cut marshmallow into small pieces using scissors (to avoid stickiness, dip the scissors in cold water between cuts).

Preheat broiler. Lay marshmallows on top of the brownies and broil for 5–6 minutes. Watch carefully so marshmallows don't burn. The marshmallows should puff up but not brown. Let cool. In the double boiler, on low heat, combine icing sugar, butter, cocoa and table cream. Pour onto brownies and allow to cool.

YIELD 10–12 squares

skor mandelbread

Leslie Marcus *This has always been a staple in our home. The Skor bits add another crunchy, sweet element to the traditional "mandel" bread. These are easy to prepare and always enjoyed.*

1 cup oil

3 eggs

1 cup plus 5 teaspoons sugar, divided

3 cups flour

1 teaspoon baking powder

1 cup Grapenut flakes

1 cup almonds, finely chopped

1 cup Skor bits

1 teaspoon vanilla

1 teaspoon cinnamon

Preheat oven to 350°F. In a large bowl, mix oil, sugar and eggs. In a separate bowl, sift together flour and baking powder. Combine flour mixture into egg mixture and stir together. Add Grapenuts, almonds, Skor bits and vanilla and mix by hand. Separate the dough into 3 equal portions and make log rolls on a baking sheet. Mix 5 teaspoons sugar with cinnamon. Sprinkle the top of the rolls with cinnamon sugar. Bake for 25 minutes. Slice the rolls into 1" thick slices and turn on their sides. Bake at 325°F for another 15 minutes.

YIELD: Approximately 30 pieces

sweets

earliest immigrants; "what is old is new again". Today, Toronto's Jewish →

marshmallow rolls

Frances Mandell-Arad *I found this recipe at the NCJW Brides Group in 1951 and began to make the rolls as often as possible. These keep well in the refrigerator for many weeks if they are well hidden! These are my grandson's favourite treat.*

Sharon Goelman *This is my favourite Passover recipe that I make all year round. I adapted this from a similar recipe shared by my close friend Mena Glustein who now lives in Jerusalem. I have been making this recipe for 40 years.*

3 ounces unsweetened chocolate

¼ cup margarine

40 large and coloured kosher marshmallows, quartered

1 cup icing sugar

1 egg

1 teaspoon vanilla

½ cup walnuts, chopped

sweetened and unsweetened coconut, shredded

Special materials:

4 or 5 sheets of waxed paper, each about 16" long

In a double boiler or microwave, melt the unsweetened chocolate and margarine. Cut marshmallows into quarters with scissors dipped into boiling water and place in a large bowl. Once the chocolate and butter mixture has cooled slightly, add icing sugar, then egg and vanilla, beating well by hand until smooth. Finally, add the walnuts. Pour this mixture over the marshmallows and mix together until the marshmallows are evenly coated.

Sprinkle waxed paper with coconut. Divide mixture into 4 or 5 parts. Place one part of the mixture on top of the sprinkled coconut, using the waxed paper to shape a roll. Firm up the roll, especially near the ends. Fold in the outer ends of the waxed paper to hold the shape. Repeat until everything is wrapped. Place together in a plastic bag in the refrigerator for 24 hours. Slice as needed and rewrap any leftovers.

EDITOR'S NOTE: This recipe is so popular that it was submitted by 2 people. They each had some small tweaks, which we have incorporated here.

YIELD: 12 pieces

sweets

mexican wedding cakes

Susan Devins *I bring these ethereal Mexican Wedding Cakes to all family occasions, and even the butter-police relatives break down and relish these light treats! This is the easiest recipe to make with requisite wow factor, especially when the icing sugar is freshly sprinkled on concentric circles of Mexican Wedding Cakes on a wicker platter.*

1 cup unsalted butter

6 tablespoons sugar

1 teaspoon vanilla extract

2 cups flour

1 cup pecans, finely chopped

1 cup icing sugar

Preheat oven to 300°F. In a large bowl, cream butter and sugar until light and fluffy. Beat in vanilla. Gradually add flour until well blended. Stir in pecans. Shape into 1" balls. Place about 1" apart on parchment-lined cookie sheets. Bake for 30–35 minutes, until lightly golden. When still hot, roll in icing sugar. Cool on racks and then roll again in icing sugar.

TIPS & ADVICE: You can also use a food processor for this recipe. Simply put all ingredients into bowl of the processor and process until the mixture just comes together as a ball.

YIELD: 50 cookies

raw chocolate bliss balls

Karen Gilman *I love bliss balls as they are a healthy snack with no processed sugar or flour. They don't require baking so they are quick and easy to make. They freeze well, so you can keep a stash in the freezer.*

1½ cups walnuts

8 Medjool dates, pitted

⅓ cup cocoa powder

1 tablespoon agave syrup

½ teaspoon vanilla extract

water as needed

cayenne pepper or espresso powder, optional

In a food processor, process walnuts and dates until crumbly. Add cocoa, agave, vanilla and process until dough becomes wet enough to roll. Add small amounts of water if the dough does not come together. Roll into 1" balls and store in the freezer.

TIPS & ADVICE: For spicy chocolate bliss balls, add 1 teaspoon of cayenne pepper to dough; for coffee flavour, add 1 teaspoon ground espresso powder.

YIELD: 12–15 balls

sweets

Toronto's social and political life. Toronto boasts over two hundred Jewish afternoon →

rugelach

Lois Friedman Fine *I combined two recipes and the result seems to work well. I make these very often because everyone goes for them over any other cookie.*

2 cups flour

1 cup butter, cut into chunks

¾ cup sour cream

1 egg yolk

¾ cup pecans

¾ cup sugar

1 teaspoon cinnamon

⅓ cup apricot jam

½ cup golden raisins

Place flour and butter in the bowl of a food processor. Process for 20 seconds or until dough resembles coarse meal. Add sour cream and process 5 seconds more. Add egg yolk and process until blended. Turn onto lightly floured board and knead gently, adding flour if necessary. Form into 3 discs, wrap and refrigerate for 1 hour or overnight.

In food processor, process pecans until fine. Add sugar and cinnamon and set aside. Place jam on saucer and mash to remove large pieces.

Preheat oven to 425°F. Line 2 cookie sheets with parchment paper. Remove dough from fridge and let stand for 5 to 10 minutes. Place ¼ cup of nut mixture on board. Roll out dough on top of nuts, forming a 10" circle. Spread with ⅓ of the jam and sprinkle another ¼ cup of nut mixture on top. Pat down with a piece of plastic wrap. Cut into 16 wedges. Place 2–3 raisins on the wide edge of each wedge and roll up from there to the point. Place, point side down, on prepared cookie sheet. Repeat with other two pieces of dough.

Bake one sheet at a time for 10 minutes each; reduce heat to 350°F and bake 4 to 5 minutes longer until golden brown. Remove to rack and cool.

YIELD: 48 pieces

and day schools, synagogues and other Jewish organizations and institutions.

rugelach with cream cheese dough

Etica Levy *My daughter Anita's husband Andy and my four grandchildren love these and eat them from the freezer, which preserves their flavour.*

1 cup flour

½ cup cold butter

½ cup cream cheese

½ teaspoon vanilla

⅔ cup chocolate chips

½ cup white sugar

⅔ cup chopped walnuts

1 teaspoon cinnamon

½ teaspoon vanilla

Preheat oven to 350°F. Line a baking sheet with parchment paper. Combine flour, butter, cream cheese and vanilla in processor bowl and process until a ball is formed. Divide dough into 2 pieces to make 2 balls and refrigerate for at least 1 hour. Make filling by placing remaining ingredients in food processor and process until fine. Set aside.

Roll first ball into a 12" circle. Sprinkle with filling and press down with your hands so that it sticks well to the dough. Cut into 4 triangles and then cut each triangle into 3 wedges. Roll up each wedge and lay onto parchment. Repeat with second ball of dough. Bake for 20–22 minutes.

TIPS & ADVICE: If you wish to make this recipe nut free, the walnuts can be excluded from the filling.

YIELD: approximately 24 rugelach

kimmy's yummy freezer cookies

Kimberley Walters *I found this great recipe in the Leo Baeck cookbook, tweaked it by adding more chocolate and serving it straight from the freezer. My friends and kids' friends always know to look in the freezer for this treat. Yummy! You can make squares as big or little as possible but these are very sweet, so smaller is better.*

2 cups flour

1 cup brown sugar

1 cup butter, at room temperature

1 package Skor chips

1 package white chocolate chips

1 package semi-sweet chocolate chips

Preheat oven to 350°F. Line a cookie sheet with parchment paper. Crumble flour, sugar and butter together. Add Skor, white and semi-sweet chips. Gently press all ingredients onto lined cookie sheet right to the edges. Bake approximately 20 minutes or until centre bubbles. Remove and let sit for 5 minutes. Cut into squares but leave on cookie sheet until cool. Serve chilled from fridge or freezer.

YIELD: 24–36 cookies

sweets

 It is a strong supporter of Israel, contributes to many charitable causes and is →

the best chocolate chip cookies

Pamela Kuhl *I make these cookies a few times a week and we still don't have enough! This recipe is great because it calls for oil instead of margarine, which gives the cookies a very chewy texture. I get asked for the recipe all the time.*

2 cups flour

½ teaspoon baking soda

½ teaspoon salt

¾ cup oil

1 cup brown sugar

½ cup white sugar

2 eggs

1 tablespoon vanilla

2¼ cups chocolate chips

Preheat oven to 325°F. Mix together the flour, baking soda and salt, and set aside. Cream the oil and both sugars together using an electric mixer. Add in the eggs and vanilla and mix well. Add in the flour mixture and mix just until combined. Add in chocolate chips and mix by hand. Form balls the size of a quarter cup scoop. Place on a baking tray lined with parchment paper. Bake for 16 minutes. Cool on a wire rack.

TIPS & ADVICE: These double quite easily.

YIELD: 16 cookies

south african crunchies

Lauren Barrett *This was adapted from my Granny's favourite cookie recipe. She always had some Crunchies ready for us in her home and it was the first thing she taught me to bake as a little girl. When I think of her warm farmhouse kitchen in Bulawayo, this is the smell that I remember. These are soooo easy to make and disappear faster than I can make them.*

just under 1 cup margarine

1½ tablespoons golden syrup

1 teaspoon baking soda

¼ teaspoon vanilla or almond essence

2 cups oats

1 cup flour

1 cup sugar

Preheat the oven to 325°F. Boil margarine and syrup. When boiling, add baking soda and vanilla/almond essence and mix well. Add to dry ingredients. Pack tightly into greased 9 x 13" biscuit pan. Bake for 15 minutes. Cut in pan while warm and lift out when cool.

TIPS & ADVICE: Golden syrup can be found at many specialty stores. A substitute is equal parts honey and corn syrup.

YIELD: 30 squares

apple tart

Rhoda Katz *This apple tart not only looks beautiful, but is delicious too. Of all the pies I make, this is the most outstanding. It looks like something out of one of the finest French pastry shops in Europe. I make it for special occasions, like the holidays. Sometimes, I will make chocolate leaves and decoratively put them on top.*

Pastry:

1 cup flour

½ cup unsalted butter, cold and cut in small cubes

2 tablespoons sugar

¼ teaspoon salt

1 tablespoon white vinegar

Filling:

5 or 6 medium Granny Smith apples, peeled and thinly sliced

¾ cup sugar

2 tablespoons flour

1 teaspoon cinnamon

Glaze:

1 cup apple jelly

Preheat the oven to 400°F. Add flour, butter, sugar and salt to a food processor and, using the metal blade, process until butter is cut into flour and small granules are formed (about 10 seconds). While the machine is running, pour vinegar through the feed tube and process until the dough forms a ball. Remove carefully. If the dough is soft, flour your hands and handle gently. Press into the bottom and sides of a 9" flan pan with a removable bottom.

Place the sliced apples into a large bowl and add sugar, flour and cinnamon. Mix well.

Arrange apples on the pastry in concentric circles, ending up with the smallest apple slice in the centre. Bake 50-60 minutes or until apples turn golden brown. Melt apple jelly in a small pan on stove for 3-5 minutes; do not boil. Remove from the heat and let the jelly cool slightly before brushing or spooning over the tart.

TIPS & ADVICE: For an 11" pan, I use 1½ times the ingredients.

YIELD: 1 tart

visit our website
www.JewishToronto.com/BathurstStreetKitchen

sweets

its Tomorrow Campaign, building and improving facilities and services across three beautiful →

blueberry crunch

Lis Wigmore *Although I'm not Jewish, my life and my family's lives are forever enriched by our many dear friends in the Jewish community. Our family lives, works, studies and plays in Forest Hill. Both my husband and I have been to Israel and look forward to bringing our children there. We proudly support several Jewish charities and we love this community! I often bring this dessert to dinners in town or at the cottage. It really is delicious and sort-of-healthy.*

1½ cups walnuts (or any mix of other nuts), lightly toasted, then chopped

12 cups (approximately 6 pints) fresh blueberries

1 cup sugar

1 tablespoon cinnamon

1 teaspoon mace

2 lemons, zested and squeezed to give 2 tablespoons juice

1½ cups unbleached flour (or 1 cup rolled oats and ½ cup flour, mixed)

1 cup dark brown sugar, packed

1 teaspoon salt

1 cup unsalted butter, cold (for pareve/vegan use Earth Balance or other margarine, cold or frozen)

Preheat oven to 350°F. Lightly toast walnuts and chop into pieces. Wash and dry blueberries and transfer to a round, non-stick, deep dish pizza pan or a large shallow casserole (berries should cover the bottom of the dish). In a small bowl, combine sugar, cinnamon and mace and add to berries. Sprinkle lemon zest and juice over berries, gently mix together with a rubber spatula and spread out evenly. Sprinkle nuts overtop and set aside.

In a bowl, mix flour, brown sugar and salt. Cut butter into pieces and add to dry ingredients. With a pastry blender (or two knives) cut mixture until it resembles coarse meal. Then use fingertips to work into a crumbly texture. Sprinkle evenly over berry mixture and bake for 25 minutes or until a lovely golden brown on top.

TIPS & ADVICE: This recipe can easily be divided in half and baked in a shallow casserole or cake pan. If needed, spray dish with non-stick spray. Can be reheated; just be careful not to overcook.

NUMBER OF SERVINGS: 10–12

sweets

max's apple berry crisp

Rona Cappell *As a child, my son Max was a finicky eater. I made this for dessert one night and he gobbled it up. I started to make double batches and served it to him for breakfast with yogourt and honey. He lives in Miami now, so when he visits, I have this on hand.*

¾ cup sugar

½ cup whole wheat flour, divided

1 lemon, zested

4 cups apples, peeled and sliced

1 (600 g) package frozen mixed berries

1½ cups quick cooking oats

¾ cup brown sugar

2 teaspoons cinnamon

¼ cup butter, melted

Preheat the oven to 375°F. In a large mixing bowl, combine sugar, ¼ cup flour and lemon zest. Add apples and berries and stir to combine. Spoon into a 9 x 13" pyrex dish that has been sprayed with cooking spray. In a medium mixing bowl, mix oats, brown sugar, cinnamon and remaining flour. Drizzle with butter and stir to combine. Spoon over fruit. Bake 40-50 minutes or until bubbly and golden.

TIPS & ADVICE: You don't necessarily have to use apples. Depending on what's in season, I have replaced apples with peaches or pears.

NUMBER OF SERVINGS: 4

sweet bread pudding

Myrna Hurwich Silver *This recipe has been enjoyed by family and friends for many years and is often requested. My kids and grandkids love coming to the cottage or the house for dinner as they know they are going to get this dish for dessert. I'm sure one day after I'm gone, someone will say that this is one of the things they are going to miss about me!*

2 eggs, beaten

½ cup white sugar

2 teaspoons vanilla or ½ cup sherry

½ teaspoon salt

½ teaspoon cinnamon

2¾ cups milk, scalded

10 slices stale challah, cubed

¼ pound melted butter

1 apple, grated

Preheat oven to 375°F. Beat eggs, sugar, vanilla, salt and cinnamon. Place stale bread in greased 8 x 10" pyrex. Pour milk over stale bread. Add egg mixture to bread cubes and add melted butter. Add apple and mix well. Place pyrex in a larger roasting pan filled with water and bake for 1 hour.

NUMBER OF SERVINGS: 8–10

sweets

Bathurst and Sheppard, and the Joseph and Wolf Lebovic Jewish Community Campus in the heart →

lemon meringue flan

Johanna Samuel *This is a favourite dessert in France and a gorgeous addition to any dinner. It's light and goes with everything. The crust dough and the curd can be made in advance and then assembled, but the meringue must be made the day the tart is served. This tart is just as delicious without the meringue. The lemon curd is based on a recipe for "The Most Extraordinary Lemon Tart" by the great Dori Greenspan. She calls the curd "lemon cream"; it can be refrigerated for four days and frozen for up to two months prior to assembling in the tart crust.*

Crust:

1⅔ cups unbleached, all-purpose flour

¼ cup sugar

¼ cup almonds, slivered

10 tablespoons (1¼ sticks) chilled unsalted butter, cut into ½" cubes

1 large egg, lightly beaten

Curd:

1 cup sugar

finely grated zest of 3 lemons

4 large eggs

¾ cup freshly squeezed lemon juice (from 4 to 5 lemons)

2 sticks plus 5 tablespoons (10½ ounces) unsalted butter, room temperature, cut into 1" pieces

Crust: Blend the flour, sugar, and almonds in a food processor until the nuts are finely ground. Using on/off turns, cut in the butter until a coarse meal forms. Add the egg and blend just until dough forms. Gather dough into ball; flatten into a square 1" thick, wrap in plastic, and chill 1 hour.

Line the bottom of a 10" round removable bottom tart pan with parchment paper. Cut the dough into 1" slices. Lay the slices in the bottom of the pan and up the sides, and push them together, closing all fissures. Press the bottom of a glass against the dough to flatten and smooth. Refrigerate the crust for one hour.

Preheat oven to 375°F. Bake the crust until golden brown, about 17 minutes. Remove the crust from the oven. Tamp down bubbles with the bottom of a glass. Cool the crust and then remove the fluted ring by setting the tart pan over a jar and letting the ring fall to the counter. Use a flat metal spatula to place crust on a plate.

Curd: Have a thermometer, preferably an instant-read, a strainer, and a blender (first choice) or food processor at the ready. Bring a few inches of water to a simmer in a saucepan. Put the sugar and zest in a large metal bowl that can be fitted into the saucepan of simmering water. Off heat, work the sugar and zest together between your fingers until the sugar is moist, grainy and very aromatic. Whisk in the eggs followed by the lemon juice.

sweets

Meringue (optional):

4 egg whites, at room temperature

⅛ teaspoon cream of tartar

1 cup sugar

Powdered sugar for garnish

Fit the bowl into the saucepan (water can't touch the bottom of the bowl) and cook, stirring with the whisk as soon as the mixture feels tepid, until the cream reaches 180°F. Whisk constantly to keep the eggs from scrambling—the cream will start out light and foamy, then the bubbles will get bigger, and then, as the cream is getting closer to 180°F, it will start to thicken and the whisk will leave tracks. The tracks mean the cream is almost ready. Keep whisking and checking the temperature. Getting to the right temperature can take as long as 10 minutes.

At 180°F, remove from the heat and strain it into a blender; discard the zest. Let the cream rest, stirring occasionally, for about 10 minutes.

With blender on high, with the machine going, add the butter, about 5 pieces at a time. Turn off the blender and scrape down the sides of the container as needed. Once the butter is in, continue to beat the cream for another 3 minutes.

Pour the cream into a container, press a piece of plastic wrap against the surface, and chill at least 4 hours or overnight. When you are ready to construct the tart, just whisk the cream to loosen it and spoon it into the tart shell.

Meringue (optional): In a mixer fitted with the whisk attachment (or with a hand mixer), beat the (room temperature) egg whites with the cream of tartar just until soft peaks form. Pour ¼ cup of the sugar in as the whites are beating. Add the sugar, ¼ cup at a time, slowly, until it is all incorporated and the whites are shiny and stiff.

Using a ½" piping tip, pipe or spoon the meringue on the tart, making swirls and indents with the back of the spoon.

Brown the meringue either with a kitchen torch, or by placing the tart in a 350°F oven just until the meringue is lightly browned. Sprinkle powdered sugar around the edge of the tart, and serve chilled.

YIELD: 1 (10") flan

sweets

banana orange ice cream pie

Judy Naiberg *Affectionately called "BOICP," our family has been making this pie since 1968, a time when every freezer in the nation was well-stocked with frozen concentrated orange juice. The combination of the tart orange with the creamy banana and the crunchy chocolate crust is sublime. My brother, the foodie, still insists on this as his birthday cake every year.*

1 box chocolate wafers (or two rows of Oreos in which case, omit ⅓ cup sugar)

⅓ cup plus ½ cup sugar

7 tablespoons butter, melted

½ can undiluted orange juice concentrate

⅓ cup lemon juice

3 peeled bananas (4 if small)

1½ cups whipping cream

Preheat oven to 350°F. Make the crust by mixing the chocolate wafers, ⅓ cup sugar and butter in a food processor. Once mixed, pat crust into a 10" pie plate. Bake for 8 minutes; let cool. Make filling by combining orange juice concentrate, lemon juice, ½ cup sugar, bananas and whipping cream in a blender and blending until smooth. Pour filling into the shell and freeze.

YIELD: 1 (10") pie

did you know?
Through UJA Federation, 2200 children attend Jewish Day School because of a $10M+ allocation towards tuition subsidies annually.

sweets

sour cream apple pie

Johanna Samuel *This is a delicious favourite dessert.*

Crust:

2½ cups + 3 tablespoons flour, divided

½ cup sugar

1¾ teaspoons cinnamon

¾ teaspoon salt

6 tablespoons unsalted butter, chilled

6 tablespoons shortening, chilled

4–6 tablespoons apple cider or apple juice, chilled

Filling:

5–7 tart apples, peeled, cored and thinly sliced

⅔ cup dairy sour cream

⅓ cup sugar

1 egg, lightly beaten

1 teaspoon vanilla extract

¼ teaspoon salt

Topping:

3 tablespoons brown sugar

3 tablespoons white sugar

1 cup shelled walnuts or pecans, chopped

½ teaspoon cinnamon

Crust: Sift 2½ cups flour, ½ cup sugar, cinnamon and salt into a bowl. Cut in butter and shortening with a fork until mixture resembles rolled oats. Moisten with a bit of cider or juice, tossing lightly with a fork. Form dough into a ball, wrap and refrigerate 2 hours. Preheat oven to 350°F. Cut off ⅓ of the dough and return this piece to the fridge. Roll out the other ⅔ between 2 sheets of wax paper. Line a greased 9" pie pan with the dough. Trim overhang and crimp.

Filling: Drop apple slices into a mixing bowl. Whisk together sour cream, ⅓ cup sugar, egg, vanilla, salt and the remaining flour in a small bowl. Pour mixture over apples and toss well. Spoon apples into pastry lined pie pan.

Topping: Mix nuts, brown sugar, sugar and cinnamon together and sprinkle evenly over apple mixture. Roll out remaining pastry to form a 10" circle. Cut into ½" strips and arrange these lattice fashion over apples; trim ends of strips and crimp edge of crust.

Set pie on the middle rack of the oven and bake for 55–65 minutes. Pie is done when juices are bubbling and apples are tender.

YIELD: 1 pie

sweets

basil's rice pudding

Helaine Robins *Basil's was a restaurant near Yonge Street and Gerrard that closed in the '60s. While not a Jewish restaurant, it was one that many Toronto Jews frequented. My aunt made this recipe to break the fast on Yom Kippur. Now I do the same.*

½ cup short grain rice, well washed

1 quart skim milk

½ cup sugar

½ teaspoon salt

1 egg

2 teaspoons vanilla

½ cup raisins

Wash rice with cold water until water runs clear. Put rice, milk, sugar and salt in saucepan and cook on low heat for 1 hour till rice is soft, stirring every 10 minutes. Remove from stove. Beat egg in a small dish and add vanilla. Slowly add to rice and continue to stir until the egg is set. Add raisins. Can also sprinkle with sugar and cinnamon.

TIPS & ADVICE: The original recipe calls for 2 eggs and whole milk. I use skim and 1 egg. You can also use 2 egg whites. You can add more milk to make the pudding thinner.

NUMBER OF SERVINGS: 8

chocolate mousse (pareve)

Eveline Berger *This is a great pareve dessert to serve after dinner. It is easy to prepare, looks great and can be made ahead of time.*

4 eggs, separated

1 cup semi-sweet chocolate pieces

6 tablespoons boiling water

1 tablespoon vanilla, dark rum or water

Beat egg whites in mixer until stiff. Put chocolate pieces in food processor and grind until fine powder (about 5 seconds). Add boiling water and blend until smooth (10 seconds). Add egg yolks and vanilla and blend until smooth (5 seconds). Fold chocolate mixture into egg whites. Pour into serving dish. Refrigerate for at least 6 hours before serving.

TIPS & ADVICE: I usually refrigerate overnight.

NUMBER OF SERVINGS: 6

sweets

crème caramel

Kathy Green *This recipe is an adaptation of my mother-in-law's recipe. It is delicious and the ingredients are generally handy in anyone's fridge.*

1 quart homogenized milk

8 large eggs

1½ cups sugar, divided

½ teaspoon vanilla

½ cup water plus more for water bath

Preheat oven to 325°F. Bring milk to a boil on the stove in a saucepan. Cool, then whisk in the eggs and ¾ cup of the sugar and vanilla. In another saucepan, bring ¾ cup of sugar and ½ cup of water to a boil. Boil until caramelized; then immediately pour the caramel into an ovenproof glass dish. Swirl around.

Heat a large pan of water in the pre-heated oven. Pour milk and egg mixture overtop of caramel through a sieve. Set dish within pan of heated water and bake for about 1 hour. Test with a knife to make sure it is set. Chill and serve, spooning some of the caramel liquid from the bottom of the pan over the custard.

NUMBER OF SERVINGS: 10

halva ice cream

Laura Orzy *Growing up in South Africa, almost everything good was made from scratch. Who doesn't love ice cream and who doesn't love halva? Together they make for a most delicious dessert.*

6 extra large eggs, separated

⅔ cup sugar

1 pint heavy cream

½ pound halva

1 milk chocolate bar, regular size, nut free

1 can Carnation evaporated milk

1 cup berries, sliced

Lightly oil a springform pan or Tupperware mould. Beat egg yolks and sugar until light and fluffy and set aside. Whip cream until stiff and fold into egg yolk mix. Beat egg whites until stiff peaks form and fold into cream and yolk and sugar mixture. Flake halva and fold into mixture. Pour into prepared mould and freeze overnight.

Three hours before serving, melt chocolate in the microwave for 60 seconds and add 1 can of Carnation milk and mix. Take frozen ice-cream out of the mould. Drizzle chocolate mixture over and add berries around the plate and ice cream.

NUMBER OF SERVINGS: 10

innocent crème caramel

Judith Gabor *I developed this recipe because I love crème caramel but not the fat and calories. I have given this recipe to many people who are all now converts to the lower fat crème caramel. It's easy and fun and looks gorgeous on a large elongated platter. It is now my claim to fame with family and friends.*

2 tablespoons sugar

1 can condensed milk

12 egg whites

1 litre skim or 1% milk (approximately)

dash vanilla extract

dash almond extract

Preheat oven to 375°F. In a pot, on medium low heat, slowly caramelize the sugar, adding a few drops of water, making sure not to burn it. Cool the pot in cold water. Combine the condensed milk, egg whites, milk, vanilla, and almond extract in a mixing bowl and mix with a hand beater until well combined. Put the cooled caramel mixture into a loaf pan and then, add the egg/milk mixture to the caramel pan. Half-fill a baking dish larger than the loaf pan with cold water.

Place the loaf pan into the water-filled pan and transfer to oven. Bake 40 minutes, then check to see if the mixture has thickened. You should be able to shake the pan and see movement but no liquid. Remove the pan from the oven and place uncovered in the refrigerator. Allow to cool completely.

TIPS & ADVICE: When ready to serve, run a knife around the edge of the pan and turn out onto an appropriate sized serving dish. Garnish with berries on top and around the edges of the crème caramel. The amount of milk depends on the size of your loaf pan. If you are using a larger loaf pan, add more milk. The milk/egg mixture should come about ⅔ of the way up the inside of the pan. If a skin has formed at the top of the dessert after baking, that's fine, as it adds to the flavour. If you use a higher temperature oven, the texture of the dessert will be less smooth. If you want a very smooth texture, bake it at 325°F until the mixture solidifies.

NUMBER OF SERVINGS: 8–12

sweets

the most delicious pareve ice cream

Phyllis Flatt *This is a favourite Flatt Family Shabbat dessert. I love to serve it on top of a warm apple pie or a summer berry crisp. This recipe is very quick and easy and can be made several days ahead. It also works well for Passover.*

4 eggs, separated

½ cup sugar, divided

1 cup Nutriwhip (regular or light)

1 packet vanilla sugar (or 1–2 teaspoons vanilla extract)

¼ cup Amaretto

2 teaspoons cinnamon

2 teaspoons cinnamon and sugar mixture

Beat egg whites with ¼ cup sugar until stiff peaks form. In a separate bowl, beat egg yolks with ¼ cup sugar until creamy. In a third bowl, beat Nutriwhip with vanilla sugar until thick. Fold whites into yolks and then fold in the Nutriwhip followed by Amaretto and cinnamon. Adjust flavourings according to taste. Pour into freezer-proof serving bowl and sprinkle with cinnamon and sugar mixture. Freeze for at least 6 hours.

TIPS & ADVICE: To change it up, this recipe can be made with cocoa and chocolate liqueur or finely ground coffee powder and Kahlua instead of cinnamon and Amaretto.

NUMBER OF SERVINGS: 12

lemon dessert

Bella Rolnick and Sherryn Roth *Bella is really the one who created the recipe. Sherryn's family loves it. We both wanted to include it! It is fast, easy and delicious. Serve it with love to your favourite people.*

1 large package lemon pudding

1 box graham crackers

1 small container (500 ml) of Nutriwhip—not the Lite

chocolate sprinkles or 2 square dark chocolate bars, curly grated

Prepare the lemon pudding according to package directions. Line the bottom of a baking dish with graham crackers—do not crush into crumbs, leave whole and break to fit the contour of the baking dish. Pour lemon pudding over the graham crackers before it cools and sets. Spread evenly. Add another layer of graham crackers over the lemon pudding. Allow to cool.

Whip the Nutriwhip until it forms peaks and spoon over the graham crackers. Cover and allow to cool in the refrigerator until serving. Garnish with the chocolate shavings or sprinkles just before serving. Cut into squares to serve.

NUMBER OF SERVINGS: 10–12

sweets

grandma rose's famous chocolate mousse cake

Lissie Sanders *Growing up, this was our favourite dessert made by our Grandmother Rose Strauss. She came from Poland before the war and settled with her family at 114 Montrose Avenue. She then met her future husband, Jack Strauss, and moved to the thriving metropolis of Kitchener, (then called Berlin) Ontario. She owned a restaurant there and was known as Ma Strauss to all that came there to eat. This is a family heirloom.*

2 packages kosher mini marshmallows

1 cup strong black coffee

1 pint whipping cream

2 packages round chocolate wafer cookies

2 ounces semi sweet chocolate

Melt marshmallows in a double boiler and add coffee. Mix until smooth. Take off heat and let cool. Whip the cream until quite stiff and then carefully fold it into the marshmallow mixture. Crush one package of the chocolate wafers coarsely with a rolling pin. Add crushed wafers into whipped cream and marshmallow mixture.

Line a Springform pan along the sides and bottom with remaining wafers. Pour marshmallow, whipped cream and wafer mixture into pan, being careful that the side cookies don't fall over. Grate the semisweet chocolate on the top of the cake. Put into the freezer until frozen. Remove from Springform a few minutes before serving and place on serving dish. To serve, slice as you would a cake.

NUMBER OF SERVINGS: 10

frozen lemon meringue passover torte

Adell Shneer *I adapted this torte from a recipe I found online from the Vancouver Sun when I was looking for a Passover Frozen Lemon Meringue Torte (like the one the kosher caterer Peter Graben used to make in Toronto). Although it is not originally a Passover dessert, I was able to change it to make a delicious Passover dessert. It also is dairy, so I have made recommendations for a non-dairy Passover version. It was a big hit as the grand finale for our Passover Seder.*

Meringues:

1¼ cups sugar, divided

2 tablespoons potato starch

2 tablespoons vanilla sugar or scraped seeds from ½ vanilla bean

1 tablespoon lemon zest

6 egg whites

1 teaspoon lemon juice

½ cup ground almonds

Curd:

1½ cups sugar

⅓ cup butter or pareve margarine

1 cup lemon juice (fresh)

2 tablespoons grated lemon rind

6 egg yolks

2 eggs

1½ cups whipping cream or non-dairy topping

Meringues: Trace 4 (8") circles on parchment paper and place on baking sheet. Mix ¾ cup sugar, potato starch, vanilla sugar and lemon zest; set aside. Beat egg whites and lemon juice to soft peaks; beat in remaining ¾ cup sugar, 2 tablespoons at a time, until stiff peaks form. Fold in reserved lemon-sugar mixture and ground almonds. Spoon or pipe onto parchment circles, smooth tops. Bake at 300°F for 1 hour. Cool completely. Remove from parchment and reserve.

Curd: In saucepan over medium-high heat, stir together sugar, butter, lemon juice, and lemon rind. Simmer for one minute. In separate heat-proof bowl, whisk egg yolks and eggs. Slowly whisk in lemon mixture. Return to pan, reduce heat to medium and cook, stirring constantly until mixture is thick enough to coat the back of a spoon. Transfer to bowl. Cover with plastic wrap and refrigerate until chilled. Whip cream or non-dairy topping. Fold into lemon curd.

Assembly: Break least attractive meringue into shards, set aside. Fit one meringue into 9" springform pan. Pour one-third of the lemon mixture on top. Repeat layers twice. Sprinkle crumbled meringue over top. Freeze for at least 8 hours. (Make ahead: Cover with plastic wrap and freeze for up to 1 week.)

TIPS & ADVICE: To make it pareve, substitute pareve margarine for the butter, and non-dairy topping for the whipping cream. This is a great make-ahead as it is stored in the freezer. Pull it out about 20 minutes before serving. Return leftovers to the freezer (if there are any!). For a non-Passover dessert, substitute vanilla extract for vanilla sugar and cornstarch for potato starch.

NUMBER OF SERVINGS: 8–10

apricot brandy pound cake

Eileen Jadd *This unique recipe came from my maternal grandmother, Lillian Alvin. Twice a year, when she visited, she brought this with her. Sometimes we were lucky and she even shipped us the cake in between visits! I love making this recipe because it reminds me of her and our mutual love of baking. Despite its many ingredients, it's actually not too difficult to make, and is simply delicious.*

3 cups sugar

1 cup butter

6 eggs

1 cup sour cream

½ cup apricot brandy

1 teaspoon vanilla

1 teaspoon orange extract

½ teaspoon rum extract

½ teaspoon lemon extract

¼ teaspoon almond extract

3 cups flour

½ teaspoon salt

¼ teaspoon baking soda

Preheat oven to 325°F. Cream sugar and butter. Add eggs (one at a time), beating thoroughly. Combine the next seven ingredients in a separate bowl. In a third bowl, sift together flour, salt and baking soda. Add flour and sour cream mixture to the sugar mixture, alternating a little at a time from each bowl. Mix well until blended. Pour into greased and floured large tube cake pan. Bake for about 1½ hours, no peeking. Test with a toothpick.

TIPS & ADVICE: This pound cake is equally delicious pareve and can be made using margarine and non-dairy sour cream like tofutti. It also freezes well in large portions or in slices.

NUMBER OF SERVINGS: 10–12

did you know?
Healthy at Home cared for more than 1,200 isolated seniors in their own homes last year

auntie goldie's apple cake

Ruth Garbe *I tasted this cake at a Shabbat lunch at a friend's home. Her guest, Pearl Greenspan, made it and it was just so yummy that I had to have the recipe. This recipe came from Pearl's Aunt, Goldie Howard z"l. It's really delicious, simple to prepare and has become a real favourite in our home.*

Dough:

2 cups flour

½ cup sugar

½ teaspoon baking powder

½ teaspoon salt

1 cup butter or margarine or
½ margarine and ½ Crisco

2 beaten egg yolks

Filling:

8 medium apples, peeled, cored
and sliced

¾ cup sugar

¼ cup flour

1 teaspoon cinnamon

Preheat oven to 350°F. In food processor, combine dry dough ingredients, butter and egg yolks until crumbly. Divide mixture in half. Press half into the bottom of a sprayed 8 x 8" pan. Collect the other half of the dough into plastic wrap.

Combine filling ingredients. Arrange over bottom of crust. Crumble remaining dough over the apples using a grater. Bake for 40–60 minutes. Do not cover as topping will get soggy.

TIPS & ADVICE: This cake can be made in a 9 x 13" pan. The pieces will be more like apple bars than a cake. I grate the apples in the food processor instead of slicing them. I sprinkle some cinnamon sugar on top of the cake before baking.

NUMBER OF SERVINGS: 9 generous pieces

best banana loaf

Helene Korn *A delicious way to satisfy so many palates, this banana loaf recipe is very versatile. Each one of my boys elevates this recipe in his own way. My eldest prefers a double bake: a thick slice of loaf dipped into a French toast batter, fried and topped with sliced bananas and icing sugar. My youngest prefers the bread thinly sliced, toasted and topped with a fruit preserve and my middle son, as a dessert, spread with a vanilla glaze. I like mine with a blanket of vanilla ice cream. This is a great go-to that takes moments to prepare. In a bake off, my best timing . . . 6 minutes and 36 seconds!*

¾ cup vanilla yogourt

1 teaspoon baking soda

2 large eggs, room temperature

1½ cups white sugar

½ cup unsalted butter, room temperature

1 teaspoon pure vanilla extract

2 bananas, very ripe, sliced

1 tablespoon liqueur (Cointreau adds a lovely orange flavour, or Kahlua, a touch of coffee.)

2 cups all-purpose flour

1 teaspoon baking powder

Preheat oven to 375°F. In a small bowl, place the yogourt and mix in the baking soda. Set aside. It will double in volume. In a processor or mixing bowl, add together the eggs, sugar, butter and vanilla. Mix well. Scrape down bowl. While machine is running, add the bananas. Blend well. Add the yogourt mixture and liqueur. Quickly blend and then add the remaining dry ingredients. Blend using three quick on/off pulses, just until the flour disappears. Do not overmix.

Pour the mixture into a parchment lined loaf pan. Reduce the oven temperature to 350°F before putting into oven. Bake for 50–55 minutes, testing for doneness with a toothpick. Let cool until you are able to remove the loaf from the pan. Cool further and enjoy!

TIPS & ADVICE: Ripe frozen bananas are great as they will thicken the mixture and spread easily. Amazing with vanilla ice cream!

YIELD: 1 loaf

cake of three milks (tres leches)

Marlene Jaegerman *This is a Venezuelan cake. It is sooo sweet, and delicious.*

½ cup unsalted margarine

4 eggs, separated

1 cup sugar

1½ cups flour

1 teaspoon baking powder

1 can evaporated milk

1 can sweetened condensed milk

1 can regular milk (use condensed milk for measure)

1 teaspoon vanilla

Meringue:

2½ cups sugar

1 cup water

3 egg whites

cinnamon

Preheat oven to 350°F. Melt margarine very slowly at low heat (leave aside once melted). Beat the egg whites at high speed until stiff, lower the speed and add the egg yolks, one by one, followed slowly by the sugar, the melted margarine, and finally, the flour mixed with the baking powder.

Butter and flour a 9 x 13" rectangular pyrex. Pour in the mixture and bake 35–45 minutes (or until a cake tester comes out clean). Mix all 3 milks together along with the vanilla and ensure they are very well blended. Once cake is ready and at room temperature, pour the milk mixture very slowly until ALL of it is absorbed by the cake (you may need to poke with a knife in different places to help the liquid in).

Meringue: Boil sugar and water until the mixture thickens into a light syrup. Beat the three egg whites until stiff and add the syrup (water and sugar from above) very slowly on medium speed until meringue forms. Spread this meringue on top of the cake and place in the fridge until it is cold. Once cold, broil in the oven quickly until a bit brown on top. Return to the fridge again until it is time to serve. Decorate with cinnamon on top.

NUMBER OF SERVINGS: 12

sweets

carrot cake (pareve)

Rebecca Simpson *This is a great pareve cake—moist and sweet. It freezes really well. I also make it into muffins (with whole wheat flour) for my kids' lunches and it is delicious and somewhat healthy!*

2 cups sugar

1 cup canola oil or vegetable oil

4 eggs, beaten

3 cups carrots, grated

2 cups flour (all-purpose or whole wheat)

1 teaspoon salt

1 teaspoon baking soda

1 teaspoon baking powder

2 teaspoons cinnamon

Preheat oven to 350°F. In mixing bowl, blend sugar, oil, and eggs. Add carrots. Mix dry ingredients together in another bowl and add to wet ingredients. Cooking time varies. If using a bundt pan, bake for 48 minutes. If using a 9 x 13" pan, bake for 30– 40 minutes.

TIPS & ADVICE: It is a very moist, delicious cake. If you like nuts or coconut, you can throw that in too. It can be served plain or with a cream cheese icing (dairy) or a non-dairy vanilla icing for a pareve cake.

NUMBER OF SERVINGS: 12

madeleine's fruit cake

Lauren Fleischmann *This is a recipe handed down to me by my mother-in-law, Madeleine Fleischmann, and is forever associated with her, thus a favourite. It is so easy to make and so yummy.*

3 eggs

1 cup sugar

1 teaspoon vanilla

1 teaspoon oil

3 tablespoons orange juice

zest of 1 orange

1½ cups flour

2 teaspoons baking powder

2 cups any fruit

Preheat oven to 320°F. Beat eggs, sugar, and vanilla until fluffy. Beat in oil then add orange juice and zest. Add dry ingredients and beat until smooth. Put into a parchment lined 9 x 13" baking pan and scatter fruit on top. Bake for 35–45 minutes.

TIPS & ADVICE: I like it best with fresh strawberries or sour cherries from a jar. Apricots work well, too. However, you could add any fruit.

NUMBER OF SERVINGS: 10–12

sweets

chiffon cake

Andrea Cohen *This recipe was my mom's signature cake recipe and we all love it. My mom used to make this cake for everyone's birthday and we always broke the fast with it. My daughters, my sister-in-law, niece and I all make this cake now and whenever we eat it, we call it "Granny's Cake" and we remember my mom. It is very easy to make, it freezes well and is delicious.*

2¼ cups flour

1½ cups sugar

1 teaspoon salt

6 egg yolks

¾ cup cold water

½ cup oil

8 egg whites

½ teaspoon cream of tartar

3 teaspoons baking powder

icing sugar for garnish

Preheat oven to 350°F. Sift the flour, sugar and salt together. Make a well in the centre of the dry ingredients and add the egg yolks, water and oil. Beat for 5–7 minutes. Meanwhile, beat the egg whites until frothy, add the cream of tartar and continue to beat until *very* stiff. Fold the baking powder into the egg yolk mixture and then gently fold this mixture over the well-beaten egg whites, keeping as much air in the mixture as possible.

Pour into an ungreased chiffon pan and bake at 350°F for one hour. Invert over the neck of a bottle and allow to hang until thoroughly cooled. Remove from tin by sliding a metal spatula or a long thin knife between the cake and the tin. Dust icing sugar over the top of the cake.

NUMBER OF SERVINGS: 16

chocolate and vanilla swirl cheesecake

Aviva Gottlieb *My dad, Lou Winer, made this recipe any time we had a large family gathering. It was a favourite of all the kids, grandkids and even the in-laws. The big question before Yom Kippur was, "Is Zaidy Lou making his cheesecake for breaking the fast"? It is so nice that a little bit of Zaidy Lou lives on through this recipe.*

Filling:

3 ounces semi sweet chocolate

3 pounds cream cheese

1 cup sour cream

2 cups sugar

1 tablespoon vanilla

4 eggs

Crust:

14 ounces graham cracker crumbs

2¼ sticks butter, softened

¼ stick butter for coating pan

Filling: Preheat oven to 300°F. Melt chocolate in a large bowl over hot water, remove from heat and reserve. Mix cream cheese and sour cream together, scraping down and remixing several times until smooth. Add sugar and vanilla and blend well. Whisk eggs lightly and add to cream cheese mixture. Mix and scrape down a few more times. If batter is pourable, go to next step. If not, add more sour cream to mixture. Pour ⅓ of batter into melted chocolate and mix well. Reserve remaining batter.

Crust: Combine graham cracker crumbs and soft butter, mixing well. Coat the inside of a 10" springform pan with butter. Press crust mixture against the inside of the mould, starting at the sides, then covering the bottom.

Assemble and bake: Now, layer the batter: Pour ½ plain batter into the mould, then a layer using most of the chocolate, then another layer of the plain filling. In a circular pattern, pour remaining chocolate mixture into mould. With a fork, swirl the plain and chocolate mixtures into each other, forming a nice pattern. Bake at 300°F (325°F if your oven is low) for 1½ hours until it is ¾ set. The center will still shake like jello and there will be no browning. Remove cake from oven to cool. Refrigerate overnight, and cake will be ready to serve.

TIPS & ADVICE: Place a container of water in the oven when baking so cheesecake does not dry out.

YIELD: 1 full size cheesecake

european jewish cheesecake

Carole and Michael Ogus *(from* Carole's *Cheesecake Company Ltd.) We hope the community will enjoy this old time recipe from our families and from the current generation.*

Crust:

1⅓ cups graham cracker crumbs

4 tablespoons sugar

6 tablespoons butter, melted

Cheesecake:

1 pound (454 g) quark or cottage cheese. Use cream cheese for a more North American taste.

½ cup sour cream

½ cup sugar

2 eggs

1 teaspoon vanilla extract

Topping:

1⅓ cups sour cream

10 teaspoons sugar

½ teaspoon vanilla extract

Grease a 9 x 9 x 2" aluminum pan with butter and line with waxed paper. Combine crust ingredients and press into aluminum pan. In a mixer, place the cheese with the sour cream and beat for 10 minutes on high. Add the sugar and beat for 5 minutes. Add the eggs and vanilla and blend on slow for 5 minutes. Pour batter into pan. Bake in a preheated oven at 300°F for 1 hour. Blend the topping ingredients and pour over the hot cake. Return to the oven for 10 minutes. Let cool and refrigerate overnight. Cut into rectangular portions and serve with a side of fruit preserve.

NUMBER OF SERVINGS: 10

sweets

chocolate peanut butter banana cake

Susan Lindzon *I found this recipe in a magazine many years ago and adapted it to become my own. It is by far my family's favourite Shabbat and birthday dessert. Unfortunately, it can't be served when our extended family comes over because of gluten, peanut and banana allergies. This makes it an exclusive Lindzon family favourite that is loved by our children and all of their friends. This cake can all be put together in one bowl, or, if cut in half, mixed right in the pan used for baking. It keeps really moist and fresh for a number of days and it also freezes very well. If we are having just a few people over and we don't want the temptation of finishing it off ourselves over the weekend, I will often still make the full recipe but divide the batter between two smaller bundt pans and freeze one for another time.*

⅔ cup vegetable oil

4 squares semi sweet chocolate

2½ cups flour

2 cups sugar

1½ cups water or unsweetened almond milk

1 cup ripe bananas, mashed

2 eggs, lightly beaten

2 teaspoons vanilla extract

1 teaspoon baking soda

½ teaspoon salt

Glaze:

⅓ cup smooth peanut butter

2 squares semi sweet chocolate

⅓ cup toasted peanuts, coarsely chopped

Preheat oven to 350°F. Place oil and chocolate in microwave safe dish. Cover with wax paper and heat carefully, checking and stirring until the chocolate is just melted. Stir well to combine. Let cool slightly. Pour into mixing bowl. Add the next eight ingredients and blend with hand mixer or fork for approximately 2 minutes, until smooth and creamy. Pour into large bundt pan which has been sprayed with cooking spray. Bake for 40–50 minutes or until cake tester comes out clean. Let cool and invert onto a cake plate.

Glaze: Carefully melt peanut butter and chocolate in microwave until melted together. Stir well. Drizzle over cake and sprinkle with peanuts. Let sit until icing has cooled on the cake—it may have to go into the fridge for a few minutes for this to happen.

TIPS & ADVICE: You can replace the water or almond milk with regular milk if it doesn't need to be dairy free. You can make this very quickly and more like a brownie by cutting the recipe in half and mixing all ingredients in the square baking pan you will use to bake it. Spread the same amount (not half) of the icing on top and cut into squares when cool.

NUMBER OF SERVINGS: 12–18

sweets

chocolate snacking cake

Cherie Lubelski *This is a great cake for kids that have allergies to eggs or milk. It never fails me and has come in handy for many a bake sale!*

1½ cups flour

1 cup sugar

3 tablespoons cocoa

1 teaspoon baking powder

1 teaspoon baking soda

½ teaspoon salt

1 cup warm water

⅓ cup coconut oil, melted (or vegetable oil)

1 tablespoon white vinegar

1 teaspoon vanilla extract

½ cup chopped nuts, optional

Preheat oven to 350°F. In a mixing bowl, combine flour, sugar, cocoa, baking powder, baking soda, and salt. Mix thoroughly. Add warm water, oil, vinegar and vanilla. Whisk or beat thoroughly. Add nuts if using. Pour into lightly greased 8" square cake pan. Bake in preheated oven for 25–30 minutes. A toothpick should come out clean and cake should bounce back when lightly touched.

NUMBER OF SERVINGS: 10

coffee cake

Ilsa Kamen *I love making this cake as much as everyone else loves eating it. It is quick and easy. When I have the topping in the freezer already, I can whip this cake up in 10 minutes.*

4 tablespoons flour

4 tablespoons brown sugar

2 tablespoons Crisco shortening

2 cups flour

1 cup sugar

¼ pound Crisco shortening

2 teaspoons baking powder

2 eggs

orange juice

Preheat oven to 350°F. Combine flour, brown sugar and 2 tablespoons Crisco to make topping, using measurements as a guide but adjusting quantity as needed. Mix together flour, sugar, ¼ pound Crisco and baking powder. In measuring cup, break eggs and add orange juice to equal 1½ cups. Add to mixture and stir to combine. Spray tube pan. Pour mixture in. Sprinkle topping over batter. Bake 50–60 minutes, testing with a toothpick for readiness.

TIPS & ADVICE: I always have topping on hand.

NUMBER OF SERVINGS: 12–18

sweets

cinnamon coffee cake

Judy Steiner *I volunteered this cake for a Super Bowl party my husband was attending many years ago. Every year since, I have had a special request to make it. All the guys look for this cake first when they start eating . . . so much so that this year, one of the guys had a hunk of cake along with his chicken wings on the same plate.*

Crumb topping:

1⅔ cups sugar

8 teaspoons cinnamon

1 tablespoon oil

1½ teaspoons vanilla

Cake:

2 cups sugar

1 cup oil

4 eggs

1 teaspoon vanilla extract

3 cups all-purpose flour

3 teaspoons baking powder

1 teaspoon salt

1½ cups orange juice

1 cup chocolate chips

Preheat oven to 350°F. In a small bowl, make the crumb mixture by mixing the sugar, cinnamon, oil and vanilla. Set aside. In another bowl, make the cake batter by creaming together the remaining sugar, oil, eggs and vanilla. In a third bowl, combine flour, baking powder and salt and stir to blend. Add the dry ingredients to the wet ingredients, alternating with the orange juice until well mixed. The batter will be liquid.

Line a 9 x 13" baking pan with parchment paper. Pour half the batter into the pan and sprinkle evenly with the chocolate chips and half the crumb mixture. Pour the remaining batter and top with the remaining crumb mixture. Bake for 55–60 minutes until a tester comes out clean. Time varies depending on your oven.

NUMBER OF SERVINGS: 12

grandma morton's banana cake with butterscotch frosting

Julie Morton *This is a cake first baked by, and then handed down from, my paternal grandmother—Beck Morton, from Winnipeg. It is a taste of love and memory that has accompanied almost every major life event in my family.*

Cake:

2 egg whites

1½ cups white sugar

¾ cup butter

2 cups mashed bananas

2¼ teaspoons baking soda

2¼ cups cake and pastry flour

6 tablespoons milk

1½ teaspoons baking powder

1½ teaspoons vanilla

Frosting:

3 cups brown sugar

14 tablespoons butter

⅔ cup plus 2 tablespoons milk

3 cups sifted icing sugar

vanilla extract to taste

Cake: Preheat oven to 350°F. Beat egg whites in a bowl until soft peaks form. Beat butter and sugar together in a mixing bowl until smooth. In another bowl, mix together bananas and baking soda. Add beaten egg whites to bananas. Add rest of ingredients except bananas to butter/sugar mixture. Beat well. Add banana mixture and stir gently to combine. Bake 15–20 minutes in 2 lightly greased round cake pans.

Frosting: Combine brown sugar and butter in a saucepan. Bring to boil over low heat. Stir constantly. Add milk and bring to boil for 3 minutes. Set aside to cool until lukewarm. Add sifted icing sugar, one cup at a time, and beat until thin enough to spread. (Don't overbeat). Add a little vanilla. Frost cake.

TIPS & ADVICE: This cake is even better on day two or three (if there is any left). With a cold glass of milk—there is nothing more delicious!

YIELD: 1 double layer round cake

sweets

holder's coconut bread

Ruby Kreindler *My Eastern European in-laws met and married in Barbados, where they lived for many years. My husband and his siblings were born on this beautiful, tropical island. One by one, the family gradually moved to Montreal and then Toronto. In Barbados, Holder was my in-laws' cook/housekeeper, and her Coconut Bread (cake) was a family favourite. I have added some ingredients, and also adapted her recipe with help from the website, "just bajan.com". This recipe is not difficult to prepare, but the appearance of the dough before it is baked may make the baker wonder if he/she has done something wrong because it looks unusual. Don't worry. It will turn out fine! This coconut cake reminds my family of good times spent visiting my in-laws in Barbados. They lived on the Atlantic coast where there was a constantly-blowing, salt-laden warm breeze. Coconut bread makes us smile and begin to tell stories of Barbados to one another.*

1¼ cups sugar

¾ cup applesauce

¾ cup canola oil

2 eggs

1¼ teaspoons cinnamon

½ teaspoon ground nutmeg

2 teaspoons coconut extract

1 teaspoon vanilla extract

4 cups coconut, finely grated

¾ cup raisins, golden

7¼ cups all-purpose flour

1½ teaspoons baking powder

1 cup water, approximately

Preheat oven to 350°F. In mixing bowl, beat together sugar, applesauce and oil. Add eggs and beat well. Then mix in cinnamon, nutmeg, vanilla, and coconut extract. Next, mix in the coconut and raisins. Pour all these ingredients in a very large bowl. Add the flour. Sift the baking powder over the flour. Add water, adding as much liquid as is necessary for dough to stick together. Knead a little. Dough will be stiff. Turn batter into 2 well-greased loaf pans. Bake at 350°F about 45 minutes until light, golden brown.

TIPS & ADVICE: This freezes well. I find that freezing in ziploc bags with the air pushed out does the job best. To make this recipe healthier, I cut out the butter, which was in the original recipe and substituted canola oil plus applesauce (Ratio is 1:1).

YIELD: 2 loaves

honey cake (healthy)

Marla Hertzman *Honey cake is traditionally made with lots of oil, eggs, white flour, sugar and of course, honey. I wanted to make a healthy honey cake for a sweet new year— without using too much oil and refined sugars so for Rosh Hashanah, I tested this cake on my family. Both Gordy and Zach said it was good but I could tell by how quickly they gulped a glass of water that it must have been a little dry. Yale told me to make it again and try adding zucchini. Guess what...?! This cake is now perfectly moist. The spelt flour makes the cake mildly sweet and gives it a slight nutty flavour that adds real character. The additions of applesauce and zucchini make it light and moist. Happy New Year.*

2½ cups spelt flour

1 tablespoon baking powder

2 teaspoons baking soda

1 teaspoon cinnamon

¼ teaspoon ground ginger or fresh

¼ teaspoon ground cloves or allspice

1 cup honey

1 cup applesauce

1 medium zucchini, shredded

½ cup safflower or grapeseed oil

2 teaspoons vanilla extract

¼ cup sliced almonds, optional

Preheat oven to 325°F. Combine the first 6 dry ingredients in a mixing bowl. Make a well in the center of the dry ingredients and pour in the wet ingredients. Stir together until the wet and dry ingredients are thoroughly combined.

Cut two pieces of baking parchment to fit the bottoms of two 8" loaf pans. Lightly oil the pans. Divide the batter between the two loaf pans. Sprinkle the almonds over the tops of the loaves. Bake for 35–40 minutes, or until a knife inserted in the center of a loaf tests clean. Allow the cakes to cool completely. Remove the loaves from the pans. Cut each loaf into 10 slices to serve. If you want to make this cake vegan, substitute ½ cup of agave and ½ cup of maple syrup for the honey.

TIPS & ADVICE: I like to make this honey cake at least a day or two before serving as the taste gets better. If not using, store in the fridge.

YIELD: 20 slices

sweets

honey cake

Robin Farb-Eckler *This honey cake is adapted from Lottman's Bakery, a landmark on Baldwin Street in Kensington Market, in Toronto's Jewish neighbourhood. I got this recipe from our family friends, Pearl (Lottman) Godfrey and her sister, Katie, who got this recipe from their parents, Emma and Sam Lottman, the owners of Lottman's. As landmarks disappear, we keep these recipes and the memories that go with them.*

1¾ cups honey

1 cup strong coffee

3 tablespoons cognac

4 tablespoons vegetable oil

1¼ cups dark brown sugar

4 eggs

3½ cups all-purpose flour

3 teaspoons baking powder

1 teaspoon baking soda

1 teaspoon cinnamon

½ teaspoon ginger

¼ teaspoon nutmeg

¼ teaspoon cloves

zest of 1 lemon

handful sliced almonds for garnish

Preheat oven to 325°F. Mix together honey and coffee, then bring to a boil. Let cool, then add cognac. Beat oil, eggs and sugar together; set aside. Sift dry ingredients together, in a separate bowl. Fold the zest into the egg mixture, then fold in ⅓ of the dry mix. When flour is mixed in, add about half the coffee/honey mixture and blend well, repeat with the flour, the liquid, and lastly the remaining flour. Divide into 2 prepared loaf pans and top with the sliced almonds. Bake for 70–75 minutes.

NUMBER OF SERVINGS: 10–15

sweets

hot water chocolate cake

Julie Levin *This was a recipe found by my mother, Myrna Levin, in 1938 or 1939, either from a newspaper article or a magazine. My mom first made this cake when her sister traveled from Saskatoon, Saskatchewan, through Winnipeg on her honeymoon trip. The cake has become a family staple, enjoyed by several generations and extended family members for many occasions. When we were children, my mother made this for our birthday parties. As there were 5 of us, we ate it frequently! When my sons were small, I baked the cake with them a week ahead, froze the layers and then they were able to ice and decorate the cake easily for their birthday parties. My sister and I made 3 of these cakes, double recipe for each, for our niece's wedding. A family favourite because it is easy to do, this cake has lovely rich chocolate flavour. My sister's lament was that she could not have it for her birthday, which often coincided with Pesach.*

Cake:

⅔ cup butter, room temperature

2 cups sugar

2 eggs, room temperature

2 teaspoons vanilla

4 ounces (4 squares) unsweetened chocolate, melted

2⅔ cups cake flour

2 teaspoons baking powder

2 teaspoons baking soda

½ teaspoon salt

2 cups boiling water

Icing:

2 squares unsweetened chocolate

1 tablespoon butter

1 cup icing sugar

¼ cup milk

1 egg

1 teaspoon vanilla

Preheat oven to 350°F and grease either two 9" round pans or one 9 x 13" pan. In the large bowl of an electric mixer, cream butter with sugar and beat until mixture is light and fluffy. Add eggs and vanilla and then add melted chocolate. Sift dry ingredients 3 times into a separate bowl.

Add dry ingredients alternately with the water: ⅓ of flour mix, ½ water, ⅓ flour, remaining water, last ⅓ of flour, starting and ending with dry and mixing on low speed until all the flour is absorbed. Pour into prepared pan(s). Bake 20-25 minutes for round pans or 30-40 minutes for a rectangular pan.

Icing: Melt chocolate and butter together in double boiler or very gently on very low heat. Place a small mixing bowl with the beaters, sugar, milk, egg, and vanilla in the fridge to cool. Once chocolate is ready, take small bowl out of the fridge. Place it into a larger mixing bowl filled with ice so that the ice surrounds the smaller bowl. Very slowly, add the chocolate and butter mixture and beat until fluffy, forming soft peaks. Use to ice Hot Water Chocolate Cake.

TIPS & ADVICE: Don't overbeat icing or it will become liquid. If that happens, remove some of the icing, reheat and add again. Watch very carefully as this is a soft rather than stiff icing. Wait until the cake has cooled well before icing.

NUMBER OF SERVINGS: 10–12

sweets

lemon pudding cake with strawberry sauce

Lois Friedman Fine *I love this recipe because it is light, refreshing and very well received.*

Cake:

¾ cup sugar, divided

¼ cup flour

¼ teaspoon salt

3 large eggs, separated

1 cup milk

5 tablespoons fresh lemon juice

zest of 1 large lemon, finely grated

Strawberry sauce:

1 pint strawberries

½ cup sugar

1 teaspoon lemon juice

Cake: Preheat oven to 350°F. Place ½ cup of sugar, flour and salt in a bowl and mix well. In another bowl, beat egg yolks lightly and add milk, lemon juice, and zest. Add to dry ingredients and whisk until well blended. Beat egg whites in a large bowl with electric mixer until they hold soft peaks. Gradually add remaining ¼ cup sugar, beating until whites hold stiff, glossy peaks. Whisk ¼ of whites into batter to lighten it, then fold in remaining whites, gently but thoroughly.

Pour into lightly greased 1½ quart gratin or other shallow baking dish, place in a hot water bath and bake for 40–45 minutes.

Sauce: Hull and slice berries (if berries are large, cut slices in half). Place in saucepan with heavy bottom along with sugar and lemon juice. Cook over medium heat until it comes to a boil. Reduce heat and simmer for three minutes. Pour into bowl and refrigerate. Spoon over cake to serve.

NUMBER OF SERVINGS: 6

did you know?
UJA Federation's Global Seder to Fight Hunger ensured that 1,200 of the most disadvantaged members of our community celebrated Passover in dignity.

shirley's mystery mocha cake

Lou Dale *My mother, Shirley Albright, has been making this terrific cake forever. This is the only cake that my husband, Shelly Dale, requests for his birthday!*

1 package any flavour cake mix

½ cup brown sugar

½ cup white sugar

5 tablespoons cocoa

1¼ cups strong cold coffee

Preheat oven to 350°F. Prepare the cake mix following the instructions on the box. Pour the batter into a bundt pan. Mix the sugars and cocoa and sprinkle over the cake batter. Pour the cold coffee over the batter. It will look very liquidy, but do not worry. Bake at 350°F for 50 minutes. Do not test the cake for readiness.

Here is the tricky part . . . once the cake comes out of the oven, you must invert the pan immediately onto your serving plate. The hot mixture of sugars, cocoa and coffee will become the icing on the cake.

TIPS & ADVICE: It is difficult to hold the hot pan with your oven mitts and then to flip the pan. You must be very quick when you flip the pan, otherwise the icing will end up on the counter.

NUMBER OF SERVINGS: 10–15

orange pareve cake

Maureen Zieper *This recipe was given to me by my late mother-in-law, Dolly Zieper, when I married 53 years ago. I've been making it ever since. My whole family enjoys this cake and we always talk about Granny Dolly when I serve it. My mother-in-law was one of 8 brothers and sisters, and each and every one of those aunts made the same recipe. This is such an easy cake to make for a special dessert. I usually make extra sauce to put on or at the side of each slice, as the sauce only penetrates about halfway down the cake and it looks great with the grated rind on the top. It freezes nicely as well.*

Cake:

1 cup sugar

2 eggs

½ cup orange juice

⅓ cup plus 2 tablespoons canola oil

2 cups flour

2 rounded teaspoons baking powder

Sauce:

1 cup orange juice

½ cup sugar

rind of 1 large orange, grated coarsely

Cake: Preheat the oven to 350°F. Cream the sugar and eggs well with electric beaters. Slowly add orange juice and oil. Sift flour and baking powder and fold into wet ingredients. Pour into well-greased bundt pan and bake for 45 minutes in the middle rack of the oven.

Sauce: In a small saucepan, boil the orange juice and sugar together. Add the grated rind of the orange and cook for half a minute. Remove from heat.

Turn out cake onto wire rack. Don't let it cool down. With a dessert spoon, slowly pour the hot sauce all over the cake so that it gets absorbed. Using a fork, prick the top of the cake and the sides so that the juice gets well absorbed. I put a glass plate under the wire rack so that the juice that runs off the cake can be used again to pour over. You can make a little extra sauce to serve on the side when you slice the cake.

NUMBER OF SERVINGS: 8–10

plum cake with streusel (also known as Flomen Kuchen)

Julia Koschitzky *I adapted this wonderful recipe from my friend, Helene Green. This is a recipe that her mom used to make. Helene's 7 year old son submitted it to The Associated Hebrew School Kids' Kosher Cookbook in 1979. It is a seasonal cake, which I make for my family for Rosh Hashanah when the plums are purple and ripe. It is a delicious dessert (good even for breakfast) and freezes well. When I make it, I am reminded of my friend, Helene.*

Streusel:

1 cup flour

½ cup margarine or butter

½ cup brown sugar

½ cup sugar

Cake:

2 eggs

1 cup sugar

1 cup margarine or butter, melted

1 tablespoon orange juice or milk

1 teaspoon lemon juice

1 teaspoon vanilla

2 cups flour, sifted

2 teaspoons baking powder

4–5 cups purple prune plums, pitted and sliced in half

2 teaspoons cinnamon

Mix together the ingredients for the streusel topping until crumbly and set aside. For the cake batter, beat the eggs and sugar until light and lemony colour. Add butter (or margarine), orange juice, lemon juice, vanilla, flour and baking powder. Mix well.

Spread batter in greased 9 x 13" pan. Arrange plums on top of batter, sprinkle cinnamon, then add the prepared streusel topping. Bake for 1 hour at 350°F, unless you are using a pyrex dish, in which case, reduce the temperature to 325°F .

TIPS & ADVICE: Other fruit such as apples or peaches can be used instead of the prune plums, but the plums really make the best cake.

YIELD: 1 cake (9 x 13" cake pan)

sweets

plum torte

Helen Silverstein *This was my grandmother, Celia Gitter's recipe and now no Silverstein/ Gitter/Rubin simcha is complete without this plum torte. We all buy many pounds of prune plums when in season at the end of the summer, wash, half, pit and freeze in 4 cup quantities so we can make this torte year round. This recipe always looks beautiful with the fruit showing through the top crust. All the women in my family make this recipe but it looks different depending on how the dough was mixed. Always a hit!*

2 cups flour

¾ cup sugar

¼ pound butter, room temperature

1 teaspoon baking powder

2 eggs, lightly beaten

1 teaspoon vanilla

4 cups prune plums, halved and pitted

¾ cup sugar

2 tablespoons minute tapioca

Preheat oven to 400°F. Mix the first 4 ingredients by cutting butter into dry ingredients or crumbling between fingers. Add eggs and vanilla. Pat into bottom and sides of a 9" springform pan, saving some flour mixture to put on top. Mix approximately 4 cups of prune plums with sugar and tapioca. Fill the springform pan with the fruit mixture and then crumble remaining crust on top. Bake for 15 minutes at 400°F and then lower the temperature to 375°F for one hour.

TIPS & ADVICE: You can substitute any fresh fruit filling you would use for a 9" pie. It is always nice to use whatever fruit is in season. You can sift icing sugar on top for a lacy effect. Freezes well.

NUMBER OF SERVINGS: 8–10

tubby's maple cream fudge

Ellen Cole *I learned to make this recipe in grade school and I have been making it with great success ever since. It is a family favourite. It is called maple fudge even though it has no maple flavouring—I'm not sure why!*

2 cups brown sugar, light or dark

2 tablespoons butter

⅔ cup whole milk

½ teaspoon vanilla

In a saucepan, mix the sugar, butter and milk on medium heat until the sugar dissolves. Keep stirring until the mixture forms a soft ball when dropped in cold water (238°F on a candy thermometer). Cool mixture down a bit and add the vanilla. Beat with a hand mixer until smooth. Pour into a greased 8 x 8" pyrex and cool. Cut into 1" inch squares.

NUMBER OF SERVINGS: 12 (1") pieces

sweets

pumpkin loaf

Dani Palter *This recipe came from a friend of my parents that they met at business school in Boston. We are still good friends today, almost 25 years later! We all love this recipe because it gets better and more moist every day. Often when we go on a long trip somewhere, we will bring one of these to nibble on when we need something sweet.*

2 cups canned pureed pumpkin

3 cups sugar

3⅓ cups all-purpose flour

4 eggs

1 cup vegetable oil

½ cup water

1 teaspoon baking soda

½ teaspoon baking powder

1 teaspoon cinnamon

1 teaspoon cloves

1 teaspoon nutmeg

Beat all ingredients in mixer or with hand-mixer or whisk. Grease and flour 2 loaf pans and bake 1¼ hours at 325°F. Check at 1 hour.

TIPS & ADVICE: Do NOT use pumpkin pie puree. Can substitute whole wheat flour for up to 2 cups of the all-purpose flour.

YIELD: 2 loaves

swiss almond bits

Andrea H. Cohen *Makes a wonderful hostess gift with recipe attached.*

1¼ cups almonds, coarsely chopped, divided

1 cup butter

1⅓ cups sugar

3 tablespoons water

1 tablespoon corn syrup

⅔ cup semi-sweet chocolate chip pieces

Toast almonds in a 350°F oven for approximately 8 minutes, watching carefully to make sure they don't burn; let cool. In a large saucepan, melt butter. Add sugar, water and corn syrup. Cook to hard crack stage (300°F on a candy thermometer). Quickly stir in 1 cup toasted almonds. Pour into lightly oiled or buttered 9 x 13" baking pan. Sprinkle chocolate pieces over hot mixture. Cover with kitchen towel for a few minutes until chocolate chips are melted. Spread chocolate evenly and then sprinkle with remaining nuts. Press lightly into chocolate. Cool in refrigerator for one hour. Break into irregular pieces.

NUMBER OF SERVINGS: about 24 pieces (depending on size)

sweets

rich chocolate cupcakes

Paula Barsky *I have adapted this rich, moist and delicious cupcake with its complementary icing from a recipe by Emily Luchetti, Desserts from America's Top Chefs Magazine 2007. I have served them at many parties in a mini format.*

Cake:

½ cup cake flour

½ cup all-purpose flour

⅓ cup unsweetened cocoa powder (prefer Ghirardelli)

½ teaspoon baking soda

¼ teaspoon kosher salt

1 large egg

½ cup dark brown sugar, firmly packed

½ cup sugar

½ cup buttermilk

½ cup brewed coffee

⅓ cup canola oil

Frosting:

2 ounces unsweetened chocolate, chopped

1 ounce bittersweet chocolate, chopped

4 tablespoons unsalted butter, softened, divided

1½ cups powdered sugar or more

large pinch kosher salt

⅓ cup milk

Preheat the oven to 350°F. Grease 12 regular muffin cups. Sift the cake and all-purpose flour, cocoa, baking soda, and salt into a bowl. In a large bowl, whisk egg and sugars. In a small bowl, mix the buttermilk, coffee, and oil. In three additions, alternately stir the wet and dry ingredients into the egg mixture. Spoon batter into the muffin cups. Bake until a skewer inserted in the centre of a cupcake comes out clean—approximately 15 minutes. Cool on a wire rack 15 minutes. Remove from pan. Cool completely.

Frosting: Melt the chocolates and 2 tablespoons of the butter in a double boiler over hot water. Stir until smooth. Sift the powdered sugar and salt into a bowl; add the milk. Stir in the melted chocolate mixture, mixing until combined. Add the remaining 2 tablespoons butter in four pieces, mixing in each piece before adding another, until smooth and spreadable. More powdered sugar may be required to ensure the consistency is thick enough to spread. Pipe or spread frosting on each cupcake.

TIPS & ADVICE: Since these are "melt in your mouth" cupcakes, you can also make "mini" cupcakes with a baking time of 10 minutes.

YIELD: 12 full-size cupcakes or 36 mini cupcakes

rock cakes

Ellen Moss *We have revised this Rock Cake recipe from Florence Greenberg's Cookery Book, London, 1947. My husband's mother used to make this recipe in England, whenever company came over on short notice. Now, we make it with some revisions and everyone always asks me for the recipe. It is so easy and fast to prepare if you need something in a hurry for dessert. It is delicious with butter, jam or just plain.*

1 cup self-rising flour

½ cup butter or margarine

½ cup sugar

½ cup currants

1 egg, beaten

1–2 tablespoons milk or orange juice as a pareve option, if needed

Preheat the convection oven to 375°F or regular oven to 425°F. Cut the butter into the flour. It will be crumbly. Add the sugar, currants, egg, and sufficient milk or orange juice to form a dry stiff mixture. Put in rough heaps on a greased baking sheet and bake 375°F (convection) oven for approx 12–15 minutes or until golden on top. (regular oven 425°F for approx 20 minutes)

TIPS & ADVICE: It stores well for a few days in a covered tin.

YIELD: 10–12 cakes

sari's banana bread

Julie Keshen *Sari, our family's helper when the kids were young, would make this on a regular basis and we all LOVED it! It was a household favourite. It would be devoured the same day it was made. I hope you enjoy it as much as we did, and still do.*

½ cup 2% milk

1 tablespoon white vinegar

6 bananas, ripened and mashed

1½ tablespoons baking soda

¼ teaspoon salt

4 eggs

½ cup oil (canola or vegetable)

2 cups sugar

2 cups all-purpose flour

Preheat oven to 275°F. First, add vinegar to milk to make sour milk. Mix the bananas, sour milk, baking soda and salt with wooden spoon or hand mixer until just blended. Mix in the eggs, oil, sugar, and flour. Pour into lightly sprayed 4 x 8" loaf pan. Bake for 2½ hours.

TIPS & ADVICE: You can cut back on the sugar but I suggest making the recipe once as is and then adjust accordingly.

YIELD: one loaf

sweets

shirley steinberg's delicious carrot cake

Ellen Levine *This is a recipe from my late Mom, Shirley Steinberg. I don't know where she got it from but it was everyone's favourite. When Michael Bregman was opening up Bregman's, he tried to see if it could work on a large scale to serve in his restaurant. Unfortunately, it did not translate well to a large scale. I'm pretty sure it's one of the reasons my husband married me—to get my Mom's carrot cake.*

Cake:

1 cup sugar

1 cup oil

3 eggs

1⅓ cups cake flour

1 teaspoon baking powder

1 teaspoon baking soda

1½ teaspoons cinnamon

½ teaspoon salt

2 cups carrots, grated

¾ cup walnuts, chopped

raisins (optional)

Icing:

1 (8 ounce) package cream cheese

¼ cup butter

1 tablespoon icing sugar

2 teaspoons vanilla

Preheat oven to 300°F. Mix sugar, oil, and eggs on low speed with an electric mixer. Sift dry ingredients together all at once and add to oil mixture. Add carrots and walnuts. Bake in greased tube pan for 45–60 minutes (depending upon oven). Let cake cool.

Mix cream cheese, butter, icing sugar and vanilla with an electric mixer until creamy.

Ice cooled cake. Enjoy!

NUMBER OF SERVINGS: 10

visit our website
www.JewishToronto.com/BathurstStreetKitchen

sour cream coffee cake

Susan Silverberg *This recipe was my grandmother's and was then handed to my mother, which is why it is so special to me. In turn, I will give it to my children.*

Cake:

butter (for greasing the pan)

2 cups sugar

1 cup butter

2 eggs

2 cups cake flour

1 teaspoon baking powder

½ teaspoon salt

1 cup sour cream

½ teaspoon vanilla

Topping:

8 pecan halves, chopped

2 tablespoons sugar

1 teaspoon cinnamon

Preheat oven to 350°F. Cream sugar and butter in large mixing bowl. Beat in the eggs. Sift together flour, baking powder, and salt. Gradually add the dry ingredients to creamed mixture. Fold in sour cream and vanilla. Mix together topping ingredients and sprinkle 2 tablespoons in bottom of a greased bundt pan. Cover with ⅓ of cake batter then alternate topping and batter until done. Bake for 45–60 minutes. Cool, then invert.

NUMBER OF SERVINGS: 10

best ever applesauce

Hinda Silber

10 Macintosh apples, peeled and sliced

1½ cups water

1 package 'Sweet and Low' or 'Splenda'

1 pint raspberries or strawberries

cinnamon

Place apples in a pot filled with water and add sweetener. Cook for around 15 minutes on medium to high heat. Cool. Put cooked apples into a food processor, add berries and cinnamon. Process until smooth. Add cinnamon to taste. Refrigerate.

TIPS & ADVICE: Can use a package of frozen berries as well once they are thawed.

NUMBER OF SERVINGS: 10

sweets

strawberry lemon cake

Mireille Roffe *This recipe was one of the many my mother, Hilda baked. I found this handwritten recipe while looking through some of her old cookbooks. The wonderful scent that emanates from this cake when it comes out of the oven brings back some sweet memories of my youth!*

1½ cups flour

¼ teaspoon salt

¼ cup plain yogourt (not low fat)

1 teaspoon baking soda

2 cups fresh strawberries, quartered

1 tablespoon flour

½ cup unsalted butter, room temperature

1 cup sugar

¼ cup maple syrup

2 eggs plus 1 egg white

1 teaspoon vanilla extract

grated zest of 1 whole lemon

1 tablespoon sugar

Preheat oven to 350°F. Grease and flour a 9"springform pan. Line the bottom of the pan with waxed paper. In a small bowl, mix flour and salt. In another bowl, mix yogourt and baking soda. In another bowl, combine strawberries with 1 tablespoon of flour. In a large bowl, whisk the butter with sugar and maple syrup for about 5 minutes until the mixture becomes light. Stir in eggs, vanilla, and lemon zest while beating.

At low speed, add the dry ingredients alternating with the yogourt mixture. Spread half of the batter in the prepared pan and cover with half the strawberries. Add the rest of the batter followed by the strawberries decoratively placed and pushed lightly onto the batter. Sprinkle with 1 tablespoon sugar. Bake for 50-60 minutes depending upon your oven. Place the cake on a wire rack to cool for approximately 15 minutes, then remove from pan to cool completely.

TIPS & ADVICE: This recipe can be prepared a day in advance. Yogourt can be replaced by 10% cream. If the strawberries are very sweet, the amount of sugar can be reduced to your liking. Powdered sugar can be sprinkled on the cake just before serving.

NUMBER OF SERVINGS: 8

apple dapple cake

Penny Offman *I have been making this cake for many years and it has become a favourite of my children, grandchildren and of their many friends who drop by.*

2 cups sugar

1½ cups corn oil

3 eggs

3 cups flour

1 teaspoon baking soda

1 teaspoon salt

1 teaspoon cinnamon

3 cups apples, peeled and diced

2 cups pecans, chopped

2 teaspoons vanilla extract

Glaze:

1 cup dark brown sugar

½ cup butter

½ cup heavy cream

Preheat the oven to 350°F. Combine sugar and oil and beat well. Add eggs one at a time. Sift dry ingredients and stir into egg mixture. Beat in apples, pecans and vanilla. Pour into a buttered springform tube pan and bake for 1 hour or until a toothpick inserted in the center comes out clean. Combine glaze ingredients and boil for 3 minutes. Reserving ⅓ cup, pour over the hot cake. Cool and remove from pan. Just before serving, pour remaining glaze over.

TIPS & ADVICE: For a nut free version, omit the nuts and add 1–2 more cups of apples. I prefer to use a softer apple such as Matsu, Spy or Jonah Gold.

NUMBER OF SERVINGS: 12–14

chocolate-covered matzah

Sheri Kagan *Best chocolate-covered matzah, hands down, and so easy to make.*

4 pieces egg matzah

1 cup butter or margarine

1 cup brown sugar

2 cups chocolate chips

½ cup ground almonds (optional)

Preheat oven to 350°F. Line a cookie sheet with foil and spray with non-stick spray. Lay matzah flat on the foil. Bring butter/ margarine and brown sugar to a boil in a saucepan (do not burn). Pour evenly over matzah pieces. Bake at 350°F for 8– 10 minutes. Watch carefully to make sure it does not burn. Remove from the oven.

Sprinkle chocolate chips over matzah. When they start to melt, spread smoothly with a knife. Sprinkle with ground almonds. Let cool and cut into pieces.

NUMBER OF SERVINGS: 8–10

sweets

drop cake

Theresa Mersky *This is a challenging cake which, for reasons I can't imagine today, I decided to make with much help from 6 year old Kyle, 4 year old Zane and 2 year old Leah for my husband Seth, who had to work on his birthday. We pretty much destroyed the kitchen. After the entire thing was baked and iced, we went to put it on the table for Dad's surprise. Everyone wanted to help. The cake went flying off the plate but miraculously landed intact on the floor. We put the cake back on the plate and I cautioned the kids that cakes that fall on the floor should be a secret. We called Dad to sing Happy Birthday, a recording he still has. Dad asked what kind of cake was waiting and Leah said "a Drop Cake". Drop Cake was born!*

5 large egg whites

1 cup milk, divided

2¼ teaspoons vanilla

3 cups sifted cake flour

1½ cups sugar

1 tablespoon plus 1 teaspoon baking powder

¼ teaspoon salt

12 tablespoons unsalted butter (softened)

One jar raspberry puree to use with raspberry buttercream frosting (recipe below)

Raspberry buttercream:

3 cups sugar

12 large egg whites, room temperature

8 sticks butter, room temperature

1 teaspoon pure vanilla extract

1 pint fresh or frozen raspberries, pureed and strained, to make 1 cup

Prepare 2 (9 x 1½") cake pans by greasing them, lining bottoms with parchment or wax paper, and then greasing & flouring. Preheat the oven to 350°F. In a medium bowl, lightly combine the egg whites, ¼ cup milk and vanilla. In a large bowl, combine the dry ingredients and mix on low speed for 30 seconds to blend. Add the butter and remaining ¾ cup milk. Mix well for a couple of minutes.

Gradually add the egg mixture and scrape down the sides. Scrape the batter into the prepared pans and smooth the surface with a spatula. The pans will be about ½ full. Bake 25–35 minutes or until a tester inserted near the center comes out clean and the cake springs back when pressed lightly in the center.

Let the cakes cool in the pans on racks for 10 minutes. Loosen the sides with a small metal spatula and invert onto greased wire racks. To prevent splitting, reinvert so that the tops are up and cool completely before wrapping airtight. Each layer should be about 1" high. Layer cake with raspberry puree (you can buy this already made) and ice with purchased buttercream or recipe below.

Buttercream: Bring a saucepan with about 2" of water to a simmer. Combine sugar and egg whites in a large heatproof mixing bowl set over (not in) simmering water and whisk until whites are warm to the touch and sugar is dissolved, 2–3 minutes. Place bowl on mixer stand; whisk on low speed until mixture is foamy. Raise speed to medium high; whisk until stiff, glossy peaks form and mixture is cooled completely, about 10 minutes.

Raspberry buttercream, continued

Reduce speed to medium-low, add butter, 2 tablespoons at a time, whisking to incorporate fully well after each addition (if buttercream appears curdled, at this point simply beat until smooth). Whisk in vanilla and raspberry puree. Switch to paddle; beat on low to reduce air bubbles, approximately 3–5 minutes. Frost cake.

TIPS & ADVICE: The buttercream is challenging, but you can use any frosting. This cake has raspberry puree between the layers, easy to find and buy. The best piece of baking advice from Nana Miriam is to bring your eggs to room temperature. Layers can be stored airtight for 2 days at room temperature, 5 days refrigerated, or 2 months frozen.

NUMBER OF SERVINGS: 12

"generation" chocolate rice krispie candy

Joy D. Kaufman *I did not know until very recently that this recipe originated from my grandmother, Sylvia Silverberg z"l. When I was a young child, my mother, Nora Kaufman, would make this often and warn my brother and me, who each had a capped tooth, to "be careful"! It is fast and easy to prepare and so good! We (Ex) Winnipeggers are great cooks and bakers; this one is an oldie but a goodie.*

2 tablespoons butter, or pareve salted margarine

1 square Baker's unsweetened chocolate

¼ cup plus 3 tablespoons dark corn syrup

¾ cup brown sugar

2 teaspoons real vanilla extract

3 cups regular or gluten-free Rice Krispies cereal

In a large pot, melt butter on medium–low heat. Once melted, add chocolate until the mixture is completely melted. Turn heat to low and add corn syrup, followed by brown sugar, and then vanilla extract. Add Rice Krispies and stir with a large wooden or spatula until blended well with chocolate mixture. Pour into a lightly greased 8 x 8" pan.

Do not refrigerate or it will become too hard to cut, as well as to eat. Let sit for about an hour and cut into squares; store in a cool, dry place. One pot, easy to clean, no mess!

YIELD: 20–25 pieces

sweets

cornflour coconut halva

Sinnora Moses *For generations, Indian Jews (Bene Israel) have made this traditional Rosh Hashanah dessert. Both my mother, Leah Bhastekar z"l, and my mother-in-law, Rosy Moses, made it and now so do I. Years ago, when there was no such thing as canned coconut milk, we first had to grate fresh coconut, then blend it and finally strain it to produce the milk. Now it's much easier but the recipe still requires continuous stirring to ensure a smooth consistency. The result is yummy and well worth the effort. You can make the coconut halva ahead of time and keep it in the refrigerator for at least a week. This is a great pareve dessert. The reference to cornflour in the name actually refers to the cornstarch that is used in the recipe.*

2 cans coconut milk (regular not light) plus two cans of water

½ cup cornstarch

1½ cups sugar

⅛ teaspoon edible food colouring—pink/orange/red

pinch salt

1 tablespoon pareve margarine

2 tablespoons chopped raw nuts (almonds and pistachios, optional), divided

¼ teaspoon nutmeg

¼ teaspoon cardamom

Place the coconut milk into a large pot and use empty cans to add two cans of water so as to make 2 litres of mixture. Add cornstarch to the coconut milk mixture. Add sugar, salt, and colour to the mixture. Stir very well to make sure there are no lumps in the liquid. Turn the burner on high and stir the mixture continuously for about 30 minutes to avoid lumps and sticking to the bottom. Add the margarine, half the nuts and all of the cardamom, and nutmeg.

Mix well and keep stirring for another 15 minutes until when dropped from a spoon onto a plate, the mixture does not stick to the plate or to your hand (after it has cooled for a couple of minutes). If you can pick it up as a solid piece, then it is ready; if it sticks, it needs to be cooked longer. The consistency will be a thick liquid batter.

Once ready, pour hot mixture into 2 greased 8 x 10" pyrex baking dishes. Spread evenly and sprinkle the remaining nuts on top. Cool on the counter and cut into squares or diamonds. Keep refrigerated.

NUMBER OF SERVINGS: 8

fruit salad crunch and topping

Hailey Remer *My husband and I got married and moved to Israel for a year so he could learn in Yeshiva. My first week there was Sukkot and I had 6-10 people at every meal. Being a basic baker, with few to no utensils, I needed to find something fast and easy. Fruit! That's always good. I cook according to colour; my motto is if it looks good, it will taste good. I chose mango, blueberries (a major treat in Israel) and pomegranate seeds; all vibrantly coloured fruits with flavours that work well together. To jazz up the fruit salad a bit, I asked my South African and English neighbours for some ideas. They were better stocked and voila—crunch and a great sauce that my friends often serve over cheesecake. Nowadays, I usually have some crunch in my fridge and make this when I need something quick or have surprise guests. I also serve it with vanilla ice cream (dairy or pareve). It makes for a crowd pleasing, colourful, easy and refreshing dessert.*

Crunch topping:

1 cup Rice Krispies

¾ cup almonds, crushed

½ cup brown sugar

1 tub soft Earth Balance (vegan buttery spread)

Strawberry coulis:

½ cup orange juice

1 bag frozen strawberries

2 tablespoons icing sugar

fruits of your choice, in season

Topping: Mix Rice Krispies, almonds, brown sugar, and margarine. Lay flat on parchment lined cookie sheet and bake in the oven at 350°F for 10 minutes. Let cool.

Coulis: Blend orange juice, frozen strawberries, and icing sugar in a blender until pureed.

Cut fruit into small chunks and put in a bowl. I like using pears, strawberries, blueberries, mango, nectarines, pomegranate seeds etc.

Serve in individual cups with fruit salad, crunch layer and the strawberry coulis on top.

TIPS & ADVICE: Crunch layer can be made ahead of time and stored in an airtight container. Sometimes, I add a bit of juice to the fruit salad for some extra flavour.

NUMBER OF SERVINGS: 6-8

sweets

pretty in pink cake

Estee Kafra *When rhubarb is in season, I like to take advantage of those elegant red stalks and bake and cook as much as I can. I developed this recipe and I now have a favourite rhubarb cake, hands down. I plan to try it with pineapple when rhubarb isn't in season.*

Rhubarb topping:

¾ pound rhubarb, trimmed and cut into 1½" pieces

1 cup sugar

2 tablespoons butter or oil

1 tablespoon fresh lemon juice

1½ teaspoons ground vanilla bean

½ teapoon kosher salt

Cake:

½ cup margarine or butter

½ cup sugar

½ cup oil

2½ cups flour

⅓ cup orange juice

2 eggs

2 teaspoons baking powder

1 teaspoon lemon zest

Preheat oven to 350°F. Combine the ingredients for the rhubarb topping in a heavy saucepan and cook until softening, about 8–10 minutes. Let cool. Strain the excess juice.

Beat the margarine or butter with the sugar, add oil and beat until fluffy and light in color, slow the mixer and add remaining ingredients. Place the rhubarb topping at the bottom of a parchment lined spring-form pan and spoon batter on top of it, smoothing the top with the back of a spoon.

Bake for 50 minutes. Let cool and flip onto plate.

NUMBER OF SERVINGS: 10–12

did you know?

Toronto has the only growing Holocaust survivor population in the world, outside of Israel. The demand for emergency funds has increased from 180 survivors in 2007 to over 500 in 2012.

SECOND HELPINGS, PLEASE!

REVISED EDITION

best borrowed recipes

No young bride, from 1968 on,
left home without this cookbook

MT. SINAI CHAPTER #1091
MONTREAL   B'NAI B'RITH   WOMEN
DISTRICT 22

best borrowed recipes

The following "best borrowed" recipes are some of our community's 'go-to' dishes which they have found published in other cookbooks, magazines or online. Try these recommended favourites!

SALADS

Heidi Solomon—Grilled Corn, Avocado & Tomato Salad with Honey Lime Dressing,
http://www.fortheloveofcooking.net/2009/07/grilled-corn-avocado-and-tomato-salad.html.
This is a favourite summer salad that I make all year round. Feta cheese or black beans can also be added for extra protein.

Cindy Berg—Green Salad, The Forest Feast, 2014, pages 118–119. Erin Gleeson. *This has edamame, green onions, pistachios, basil, and other great green ingredients.*

Cyrel Troster—Salade d'oranges aux Olives or Orange Salad with Olives, The Book of Jewish Food, 1996, page 249. Claudia Roden. *The combination of sliced oranges and tangy olives makes this salad a favourite. It cheers me up in the winter and gives me hope for a warm spring.*

VEGETABLES, BRUNCH, SNACKS & STARTERS

Sheryl Salter—Mini Cauliflower Pizza Crusts, Tablespoon.com, 2012 girlversusdough
http://www.tablespoon.com/recipes/mini-cauliflower-pizza-crusts/b8f4a680-6895-4202-ae91-cc0061ae258b. *These are so delicious!! You would never know that you're eating cauliflower.*

Lori Rosenthal—Spicy-Sweet Green Beans, http://markbittman.com/spicy-sweet-green-beans/. The Food Matters Cookbook. Mark Bittman. *This recipe has the best of both worlds, sweet and salty. The paste is also great with asparagus, edamame or broccoli.*

Annette Metz Pivnick—Eggplant with Buttermilk Sauce, Plenty, 2010, page 110. Yotam Ottolenghi.

Cindy Berg—Twice-Baked Sweet Potatoes, Vibrant Food, 2014, page 168. Kimberley Hasselbrink. *This is a great sweet potato recipe—and my husband who doesn't even like sweet potatoes or feta cheese, loves this dish.*

Laurie Sheff—Black Pepper Tofu, Plenty, 2010, page 44. Yotam Ottolenghi. *We have a lot of vegetarians and vegans in our family and circle of friends. Use Earth Balance to make this dish vegan.*

Laurie Sheff—Vegetable Strudel, The Hamptons Food, Family and History, 2012, page 179. Ricky Lauren. *This strudel is great for a summer lunch and is always on our table when we break the fast after Yom Kippur.*

Marilyn Gotfrid—Baked Lemony Feta Cheese with Thyme, Rosemary and Black Pepper, Two Dishes, 2009, page 51. Linda Hayes and Devin Connell. *Simple and sophisticated, the dish looks great and tastes even better! It is great for hors d'oeuvres or as a main dish served with a great salad and fresh bread.*

Barb Wiseberg—Bagel and Cream Cheese Baked French Toast, Pioneer Women Cooks a Year of Holidays. Ree Drummond http://4kowboys.blogspot.ca/2013/12/bagel-and-cream-cheese-baked-french.html. *This recipe is a natural for brunch, lunch or a dairy dinner.*

best borrowed

Emily Sanders—Fried Olives with Laban, Balaboosta, 2013, page 120–121, Einat Admony. *If I had to choose my favourite food, I think it would be olives!*

PASTA, GRAINS

Ellen Schneidman—Grandma Jeanne's Macaroni Casserole, The Oy of Cooking, 2003, page 117. Susie Weinthal. *My kids' favorite comfort food.*

Cindy Berg—Camargue Red Rice and Quinoa with Orange and Pistachios, Ottolenghi, 2013, page 76. Yotam Ottolenghi and Sami Tamimi. *This is a family favourite that is served as a side dish or definitely sweet enough to be served as a dessert.*

Vera Sanders—Broccoli Cauliflower Kugel, Whole Foods Kosher Kitchen: Glorious Meals Pure and Simple. Levana Kirschenbaum. *This is a yummy use of vegetables and a great dish for Passover.*

Debbie Gorman-Sadja—Carrot Kugel, The Kosher Palette, page 197. Susie Fishbein and Sandra Blank. *This is a family favourite that goes well with everything. You can even serve it for dessert!*

Valerie Fish—Israeli Couscous with Roasted Eggplant and Cinnamon-Cumin Dressing, http://www.bonappetit.com/recipe/Israeli-couscous-with-roasted-eggplant-and-cinnamon-cumin-dressing. *I like this recipe so much because it has complex, interesting flavors.*

Ronnie Oelbaum—Fantastic 4 Mushroom and Cheese Lasagna, Bite Me, 2009, page 114. Julie Albert and Lisa Gnat. *My aunt, Michelle Roth, made this at a family gathering and I was hooked!*

FISH

Ellen Schneidman—Baked Halibut with Cheese Sauce, The Good Table, Mount Sinai Hospital Auxiliary, 1985, page 138. *Finally got me to eat fish and love it.*

Reeva Solomon—Basil and Lime Salmon, http://www.thehomechannel.co.za/food/sharons-simple-stylish-meals/basil-and-lime-salmon. *This recipe by famous South African chef, Sharon Glazer, is very easy, very tasty and always turns out perfectly.*

Gail Fenwick—Parmesan Crusted Fish, Canadian Living Magazine, January 2012. Amanda Barnier and The Test Kitchen, www.canadianliving.com. *I have made this recipe many times with both halibut and cod.*

Leigh Ann Brenman—Jack Daniels (™) Salmon, Simply Southern, With a Dash of Kosher Soul—2009, page 159. MHA/FYOS Project (Day and High school in Memphis, Tenn). *I am an expat from Memphis, so what could be better than whisky from Tennessee in the marinade?*

POULTRY

Annette Metz Pivnick—Chicken with Shallots, http://www.foodgal.com/2014/09/a-most-excellent-chicken-dish-from-the-wife-of-andrew-zimmer. *Adapted from Andrew and Rishia Zimmern by way of Martha Stewart. I substitute margarine for the butter in ingredients; wonderful!*

Michelle Brandes—Michal's Gallilean Chicken & Beef, "More Please—Totally Scrumptious Home Cooked Meals"—the Associated Hebrew Schools cookbook, 2013, page 118. *My friend, Michal Amsalem from Israel, made this for my family when she lived in Toronto and it's absolutely delicious.*

Michelle Brandes—Chicken Tagine with Green Olives & Preserved Lemons, Friday Night Dinners, 2008, page 68. Bonnie Stern. *I love anything Bonnie Stern does but this is a dish that I especially love and we've made it at our Passover seder for the past many years.*

Ellen Schneidman—Sticky Garlic Chicken, In Good Time—Fine Food in Under An Hour, 1986, page 65. Barbra Schlifer Commemorative Clinic. *Reminds me of my beautiful mother—it was her favorite Friday night go-to recipe.*

Judy Laxer—Grilled Moroccan Chicken, The Kosher Palette, 2000, page 16, Joseph Kushner Hebrew Academy, Livingston, New Jersey. *Delicious and makes the house smell wonderful!*

Rebecca Isenberg—Judgja Bil Zeitoun (Chicken and Olives), Sephardic Cooking, 1994, page 445. Mark Copeland. *I love this dish because it always comes out so flavourful, colorful, and savory.*

MEAT

Deborah Hoffnung—Southwestern Barbecued Brisket, Bonnie Stern Heart Smart Cook Book, 2006, page 286. Bonnie Stern. *So easy and yummy.*

Barb Wiseberg—Bobotie (spiced meat), http://www.food.com/recipe/bobotie-from-the-cape-204300. Zurie (reader of food.com). *To kosher the original recipe, just substitute almond or soy milk for the dairy milk.*

Valerie Fish—Miso-Glazed Lamb Chops with Caramelized Soy Drizzle, HeartSmart Cooking for Family and Friends, 2000, page 208. Bonnie Stern. *This recipe is delicious and I never have even one chop left, no matter how many I prepare!*

Rebecca Isenberg—Albondigas (Meatballs), Jewish cooking in America, 1995, page 172. Joan Nathan. *I make these for Rosh Hashanah because they are delicious, round and sweet for the new year.*

Barb Weisberg—Dry-Spice Rub Recipe, http://www.levanacooks/dry-spice-rub/. Levana Kirschenbaum. *This is my go-to spice rub. I make two full batches of the recipe so I have enough to pass around for friends and family.*

SOUPS

Shari Wert—Potato Corn Chowder, Rose Reisman's Family Favorites, 2011, page 134. Rose Reisman. *My kids devour this soup. They love the creamy taste with a bit of spice and I love that it's made with fresh vegetables and evaporated milk instead of cream!*

best borrowed

Shari Silverstein—Cold Avocado Corn Soup, Epicurious http://www.epicurious.com/recipes/food/views/Cold-Avocado-Corn-Soup-with-Cilantro-Oil-231993. *Delicious cold soup! Amazing summer recipe.*

Julie Keshen—Creamy (Creamless) Zucchini and Potato Soup, The Nourishing Gourmet, 2010. Kim Harris. http://www.thenourishinggourmet.com/?s=zucchini+soup. *This recipe has delicious flavour, texture and it's dairy free.*

Ellen Moss—Mushroom Barley Soup, Meal Leani Yumm, 1998, page 83. Noreen Gilletz. *It is hearty, filling and nutritious. We add 4 more cups of mushrooms, 1/2 cup of lima beans and 1/2 cup more of pearl barley. It freezes well.*

Valerie Fish—Green Pea Soup with Tarragon and Pea Sprouts, http://www.epicurious.com/recipes/food/views/Green-Pea-Soup-with-Tarragon-and-Pea-Sprouts-352029. *This incredibly bright green soup looks and tastes like farm freshness—don't overcook it though as the bright green will turn dull.*

SWEETS

Cyrel Troster—Turn of the Century Danish Apple Macaroon for Pesach, The Book of Jewish Food, 1996, page 189. Claudia Roden. *I really like to make this dessert for Pesach. It is very fresh tasting with the cooked apples and a nice almond crust.*

Madelin Daviau—Triple Chocolate Brownies with Cream Cheese Frosting, The Complete Light Kitchen, 2007, page 351. Rose Reisman. *These are so yummy and half the calories of regular brownies!*

Jacqui Strauss—Pecan Flan, Passover, A Kosher Collection, 2010, page 179. Pam Reiss. *This is a delicious and elegant Passover recipe. With cake flour instead of cake meal, it works for the rest of the year too.*

Jacqui Strauss—Deep-Dish Apple Cake, Second Helpings, Please! Mount Sinai Chapter #1091—Montreal, page 128. *This apple cake is always a beautiful, delicious and warm dessert to serve in the Autumn at Rosh Hashanah or any high holiday.*

Rachel Keshen—Zucchini Brownies, Fastpaleo.com; Michelle Rock. http://fastpaleo.com/recipe/zucchini-brownies. *These are incredible, flourless brownies and they can easily be made vegan. I leave out the nutmeg and allspice.*

Elly Barlin-Daniels—Giant Zebra Fudge Cookies, Passover by Design, 2008, page 235. Susie Fishbein. *These are beautiful Passover cookies.*

Daphna Zacks—Regal Cheese Cake, For the Love of Baking, 1979, page 136. Lillian Kaplan. **Apple Crisp,** For the Love of Baking, page 93. **Old Fashioned Apple Cake,** For the Love of Baking, page 95

Susan Fremar—Oven Baked Homemade Applesauce, Barefoot Contessa, 1999, Ina Garten http://www.food.com/recipe/barefoot-contessas-oven-baked-homemade-applesauce-261455. *I also add juice of two pink grapefruits and 7 peeled, cored and quartered pears.*

Sara Bornstein—Ultra-orange cake (vegan), Joy of Cooking, 1997, page 932/933. Irma S Rombauer. *A one bowl wonder cake that is dairy and egg free.*

index

credits

Sources for The History of Our Community:

We would like to give particular thanks to The Jews of Toronto, A History to 1937, *by Stephen A. Speisman. It was an invaluable source without which "The History of Our Community" could not have been written. Also of particular assistance were the articles and information provided at www.billgladstone.ca. Thank you also to Melissa Caza at The Ontario Jewish Archives for her excellent assistance and the wonderful research conducted by Brooky Robins and Cyrel Troster.*

The Jews of Toronto; A History to 1937, By Stephen A. Speisman
© 1979 Stephen A. Speisman, McLelland & Stewart Limited, Toronto, Canada

The Rise of the Toronto Jewish Community, By Shmuel Mayer Shapiro
© 2010, Now and Then Books, Toronto, Canada

Only Yesterday; Collected Pieces on the Jews of Toronto, By Benjamin Kayfetz and Stephen A. Speisman,
© 2013, Now and Then Books, Toronto, Canada

Canada's Jews: A People's Journey, By Gerald Tulchinsky
excerpt jewishvirtuallibrary.org—joanna sloame
<http://www.jewishvirtuallibrary.org/jsource/Judaism

The Rise of the Toronto Jewish Community, From: Polyphony Vol.6, 1984 pp. 59-63
© 1984 Multicultural History Society of Ontario

http://www.billgladstone.ca/ - various articles

en.wikipedia.org/wiki/History_of_the_Jews_in_Toronto

The Defining Decade: Identity, Politics, and The Canadian Jewish Community in the 1960s
(University of Toronto Press), Harold Troper
The 1960s, when Canadian Jews found acceptance, Robert Fulford | October 16, 2010, National Post

http://ceris.metropolis.net/Virtual%20Library/Demographics/troper1/troper1.html

http://www.cjnews.com/node/80305#sthash.J53dkyOb.dpuf

Canada's immigration history one of discrimination and exclusion By: Debra Black
Immigration Reporter, Published February 15, 2013 to work on

Antisemitism in Canada (Part 1: A Disgraceful History), by Dr. Michael Keefer

UJA . . . we are at your service

Whatever services you may be looking for in the Greater Toronto Area, UJA Federation of Greater Toronto ("UJA") and its more than 100 beneficiary agencies, schools and summer camps, are here for you! Please visit UJA's comprehensive site http://www.jewishtoronto.com/ for the most up-to-date list of agencies, opportunities and programs.

SOCIAL SERVICES

BERNARD BETEL CENTRE FOR CREATIVE LIVING
Provides programming for seniors in a Jewish environment to help them live active, creative, and healthy lifestyles.
▶ Ph: 416-225-2112/email: reception@betelcentre.org/www.betelcentre.org

CHAI TIKVAH FOUNDATION
Provides Jewish, supportive, residential options, programmes, public education, and advocacy, for individuals and families affected by psychiatric disabilities.
▶ Ph: 416-634-3050/email: chaitikvah@chaitikvah.org/www.chaitikvah.org

CIRCLE OF CARE
Supports individual independence and extends and enhances quality of life of people in their own homes.
▶ Ph: 416-635-2900/ email: afoss@circleofcare.com/www.circleofcare.com

JACS (JEWISH ADDICTION COMMUNITY SERVICES)
Helps people with substance use or addiction issues and their families to explore and pursue recovery in a safe, nurturing environment; educates the community through an outreach program about substance use and addiction.
▶ Ph: 416-638-0350 / email: anna@jacstoronto.org/website: www.jacstoronto.org

JEWISH FAMILY & CHILD (JF&CS)
Supports the healthy development of individuals, children, families, and communities through prevention, protection, counseling, education and advocacy services, within the context of Jewish values.
▶ Ph: 416-638-7800 /email: info@jfandcs.com www.jfandcs.com

JEWISH FREE LOAN TORONTO
Assists Jews in need of financial assistance by providing interest-free loans which allow them to help themselves.
▶ Ph: 416-635-1217 / email: info@jewishfreeloan.ca / www.tjflc.com

JIAS (JEWISH IMMIGRANT AID SERVICES) TORONTO
Welcomes, supports and integrates new immigrants with counseling, training, referral and other support services and English language programmes.
▶ Ph:416-630-6481 / email: info@jiastoronto.org/www.jiastoronto.org

JVS TORONTO

Provides the unemployed and underemployed (including newcomers, youth, women, people with disabilities and mature workers) with employment opportunities, social and educational services and training.

▶ Ph: 416-787-1151 / email: services@jvstoronto.org/www.jvstoronto.org

KEHILLA RESIDENTIAL PROGRAMME

Identifies and champions affordable housing and implements housing initiatives for the Jewish community including seniors and mixed use non profit projects.

▶ Ph: 416-932-1212 / email: Kehilla@rogers.com/www.kehilla.ca

REENA

Enables people with developmental disabilities to realize their full potential by forming lifelong partnerships with individuals and their families within a framework of Jewish culture and values.

▶ Ph: 905-889-6484 / email: info@reena.org/www.reena.org

EDUCATION & IDENTITY

MARCH OF THE LIVING

A 2-week High School age educational experience that takes participants on a life-changing adventure in Poland and Israel.

▶ Ph: 416-398-6931 / email: asaxe@ujafed.org/www.marchoftheliving.org

THE JULIA AND HENRY KOSCHITZKY CENTRE FOR JEWISH EDUCATION

Dedicated to strengthening, enriching and promoting the quality of Jewish education for more than 70 day schools and supplementary programs, 1,500 educators and 16,000 students across the GTA.

▶ Ph: 416-635-2883 / email: dheld@ujafed.org/www.cjetoronto.com

CANADA ISRAEL EXPERIENCE (CIE)

Providing Taglit Birthright Israel trips since the year 2000 as well as other short, mid and long-term Israel programs.

▶ Ph: 416-398-6931 / email: ciec@ujafed.org/www.israelforfree.com

MASA ISRAEL JOURNEY

Connects Jewish young adults (ages 18–30) to gap year, study abroad, post-college, and volunteer programs.

▶ Ph: 1-866-864-3279/www.masaisrael.org

AMEINU

A grassroots organization reaching out to Toronto's Russian speaking community, providing Adult Education, Jewish Studies in Russian, and Russian Community Outreach.

▶ Ph: 416-736-1794 / email: ameinu@rogers.com/ www.ameinu.ca

BIRTHRIGHT ISRAEL

Strengthens Jewish identity, Jewish communities, and solidarity with Israel by providing a 10-day trip to Israel for young Jewish people.

▶ Ph: 416-398-7785 / email: birthrightisrael@ujafed.org / www.birthrightisrael.com

HILLEL OF GREATER TORONTO

Through exciting and creative programming and events, Hillel promotes Jewish identity, student leadership and religious and political diversity in a dynamic and inclusive environment for all Jewish students.
▶ Ph: 416-913-2424 / email: info@hilleltoronto.org/www.hilleltoronto.org

JEWISH CAMP COUNCIL

Promotes Jewish camping and its benefits throughout the Province of Ontario.
▶ Ph: 905-881-0018 / email: happycamper@campnbb.com / www.campnbb.com

JEWS FOR JUDAISM

Strengthens and preserves Jewish identity through education and counseling that counteracts deceptive proselytizing targeting Jews for conversion.
▶ Ph: 416-789-0030 / email: webmaster@jewsforjudaism.org/ www.jewsforjudaism.org

ONE HAPPY CAMPER

Awards a monetary incentive grant to first time campers in the GTA attending Jewish overnight camp.
▶ Ph: 416-635-2883 / www.onehappycamper.org

PJ LIBRARY

Mails free, high-quality Jewish children's books and music each month to families across the GTA as well as a monthly newsletter; transforms reading stories into Jewish experiences.. A program of the Harold Grinspoon Foundation, made possible through partnerships with philanthropists and UJA Federation of Greater Toronto.
▶ Ph: 416-621-5675/www.pjlibrary.org

THE HOUSE

Inspires Jewish young adults (ages 22–35) through dynamic and creative programming, fostering a deepening appreciation of Jewish wisdom, values, and traditions by highlighting their relevance for navigating life's important decisions and everyday life.
▶ Ph: 416-482-9025 / email: info@thehousetoronto.org/www.thehousetoronto.com

ISRAEL

ISRAEL ENGAGEMENT SHINSHINIM PROGRAMS

Brings pre-army Israeli young men and women ("ShinShinim,") to Toronto to act as peer educators and deliver a relevant and compelling message about Israel to our community's schools, synagogues, youth movements and summer camps.
▶ Ph: 416-635-2883 /email: israelengagement@ujafed.org

JEWISH AGENCY FOR ISRAEL (JAFI)

Serves as the main link between the Jewish state and Jewish communities everywhere.
▶ www.jewishagency.org

KEREN HAYESOD

A non-profit corporation, that works to further the national priorities of the State of Israel and world Jewry.
▶ www.kh-uia.org.il

UIA FEDERATIONS CANADA (UIAFC)
A national Jewish fundraising organization and community planning body working to service primarily in Canada & Israel.
▶ Ph: 416-636-7655 / email: info@jfcuia.org/www.jewishcanada.org

AMERICAN JOINT DISTRIBUTION COMMITTEE (JDC)
Works in more than 70 countries and in Israel to alleviate hunger and hardship, rescue Jews in danger, create lasting connections to Jewish life, and provide immediate relief and long-term development support for victims of natural and man-made disasters.
▶ Ph: 212-687-6200 / email: info@jdc.org/www.jdc.org

IsraAID
A non-profit, non-governmental organization which provides life-saving disaster relief and long term support with teams of professional medics, search & rescue squads, post-trauma experts and community mobilizers, who have been first on the front lines of nearly every major humanitarian response in the 21st century.
▶ Ph: 972-(0)-546-785-033 / email: israaid@gmail.com/www.Israaid.co.il

ADVOCACY

The Centre for Israel and Jewish Affairs (CIJA)
The advocacy arm of UJA Federation of Greater Toronto and other Canadian Federations, CIJA coordinates, streamlines and directs strategic, targeted advocacy programming on behalf of Canada's diverse Jewish community, including providing information, education and research on a range of key topics such as the Middle East, antisemitism, human rights and various domestic policy matters.
▶ Ph: 416-925-7499 / www.cija.ca

ARTS & CULTURE

ASHKENAZ FESTIVAL
Dedicated to fostering an increased awareness of Yiddish and Jewish culture through the arts; North America's largest celebration of Jewish music and culture.
▶ Ph: 416-979-9901/ www.ashkenazfestival.com

COMMITTEE FOR YIDDISH
Fosters and promotes Yiddish language and culture—indeed the entire Ashkenaz tradition—as a vibrant part of contemporary Jewish life and as a vital link between the Jewish past and future.
▶ Ph: 416-635-2883 / email: committeeforyiddish@ujafed.org/ www.committeeforyiddish.com

JEWISH CANADIAN MILITARY MUSEUM
Houses a large variety of war memorabilia that has been donated throughout the years and is home to a Memorial Book of Remembrance, honoring the more than 550 Jewish Canadian Armed Forces personnel who gave their lives during duty.
▶ Ph: 905-610-0500 / email: office@jcmm.ca /www.jcmm.ca

KOFFLER CENTRE OF THE ARTS
A contemporary Jewish arts and cultural institution that serves audiences of all ages and backgrounds and presents a range of artistic programs through a global lens in a specifically Canadian context.
▶ Ph: 647-925-0643 /email: info@kofflerarts.org/www.kofflerarts.org

ONTARIO JEWISH ARCHIVES, Blankenstein Family Heritage Centre
Acquires, preserves and makes available documentary sources related to Ontario's Jewish community.
▶ Ph: 416-635-5391 / www.ontariojewisharchives.org

SARAH & CHAIM NEUBERGER HOLOCAUST EDUCATION CENTRE
Through its museum and programs, the Centre generates knowledge and understanding about the Holocaust and serves as a forum for dialogue about civil society for present and future generations.
▶ Ph: 416-631-5689 / email: Neuberger@ujafed.org / www.holocaustcentre.com

TORONTO JEWISH FILM FESTIVAL
The largest Jewish Film Festival in the world, this annual event showcases the best international feature films, documentaries and shorts on themes of Jewish culture and identity.
▶ Ph: (416) 324-9121 / email: tjff@tjff.ca/www.tjff.com

THE JCC'S

MILES NADAL JCC
Serves the downtown Toronto community with recreation and athletic facilities, adult Jewish education, programming for children and teens and other community members.
▶ Ph: 416-924-6211 / www.milesnadaljcc.ca

PROSSERMAN JCC
Services include Jewish learning program, daycare and preschool, fitness centre, arts and media studios, and programs for adults age 55 and older.
▶ Ph: 416-638-1881 / www.prossermanjcc.com

SCHWARTZ/REISMAN CENTRE
Operating from the Joseph & Wolf Lebovic Jewish Community Campus campus, serving the York Region community and the Jewish community of Greater Toronto, the SRC enriches lives by providing opportunities for social, cultural, spiritual, educational and physical activities.
▶ Ph: 905-303-1821 / www.srcentre.ca